SEAPOWER ASHORE

Technology and tradition combine aboard HMS *Alexandra* at the bombardment of Alexandria in 1882: the Nordenfeldt multi-barrel machine gun with barefoot, cutlass-armed sailors and a parapet of hammocks. (National Maritime Museum, London: Neg No 58/5966)

SEAPOWER ASHORE

200 Years of Royal Navy Operations on Land

Edited by Captain Peter Hore

CHATHAM PUBLISHING
LONDON

In association with the National Maritime Museum

Copyright © National Maritime Museum, 2001. (General Editor: Captain Peter Hore)

Published in Great Britain in 2001 by Chatham Publishing,
61 Frith Street, London W1V 5TA

Chatham Publishing is an imprint of Gerald Duckworth & Co Ltd

British Library Cataloguing in Publication Data
A catalogue record for this book is available from the
British Library

ISBN 1 86176 155 4

All rights reserved. No part of this publication may be reproduced or transmitted in any form or by any means, electronic or mechanical, including photocopying, recording, or any information storage and retrieval system, without either prior permission in writing from the publisher or a licence permitting restricted copying. The General Editor and contributors assert their moral right to be identified as the authors of the work in accordance with sections 77 and 78 of the Copyright, Designs and Patents Act, 1988.

Typeset by Dorwyn Ltd, Rowlands Castle, Hants

Printed and bound in Great Britain by Bookcraft (Bath) Ltd

Contents

Foreword by Admiral Sir Jock Slater   7
Introduction: A Very British Way in War, by Peter Hore   9

1. Smith and the Siege of Acre 1799: Sea Power Decisive on Land, by Tom Pocock   26
2. 'Science and Labour': The Naval Contribution to Operations Ashore in the Great Wars with France 1793-1815, by Michael Duffy   39
3. Nelson Ashore, 1780-97, by Colin White   53
4. 'Within Cannon Shot of Deep Water': The Syrian Campaign of 1840, by Andrew Lambert   79
5. Under the Heel of Britannia: The Bombardment of Sweaborg 9-11 August 1855, by Andrew Lambert   96
6. March into India: The Relief of Lucknow 1857-59, by Richard Brooks   130
7. The Long Arm of Seapower: The Anglo-Japanese War of 1863-64, by Colin White   146
8. Admiral Beatty and Brown Water: The Sudan and China 1896-1900, by Richard Brooks   164
9. 'Ex Africa Semper Aliquid Novi': The Second Boer War 1899-1901, by Arthur Bleby   181
10. The Royal Naval Division 1914-19, by Chris Page   208
11. An Unlikely Encounter: Norway 1940, by Peter Hore   240
12. Assault on Walcheren: 1944, by Ivor Howcroft   259
13. From Tigre to Tomahawk: the Adriatic Revisited, 1999, by Dr Lee Willett   274

Index   285

Contributors

Captain Peter Hore is a former Head of Defence Studies for the Royal Navy.

Tom Pocock is Britain's leading author and authority on Nelson.

Dr Michael Duffy is Head of History and Director of the Centre for Maritime Historical Studies at the University of Exeter.

Colin White is Deputy Director of the Royal Naval Museum at Portsmouth.

Andrew Lambert is Professor of Naval History at King's College London.

Richard Brooks is a military historian whose most recent book was a history of Naval Brigades.

Arthur Bleby is a retired naval officer specialising in the study of Victorian Naval Brigades.

Captain Christopher Page is Head of the Naval Historical Branch.

Ivor Howcroft is a doctoral candidate at Exeter University researching amphibious operations in the Second World War.

Dr Lee Willett works at the Royal United Services Institute for Defence Studies.

Foreword

by Admiral Sir Jock Slater GCB LVO DL, First Sea Lord 1995-1998

As we enter a new century, the international scene has changed dramatically and the British Government has established a clear way forward for its Armed Forces based on a fundamental Review of the United Kingdom's Foreign and Defence Policy. This Review has, yet again, highlighted the inherent flexibility of maritime forces and the key contribution they make to joint operations both nationally and internationally.

During the course of the Review, there were those who spoke of a change of direction for the Royal Navy, inferring that there was something completely new in shifting the focus from open ocean operations to those near the land. This, of course, is not the case; there might be a change of emphasis but operations in the littoral are a famous part of Britain's maritime heritage.

The Royal Navy has inherited two separate traditions, one which proudly cites the decisive battle with resultant command of the sea and of which there are many fine examples in history, and another which stresses the inextricable link with operations ashore. Sir Julian Corbett wrote *Some Principles of Maritime Strategy* almost a century ago in which he emphasised the key role of the fleet in influencing events ashore. Much has changed since then, not least the advent of air power and the strategic and tactical use of space, but the basic principles remain the same.

So the Royal Navy's heritage is formed, in equal measure, from both traditions: on the one hand, a sterling and straightforward inheritance from the Nelsonic tradition of seeking battle on the sea, and on the other hand, the application of sea-based force as part of an integrated approach to operations. The first remains a glorious tradition of which the Royal Navy is justly proud but it is the second which establishes precedents for the future.

The first tradition is well studied and researched but historians often overlook or underplay the second. As the contributors to this book admirably demonstrate, there are many classic historical examples of the use of maritime power to complement and sway land operations. I welcome this collection of some of those examples from two centuries of naval warfare, which Peter Hore has edited and to which experts in their field have contributed.

INTRODUCTION

A Very British Way in War
by Peter Hore

The Royal Navy Field Gun Competition, for many years held annually at the Royal Tournament in London, was probably one of the toughest sports in the world. It was a common myth that the run, in which teams of sailors raced guns across make-believe chasms and over walls, was started a hundred years ago to commemorate the Royal Navy's participation in the Boer War. It is indeed true that in 1899 Captain Percy Scott had improvised mountings for guns taken from HMS *Terrible* and *Powerful*'s secondary armament, and that sailors had hauled these and the ship's field guns hundred of miles inland to support the British army in its war against the Boers.[1] However, Scott had already been commended for similar achievements, especially his extempore gun mountings, when a Lieutenant with the naval brigade in Egypt in 1882.[2] In London, the field gun competition itself only started in 1907, though sailors drilling at their guns had been seen at public events as early as 1881.[3] Arguably public displays of this nature are even older: for example, after the Russian War of 1854-6 the Royal Navy paraded with its guns for the presentation of medals on Southsea Common, and there were public demonstrations of amphibious landings at Southsea and at Whale Island in the late nineteenth century.

Operations like these were commonplace for the British navy in the nineteenth century, and this book opens with a description of one such. In 1799, Napoleon, cut off from France by the loss of his fleet at Aboukir in the first of Nelson's three great sea battles, had decided to march his army home long the coast of Palestine and Syria. However, Captain Sidney Smith RN first captured the French siege train, and then mounted these guns and some of his ship's guns on the walls of Acre, and led the defence in person. Sustained from

An extreme example of the employment of 'science and labour': the raising of one of two long 18-pounder guns from HMS *Centaur* to form a battery on the 600ft Diamond Rock pinnacle commanding the entrance to the harbour of Fort de France, Martinique, in 1804. Engraved by Joseph Constantine Sadler after an eyewitness sketch by John Eckstein. (National Maritime Museum, London: Neg No 2062)

the sea while Napoleon's troops had to be succoured as best they could overland, the result was inevitable. Napoleon's first defeat, and one of only few, was by a British naval officer.

The nineteenth century opened with another typical demonstration of the Navy's ingenuity and the application of science and muscle power. Diamond Rock is a sheer pinnacle rising 600 feet out of the sea off the passage to Port Royal in Martinique. The French regarded its cliffs as impossible, but under the command of Lieutenant James Maurice, seamen scaled the cliffs and swayed 18-pounder and 24-pounder guns to the summit. There, for a year and half in 1804 and 1805, Maurice and his 120 sailors and Marines signalled the movements of French shipping and did what they could to disrupt it. It must have galled Napoleon greatly, for he called the British occupation a 'symbol of insolence' and wrote that he was choked with indignation that the Rock had not been taken back, preferring to lose a ship of the line than fail to rid Martinique of the affront. Napoleon nearly had his way, because in the entire campaign of Trafalgar, the capture by two French line-of-battle ships and 3000 troops of Villeneuve's fleet of HMS *Diamond Rock*, which had been commissioned and was commanded as a Royal Navy warship, was one of the few French successes.4

More familiar operations were for the Navy to evacuate the British army, as it did Sir John Moore's army at Corunna, to raid the enemy's coasts and ports as Cochrane did in the Mediterranean, or to use access from the sea to supply the army ashore. Thus Wellington was sustained on his march into France while the French armies starved. By the end of the Great War of 1793-1815, the Navy was expert in such operations, like William Hoste's in the Adriatic. In modern doctrinal parlance, using great economy of effort Hoste conducted operations there which tied down much larger and more powerful forces, kept only a small footprint ashore, and sustained a vigorous campaign of manoeuvre warfare. Appropriately, Hoste's motto in battle was 'Remember Nelson', and, of course, Nelson himself had been no stranger to the type of operations which Hoste was waging.

It is sometimes wrongly suggested that Nelson had said something to the effect that ships are fools to fight forts, when in fact he never said this. The nearest he appears to have came to saying something like it when he was asked to help at the siege of Calvi by laying his ships alongside the forts. He declined, however, because the enemy might have had red-hot shot, and he advised the army commander, Stuart, that the shot and powder, of which the British were short, could be better directed from a battery ashore. In fact when conditions were right Nelson was frequently engaged in land operations, and his wounds which are best known, the loss of arm and damage to the sight of one eye, were both received in actions ashore. When

Although the medal was introduced during what some regard as a land campaign, the Royal Navy was deeply involved in the Russian War of 1854-6 and many of the first recipients of the Victoria Cross were naval men, as this page from *The Illustrated London News* shows. (National Maritime Museum, London: Neg No 58/1059)

other conditions were right the Navy did indeed attack forts. Returning to Acre in 1840, this time as attacker rather than defender, '... the very first broadsides were murderous ... for guns of that period, in wooden ships, something like perfection had been attained. Officers and men had been thoroughly trained under the newest system; and all matters connected with gunnery worked with the regularity of clocks'.[5] The Battle of Acre was, again in modern doctrinal parlance, a definitive act of coercion and future deterrence. Few could improve on Palmerston's assessment that as

> ... regards the interests of England not only in connection with the Turkish Question, but in relation to every other question which we may have to discuss with other powers. Every country that has towns within cannon shot of deep water will remember the operations of the British Fleet on the Coast of Syria in September, October and November 1840, whenever such country has any differences with us ...'[6]

A similar demonstration in 1855 in the Baltic, threatening the Russian capital of St Petersburg, brought the Russian War to a rapid conclusion. The remainder of the century was punctuated with events in which the Navy was increasingly committed to land operations. In Smith's and Nelson's days it had been relatively easy to land guns from ships' own broadsides, but as the size of ships' fixed armament increased the Navy started to embark field guns, rockets and other weapons specifically for operations ashore. That these operations took place as far apart as the Crimea, the Baltic, India during the Mutiny, Japan, North and South Africa, and China, was a repeated demonstration of the Navy's global reach. Only a few major campaigns are described here in this book, but there were nearly 50 such operations and many times more minor boat actions. What the Navy was doing ashore in the nineteenth century was one aspect of the so-called British way in warfare:

> Prior to approximately 1900, British grand strategy was based on the protection of her overseas Empire and on avoiding committing major British forces to do battle ... Britain sought to use her naval superiority to blockade continental enemies and to conduct raids against the enemy's homeland and overseas possession.[7]

Ingenuity in inshore waters during the Russian war: a small rocket boat (foreground), such as Colonel Congreve had proposed 50 years earlier, and a mobile raft for a ship's gun. Later, larger rafts would be armour-plated and give impetus to the idea of ironclad warships. (National Maritime Museum, London: Neg No 58/421)

A few extracts from the Navy Records Society's account of the Russian War in the Crimea serve as a typical example. In the first landings, nearly half the artillery, 74 guns of five types and 680 rockets, were manned by the Navy: '... the seamen were busy for six days landing them [the guns] with sheers and dragging them up the heights, fifty men on the drag ropes and a fiddler on the gun ...'.[8] At the Siege of Sevastopol itself, of 123 guns, 47 were the Navy's. Elsewhere sailors helped to build a railway, and at the town of Eupatoria the garrison was made up entirely of sailors and marines, the latter forming a cavalry patrol which on 12 October 1855 charged and defeated a force of Cossacks.[9] Universally, the sailors had a reputation for working with 'steadfast cheerfulness and untiring courage'. At the extreme end of the scale, two of their officers were awarded the Victoria Cross for their part in defending the Guards' colours.[10] Summing up their service, Lord Raglan wrote – a little niggardly perhaps:

> I attach the greatest value to the services of the seamen and marines, and am fully sensible of the advantage of the army has derived from their effective co-operation.[11]

The unique contribution which the Navy made to nineteenth-century warfare ashore, and recounted in these chapters, is threefold. First was the skill in improvisation and the application of science and the use of muscle-power. Next were its big guns, often the biggest available to the Army. And third was their resolve and fierce sense of identity expressed in many, often eccentric, ways. For example, in the Crimea missing ponies were always to be found in the Navy's lines; in Egypt the naval brigade's camels survived after their sores had been treated with Stockholm tar; and in South Africa the sailors employed a veritable zoo of animals to help drag their guns. The many small wars ashore also gave early experience of fighting and of command to a large number of twentieth-century admirals, Fisher, Jellicoe, Beatty and Cunningham to name but a few

In the last act of the nineteenth century, the men of HMS *Powerful* were not the only ones involved in the Second Boer War of 1899-1900, but it was their homecoming, with its public parades, in which they hauled their guns, and dinners in Portsmouth, Windsor and London, which took a grip on the public's imagination. Hubris was not far away. Since publication of his greatest and best known work, *The Influence of Sea Power*, Captain Alfred Thayer Mahan had been arguing for the massing of superior forces at sea.[12] He argued that:

> wars were won not by 'rambling operations, or naval duels', or by 'brilliant individual feats of gallantry or skill, by ships or men', but by the massing of superior forces, or by force massed and handled in skilful combination.[13]

Mahan's *Influence of Sea Power* had great impact in Britain, and *The Times* in its review chose to ignore hundreds of years of British

Seapower Ashore

Naval volunteers armed with rifles and cutlasses march past Queen Victoria in 1881: parades and displays of this nature, which were commonplace in the nineteenth century, played a part in popularising the Nvay and were eventually formalised into the Field Gun Competition at the Royal Tournament held for many years at Earls Court in London. (*The Illustrated London News* Picture Library)

The Naval Brigade heavily engaged at the Battle of El Teb in the Sudan, 4 February 1884, using Gatling and Gardner guns and supported by Highlanders. From a series of fine sketches in *The Illustrated London News* by Melton Prior. (National Maritime Museum, London: Neg No 58/6167)

practice of sea power by thundering that his book was 'a pioneer in its class, for, strange to say, the literature of the greatest Naval Power in history has no authoritative treatise on the principles of Naval Warfare'. Mahan was quickly translated into many languages, and in the German Navy the Kaiser made it compulsory reading. However, Mahan's theories were also traduced into the idea of a decisive battle between opposing fleets after which one side or the other would be left in command of the seas: this was a crude version of Mahanian theory.[14] Nevertheless, this misinterpretation of Mahan led the world's major navies to expect and to plan for a decisive battle and to ignore other aspects of naval warfare. Thus William Laird Clowes, historian of the Royal Navy, was inspired to complain in the foreword to his last volume of

> ... the frequency, previously unparalleled, with which the officers and men of the service [Navy], either with troops or alone, have been employed to do what should be purely landsmen's work, all over both hemispheres, sometimes fighting hundreds of miles from the sea – if the army, regular and irregular, were formed, organised, armed and stationed as it should be, the calls for the assistance of the Navy on shore would be fewer.[15]

However, while the Royal Navy was preparing for a new Trafalgar, it maintained the same aggressive spirit which had characterised naval operations in the Great War 1793-1815 and down through the nineteenth century. Only the scale and the technology of events were different in the First World War. For example, on Christmas Day 1914 the Navy formed the world's first ever aircraft-carrier battlegroup and with a force of just seven seaplanes raided airship hangars and ships at Cuxhaven: the results were not impressive but the ingenuity in mounting the attack was typical. Especially notable was the Navy's preparedness to employ the new-fangled seaplanes and submarines on such a daring raid. It might have been an exclusively Royal Navy affair, but one of the pilots was a Royal Marines officer.[16]

More typical of earlier operations but altogether on a larger scale were the naval operations at Antwerp, Gallipoli and on the Western Front. The term 'naval brigade' had always been loosely applied: it could be any size of force and was often applied to a force much smaller than the army would have graced with the title of brigade. However, in the First World War, there were so many men employed in brigades that they formed an entire division. Their history is summarised in a chapter of this book: it is perhaps sufficient to restate the stark fact 40 per cent of the Royal Navy's casualties in the First World War occurred not at sea but ashore in the Royal Naval Division.

In the inter-war years the view gained strength that there would and could be a decisive battle. Mackinder's theories of geostrategy, that industrialisation and especially the advent of the railway had reversed the historic advantage of maritime empires over continental ones, also gained ground. The distinction between the roles of navies, armies and latterly, air forces, was also growing. The several campaigns

For hundreds of years naval landing parties and soldiers were rowed ashore from ships and this method hardly changed, except for the introduction of steam pinnaces, until the development of specialised landing craft in the mid-twentieth century. The Navy also made itself useful by providing communications, such as this ship-to-shore telegraph at the landing at Trinkitat in the Sudan in 1884. (National Maritime Museum, London: Neg No 58/6164)

were considered quite separately and, in 1934, Admiral Professor Sir Herbert Richmond went so far as to say that major amphibious operations would be impossible.[17] If his words were judged by the fiasco of the campaign in Norway in 1940, no doubt he was right. This campaign had many of the hallmarks of previous operations of naval brigades: speed of response, ingenuity, improvisation, and great bravery. It was also the last occasion this author can detect when field guns, which for over a hundred years had formed part of the equipment of the Royal Navy's warships, were landed in earnest. It failed against the Germans who were using interior lines of communication and making effective use of their air force. However, the

Seapower Ashore

On the march to Oubat, Lord Charles Beresford (foreground) strikes an heroic pose on a donkey, while the sailors look more comfortable flying a White Ensign from their 'ships of the desert'. Animals in various naval brigades survived well, even having their saddle-sores treated with Stockholm tar. (National Maritime Museum, London: Neg No B410)

British and especially their American allies in the Second World War learned quickly, and the landings at Normandy and the Pacific War were to prove Richmond wrong. Finally the British returned to Walcheren, the scene of earlier disasters: the operation there in 1944 stands as a classic demonstration of its type, far removed from the bungling amateurism of Spring 1940.

However, in the ensuing Cold War (1945–89) strategy again tended to ossify. Even in the late 1980s a confrontation between superpowers seemed to be a permanent state of affairs, one which could only be broken by a decisive battle of unimaginably horrible scale and consequences. During the Cold War the US Navy developed a maritime strategy which can be interpreted, in a crude way, as Mahanian.[18] While ideas of decisive battle had been gaining ground, Julian Corbett had been teaching in the 1900s something rather different at the Royal Navy's War College at Greenwich. In his *Principles of Maritime Strategy*, Corbett recognised the primacy of politics in directing war and developing appropriate strategies.[19] He also distinguished between maritime strategy, the principles which govern a war in which the sea is a substantial factor, and

> naval strategy, that part of it [maritime strategy] which determines the movements of the fleet when maritime strategy has determined what part the fleet must play in relation to the action of the land forces.

Famously, he went on to say that

> since men live upon the land and not upon the sea, great issues between nations at war have always been decided – except in the rarest of cases – either by what your army can do against your enemy's territory and national life, or else by the fear of what the fleet makes it possible for your army to do.

It is not clear what Corbett's views would have been of naval brigades or the Navy taking quite such direct action as sending its sailors and marines hundreds of miles inland to help decide great issues between nations, but the Royal Navy today is very clearly Corbettian rather than Mahanian. Naturally the evolution in naval thought has been most marked and most fertile in the world's largest navy, where the influences on and the process of making strategy have been very well described in David Rosenberg's essay on making modern naval strategy.[20] The latest ideas were set out in two joint United States Navy/US Marine Corps in the early 1990s; *From the Sea – Preparing the Naval Service for the 21st Century* (1992) and its successor paper *Forward from the Sea* (1994). The former paper describes how, in the changed strategic environment, the attention of the US Navy and Marine Corps would shift towards littoral warfare and manoeuvre from the sea: the latter assesses the two Services' contribution to the totality of American armed power. These two

Tactical landings were difficult until recent times: here two 12-pounder field guns are broken down in order to fit into a cutter to be towed ashore by a steam pinnace, sometime in 1900. (National Maritime Museum, London: Neg No C7225/15)

American papers provide a high level concept compatible with the post-Cold War era from which strategy and then doctrine can be derived: they have also had a considerable influence on British naval thinking. In 1996 the then Commander-in-Chief Fleet, Admiral Abbott, argued that territorial defence was no longer necessary to Britain and Europe, who with allies in and out of NATO must now be ready to project visible and useable power in order to deter, dissuade, protect mutual interests and, if necessary, credibly coerce.[21]

In *Dimensions of Sea Power: Strategic Choice in the Modern World* I argued that the qualities and capabilities of a maritime strategy are particularly suitable for use in the unpredictable and confused situations which might threaten Britain's interests, whether these are vital, secondary or altruistic, and offer a high degree of political controllability and strategic choice.[22] Furthermore, Brigadier Fry, Royal Marines, has perceived broad and enduring rhythms of strategy, suggesting that Britain's declared foreign policy must be active and occasionally militant if it is to be relevant and credible. There is, he wrote, a growing consensus among professional military and defence academics that future operations are likely to be expeditionary, and that a 'maritime national strategy' is the appropriate response to the changed geopolitical environment.[23] This indeed is the strategy which has emerged afresh from the British government's latest review of defence, the Strategic Defence Review (1997-8).

At the end of this review, the then First Sea Lord, Admiral Sir Jock Slater, assessed the changes which have taken place since the end of the Cold War, identified how these had caught the grand strategic mood of the time, and described how the Royal Navy has responded to them with its concept of operations known as the Maritime Contribution to Joint Operations.[24] It does not take much effort of mind to see that, shorn of the modern language of doctrine, the operations described by the distinguished contributors to this book, and spanning the most recent 200 years of the Royal Navy's history, are one and the same in principle. HMS *Tigre*'s 24-pounders mounted on the walls of Acre and HMS *Splendid*'s cruise missiles fired from underwater differ only in technology.

But none of these ideas are new, having all been already outlined by Julian Corbett in his short preface to *The Successors of Drake*, as early as 1900.[25] Here he wrote '... The real importance of maritime power is its influence on military operations ... The direction of a great war can only be followed out in the mutual reaction of the two forces [the Army and the Navy] ... [there is] a point beyond which hostilities by naval action alone cannot advance ... [the successors of Drake] viewed the fleet, not as a separate entity, but as an integral part of one great force ...'. The Navy will fire cruise missiles rather haul

Seapower Ashore

Apart from their weapons, helmets and shorts, this group of sailors photographed in the Second World War is timeless. (National Maritime Museum, London: Neg No P39373)

its guns ashore in order to take part in this 'one great force', but in this sense the Royal Navy is all Corbettian now.

NOTES

1. For a recent account of this war see Tony Bridgland, *Field Gun Jack Versus the Boers: the Royal Navy in South Africa 1899-1900* (Barnsley 1998).
2. Percy Scott, *Fifty Years in the Royal Navy* (London 1919), p70. '... In the following year [1881] ... the committee [of the Naval Exhibition in London] accepted my proposal to bring 100 men up from *Excellent* and give a field gun display, such as is seen every year now at the Naval and Military Tournament'.
3. Scott, *Fifty Years in the Royal Navy*, pp46-57.
4. Vivian Stuart and George T Eggleston, *His Majesty's Sloop-of-War Diamond Rock* (Plymouth 1978).
5. Robert T Travers Young, *The House that Jack Built: the story of HMS Excellent* (Aldershot: Gale & Polden, 1955), p18.
6. Palmerston to Minto 17 Dec 1840: Minto Papers, National Maritime Museum, ELL/118.

7 Christopher Layne, 'British Grand Strategy, 1900-1939: theory and practice in international politics', *Journal of Strategic Studies* (1979), pxviii. Quoted in David French, *The British Way in Warfare 1688-2000* (London 1990). Specifically Layne was writing about a Britain and her relations with other European powers. Also Robert A Fry, 'The Future of the Maritime Contribution to Joint Operations', in Martin Edmonds and Humphry Crum Ewing (eds), *Maritime Forces in Peace & War: Joint & Combined Operations*, Bailrigg Paper 30 (Lancaster 1999), pp66-70. Or in other words '... holding someone else's coat while they go and do it [the British Way in Warfare] on our behalf'.

8 D Bonner Smith and A C Dewar (eds), *Russian War, 1854: Baltic and Black Sea* Navy Records Society, 83 (London 1943), p224.

9 A C Dewar (ed), *Russian War, 1855: Black Sea,* Navy Records Society, 85 (London 1945), pp7-9.

10 Bonner Smith and Dewar, *Russian War, 1854: Baltic and Black Sea,* p227.

11 Bonner Smith and Dewar, *Russian War, 1854: Baltic and Black Sea*.

12 Alfred T Mahan, *The Influence of Sea Power upon History 1660-1783* (Boston 1890).

13 Jon Tetsuro Sumida, *Inventing Grand Strategy and Teaching Command: the classic works of Alfred Thayer Mahan Reconsidered* (Baltimore 1997), p44. Selected quotation by Sumida from Mahan's *Sea Power in its Relation to the War of 1812*.

14 John Gooch, 'Maritime Command: Mahan and Corbett', in Colin S Gray and Roger W Barnett (eds), *Seapower and Strategy* (London 1989), pp27-46; Paul M Kennedy, 'British and American Strategies, 1898-1920', in *Maritime Strategy and the Balance of Power: Britain and American in the Twentieth Century* (Oxford 1989), pp165-88.

15 William Laird Clowes, *The History of the Royal Navy: From the Earliest Times to the Present Day* (London 1903), Vol VII, pvii. Though published in 1903, Laird Clowes concluded his seven volume history of the Royal Navy with the end of the Second Boer War 1899-1900.

16 R D Layman, *The Cuxhaven Raid: the World's First Carrier Air Strike* (London 1985).

17 H Richmond, *Sea Power in the Modern World* (London 1934), p173. '... an invasion by sea of a great modern military state may be dismissed as impracticable, even if there were no opposition at sea'. Richmond was actually discussing how far the submarine was 'an essential unit of naval forces'.

18 Norman Friedman, *The US Maritime Strategy* (London 1988). Friedman's book is a comprehensive study of the subject, which is brought up to date and developed by Stewart Fraser, *US Maritime Strategy: issues and implications*, Bailrigg Paper 25 (Lancaster 1997).

19 Julian S Corbett, *Some Principles of Maritime Strategy*, Classics of Sea Power edn, with an introduction and notes by Eric J Grove (Annapolis 1988), pp15-16.

20 David A Rosenberg, 'American Naval Strategy in the Era of the Third World War: an inquiry into the structure and process of general war at Sea, 1945-90', in N A M Rodger (ed), *Naval Power in the Twentieth Century* (London 1996), pp242-54. A longer version of this essay also appeared in James Goldrick and John B Hattendorf (eds), *Mahan is Not Enough: the proceedings of a conference on the works of Sir Julian Corbett and Admiral Sir Herbert Richmond* (Newport RI 1993).

21 Admiral Sir Peter Abbott, 'The Maritime Component of British and Allied Military Strategy', *Royal United Services Institute Journal* (December 1996), pp 6-11.

22 Eric Grove and Peter Hore (eds), *Dimensions of Sea Power: Strategic Choice in the Modern World* (Hull 1998), pp3-25.

23 Brigadier Rob Fry, 'End of the Continental Century', *Royal United Services Institute Journal*, Vol 143, no 3 (1998).

24 Admiral Sir Jock Slater, 'The Maritime Contribution to Joint Operations', *Royal United Services Institute Journal*, Vol 143, no 6 (1998).

25 Sir Julian S Corbett, *The Successors of Drake* (London 1900), ppvii-viii.

CHAPTER 1

Smith and the Siege of Acre 1799: Sea Power Decisive on Land

by Tom Pocock

The ringing of church bells, the firing of saluting guns throughout the British Isles and the drinking of toasts to Lord Nelson's victory at the Battle of the Nile expressed euphoria, relief and triumph. The invincible General Bonaparte had been defeated, his fleet destroyed and he and his army marooned in the deserts of Egypt.

Yet in France and, indeed, in Egypt, it was seen somewhat differently. The wars between Britain and Revolutionary and Napoleonic France were said to be a conflict between a whale and an elephant: to the British a victory at sea was decisive; to the French, it was what happened on land that mattered. Now, despite the wreckage in Aboukir Bay, the French army in Egypt was intact and victorious.

General Bonaparte was in Cairo and there with him, and on detachment up and down the Nile, was an army of some 35,000 trained, disciplined French soldiers. His victory over the Mameluke army at what became known as the Battle of the Pyramids had demonstrated that French tactics and fire-control could prevail against apparently overwhelming hordes of brave, indeed fanatical, warriors of the Ottoman Empire. It would be difficult to run reinforcements from France through the British blockade so his strength seemed finite; but his army could live off the land, recruit mercenaries, and his plans for the conquest of Egypt, and countries beyond, could continue. An advance on India, such as he had been considering, might be too demanding on his resources, but there were other options. One of these was to return to France overland, marching and fighting through the Ottoman Empire to Constantinople and thence to Vienna. Once the Turks and the Austrians had been subdued, France would be master of Continental Europe – for Prussia and Russia would surely be cowed – and Britain was only an offshore island. With land communications between France and the Levant secure, a new empire could be established by French armies in Africa and Asia to replace those lost to British sea power in the Caribbean and the Americas.

With satisfaction, Bonaparte could see that his most effective adversary, Admiral Nelson, was becoming embroiled, politically and personally, in Naples and Palermo. There was surely no other British commander – and it would have to be a naval officer because the British had so far failed dismally on land – whose genius for warfare and ruthless diplomacy could challenge his own. If Bonaparte considered other dangerous adversaries, the name that would surely have come to mind would have been that of Captain Sir Sidney Smith, but he had been imprisoned in Paris on a charge of espionage. Just before sailing from Toulon, he had heard that Smith had escaped from the Temple prison but he could hardly have guessed that he was already back in the Mediterranean and discussing with his brother Spencer Smith, the British minister in Constantinople, the most effective measures to be taken against the French in Egypt.

Bonaparte's mind was made up. The conquest of India would have to wait but he would return to France via Damascus, Constantinople and Vienna. In January, 1799, leaving about half his fighting soldiers in Egypt, he marched east and north into Syria with some 13,000 men in a balanced force, only his heavy artillery due to follow by sea, hugging the coast, for use in the sieges of the coastal fortress-cities of the Levant. The land forces opposing him would, he believed, be overcome as easily as he had defeated the Mameluke army. The Ottoman armies were brave and skilled in the use of personal arms but their tactics were limited to the simplicities of the charge, the ambush and defence to the last man; not for them the co-ordination of infantry, artillery and cavalry, or controlled, alternating volleys, one rank firing as the others reloaded, to produce a continuous hail of musketry.

It began as easily as expected with the capture of the fort at El Arish on the coast to the east of the Nile delta: the encampment stormed at night, the fort bombarded and its 3000 defenders killed or captured. There was one worrying development: the defenders were infected with bubonic plague, which might have been passed to the victors. On 24 February, Gaza fell without a fight and on 7 March it was the turn of Jaffa. The French artillery blew a practicable breach in the walls on the first day, it was stormed and the French indulged in the slaughter, sack and rape which the accepted rules of war allowed to be inflicted on a town so captured.

The next coastal city was Acre, originally fortified strongly by the Crusaders and likely to be a more formidable obstacle. But now the French were hampered and burdened by a shuffling column of about 3000 prisoners from El Arish, Gaza and Jaffa. A few had volunteered to fight for the French but the rest, were they to be released, would probably take up arms again; otherwise they would have to be fed and watered on the march. So Bonaparte took a decision that shocked his officers and infuriated the Islamic world: he ordered that all the prisoners be executed. This was done – first with musket-fire and then with bayonets – over two days on the beach outside Jaffa.

Bonaparte knew that Acre would be defended by the ferocious old Djezzar Pasha, the Ottoman governor of Syria, but, realising that he would soon hear of the massacre at Jaffa, sent him an ultimatum, threatening similar ruthlessness and adding, 'In a few days I shall march against Acre.' He did and on 15 March looked north from the summit of Mount Carmel to the long curving beach below, culminating with the walled city of Acre on its far headland. He also saw, anchored off the city, two ships of the line which could only be British. He did not know that they were commanded by an officer he had never met, but felt he knew: Commodore Sir Sidney Smith.

Aged thirty-four, Smith was six years younger than Nelson and, although the two shared remarkable similarities, there were also sharp differences. Both had original, lively minds and were brave, ambitious and vain; both had vivid, attractive characters, and both enjoyed dressing their slight build in theatrical uniforms. But while Nelson came from a family of country parsons, Smith's background was one of fast and fashionable living, tainted with extravagance and dis-

Captain (eventually Admiral) Sir Sidney Smith in the 1790s, wearing the star of his Swedish knighthood awarded for services as a naval mercenary in the Baltic. (National Maritime Museum, London: Neg No PU3516)

sipation. Yet the latter's enthusiasm for adventure, aided by quick wits and a flair for languages, had combined with his self-confidence to keep him at the cutting-edge of affairs. When his naval career flagged, he was off on some intelligence-gathering mission, or, memorably, serving as an unauthorised mercenary for Sweden in the war against Russia, when his feats in action won him a Swedish knighthood. This had caused resentment among his brother officers, Nelson mocking him as 'the Swedish Knight', a jibe which ceased when the latter himself accepted a Sicilian dukedom.

In 1796, Smith had been taken prisoner in a boat action off Le Havre, while involved in running Royalist agents into France. Treated as a spy rather than a prisoner of war he was held, under threat of execution, at the Temple prison in Paris. From there he wrote an open letter to General Bonaparte, whom he had opposed at the siege of Toulon three years earlier. Showing himself adept at psychological warfare, he had taunted the general, forecasting that the turn of fortune's wheel would bring triumph to himself and imprisonment to Bonaparte. Now Smith had been sent to the eastern Mediterranean both to support Nelson and act politically in concert with his brother Spencer, much to the annoyance of the former, who saw probable conflicts of interest aggravated by Smith's skill at playing one competing faction against another. 'He was ardent in his imagination and fluent in his speech', said one of Smith's friends. 'These are sometimes dangerous gifts.'

In October, 1798, he had been given command of the *Tigre* of 80 guns, from which to perform his dual naval and diplomatic role. He brought with him several French Royalist officers, who had helped him escape from Paris, including an engineer officer, Colonel Louis-Edmond Phélippeaux, and a British intelligence officer and linguist, Captain John Wright. In Constantinople, his diplomatic fluency had persuaded the Sultan to give him supreme command of all land and sea forces deployed against the French. So it was as an Ottoman commander, as well as a British naval officer and diplomat, that Commodore Smith had arrived off Acre in the spring of 1799.

Djezzar Pasha was aware that both Bonaparte and Smith were on their way. The latter had sent Captain Wright ahead to warn of the French approach and he had been followed Captain Ralph Miller – one of Nelson's 'Band of Brothers' at the Battle of the Nile – in the *Thesus* and Colonel Phélippeaux, the engineer. From them, Smith learned of the state of the defences at Acre. To defend the 15,000 inhabitants within the city, were crumbling medieval walls and towers, upon which were mounted a few old cannon, and a motley collection of some 4000 fighting men of most Middle Eastern and African types. These would stand little chance against a French army, which would be more than doubled by the addition of Druze tribesmen, whose services had been promised once Acre had been taken. As for Djezzar himself, they reported that despite his nickname 'The Butcher', he seemed more interested in preserving his wives and concubines from the invaders, than his city.

Smith at once went ashore, taking with him the first of 800 marines and seamen, who were to land some of the ships' guns, repair the defences, stiffen the resolve of the defenders and fight alongside them. Smith and his officers cannot have been what Djezzar expected. Some, including Smith himself, had grown moustaches, curling *à la Turque*, while he and several others, notably, Wright, spoke fluent French and some Arabic; instead of presenting themselves at a formal audience with the Pasha, they joined him on the piles of cushions in his palace to smoke the hookah, the long Turkish pipes. Two days after his arrival, Smith was writing to the Commander-in-Chief, Lord St. Vincent that 'the presence of a British naval force appeared to encourage and decide the Pasha and his troops to make a vigorous resistance.'

He had something else of significance to report. A few nights before, he had intercepted a French convoy off Haifa: it had been loaded with Bonaparte's siege artillery and this was already being mounted on the walls of Acre. Two French coasters had escaped into Haifa and a British attempt to cut them out had failed with heavy loss, yet that was of little consequence compared with the capture of the siege train. When this was reported to Bonaparte, he was also told that British prisoners had named the senior British officer at Acre as being the same officer who had forecast the reversal of their fortunes from a cell in Paris.

Preparing to defend Acre. Captain Smith's ship, the *Tigre*, off the fortified port which commanded the French army's route from Egypt through the Ottoman Empire to Europe. (National Maritime Museum, London: Neg No B204)

Smith deployed his forces: some 800 marines and seamen to man guns on the walls; each ship of the line to anchor so that her broadside could command the shore on either flank of the city; and gunboats and ships' boats armed with carronades to harass the enemy approaching by the coastal road. Bonaparte was deploying his forces, too. Although he had lost his heavy guns, his 12-pounder field-guns should be able to blow a breach in the old walls, which could then be stormed by his grenadiers.

On 26 March, while he watched from a hillock known as King Richard Coeur de Lion's Mount, his batteries opened fire. The 12-pound roundshot were enough to batter a breach and, although, under the direction of Smith and Phélippeaux, this was blocked with baulks of timber and more guns dragged forward to cover it,

Bonaparte decided it could soon be stormed. Two days later, at dawn, another bombardment was concentrated upon the breach, Bonaparte studied it through his telescope and gave the order for the assault.

Carrying scaling-ladders, French sappers raced forward, followed by 20 companies of grenadiers commanded by the tall, leonine Marshal Kléber; behind them massed infantry braced themselves to follow. Only as they neared the walls did the French see the dry moat at their foot, so deep that their ladders could not reach the ramparts. They tried to scramble up to the breach but were beaten back by grapeshot, musketry and hurled rocks. A bugle sounded the retreat and the survivors streamed back to their lines, leaving the moat littered with dead. 'This was the day', noted a despondent French officer, 'that Acre should have fallen.'

British officers, guns' crews and marines deployed along the walls had indeed stiffened the undisciplined raggle-taggle, giving them confidence by their calm efficiency and also determination to prove themselves as their pride was at stake. British humour – albeit gallows humour – added further confidence, as when a seaman clambered down into the moat to bury a French general, who had been killed below the walls, first shaking the corpse's hand and then, amiably but without mockery, bowing towards the French entrenchments.

Smith's control over his allies and their commander was light enough. At the end of March, a gale forced his ships to run for shelter in the lee of Mount Carmel, leaving Acre under the sole command of Djezzar. Another French attack was repelled but, in the absence of heavy naval guns to provide flanking fire from the sea, the besiegers were able to extend their trenches and saps to within half a pistol-shot of the walls. Djezzar responded by ordering that all French prisoners, including the officer who had delivered Bonaparte's ultimatum under a flag of truce, be tied in pairs, thrust into sacks and flung into the sea.

When Smith was able to return with his two ships and resume control, he found that the French were trying to drive a mine beneath the keystone of the city's defences, the Devil's Tower, and he ordered a sortie to destroy it. It succeeded, the British entering the mine to pull down the timber props so that the roof caved in, but their loss was severe. His marines and seamen had performed doughtily but there were few of them and he urgently sought reinforcements.

They came from east and west. Both he and Bonaparte heard that the Sultan had ordered an army some 20,000 strong to march from Damascus to the relief of Acre but only Smith knew that another Turkish army was on its way by sea from Rhodes. For the French, a new siege-train was making its way from Egypt, avoiding Smith's ships by being landed at Jaffa and hauled overland. While awaiting heavy guns, Bonaparte decided to deal with the threat from Damascus, sent a strong force under Kléber to meet it and, after a day-long struggle, won a decisive victory in what became known as the Battle of Mount Tabor. Soon after the whole French army reassembled before Acre, the siege-guns arrived.

French casualties had been heavy but the British suffered, too, notably with the deaths of three important officers: Colonel Phélippeaux, whose military engineering skills had been so effective, died of heat exhaustion; Major Thomas Oldfield, who commanded the marines in the *Theseus*, was killed leading the sortie that destroyed the French mine; and Captain Ralph Miller was killed by an accidental explosion in the same ship.

Smith himself was the key to the defence. Not only was he on the walls when a French assault was expected, galvanising the defenders and the Pasha, but again proved himself a master of psychological warfare. When Bonaparte prepared leaflets for distribution to the Moslem and Christian inhabitants of the Levant, promising each that he was their champion against the other, Smith turned the tables. Acquiring copies of both, he had more printed then reversed their distribution so that Moslems read that Bonaparte was a Christian champion and the Christians, a Moslem. Furiously, Bonaparte made wild accusations against Smith, accusing him – without evidence – of atrocities against prisoners and of being insane.

Now reinforcements had arrived from Rhodes and, before they could be landed at Acre, Bonaparte made frantic efforts to storm the defences. The main breach was now wider so that new tactics had to be devised to make fullest use of the Turks' fierce, if uncontrolled, courage. While Smith directed fire from the walls, the Pasha sat in his palace to exchange handfuls of ammunition for severed French heads. The storming parties were allowed to pour through the breach into the gardens of the seraglio beyond; once inside, they were cut off and slaughtered. This Smith described in a colourful mixed metaphor: 'We keep the bull penned and compare our breach to a mouse-trap.'

Smith had always been aware of the consequences of success or failure at Acre and that, when the outcome was decided, 'Constantinople and even Vienna must feel the shock.' Even after the Turkish reinforcements had been landed, Bonaparte remained determined, declaring, 'If I succeed ... I shall overturn the Turkish Empire and found in the east a new and grand empire that will fix my place in the records of posterity. Perhaps I shall return to Paris ... by Vienna after annihilating the House of Austria.'

Again Smith taunted him, writing in French to say that he knew of a secret French mission to Constantinople to discuss possible terms for a French evacuation of Egypt. 'I did not want to ask you the question, "Are the French willing to leave Syria?" before you had a chance to match your strength against ours since you could not be persuaded, as I am, of the impracticability of your enterprise ... But now you can see that [this city] becomes stronger each day instead of being weakened by two months of siege, I do ask you this, "Are you willing to evacuate your troops from the territory of the Ottoman Empire before the intervention of the great allied army changes the nature of the question?"' He had gently presented the crux of his strategy: so long as Acre survived it could be the beachhead from which an allied expeditionary force could be landed to take any further French advance in the rear.

The day after Bonaparte read this letter, he ordered another assault, the eleventh, on the walls. It began at 3am on 10 May. 'The grenadiers rushed forward under a shower of balls', recalled a French officer. 'Kléber, with the gait of a giant, with his thick head of hair, has taken his post, sword in hand, on the bank of the breach and animated the assailants. The noise of the cannon, the enthusiastic shouts, the range of the soldiers and the yelling of the Turks mingled themselves with the bursts of his thundering voice.'

Leading from the front. Captain Sir Sidney Smith rallying the defenders of a breach in the walls of Acre against repeated massed assaults by the French. (National Maritime Museum, London: PAD 5622)

Again the French erupted through the breach and almost broke out of the seraglio garden and into the city streets but again they were stopped. The assault was repeated that afternoon and, this time, it was halted when the defenders exploded a huge mine in the breach: 'the soldiers were stopped, the ditch was vomiting out flames ... and overthrew everyone ... Kléber, in a great rage, struck his thigh with his sword; but the General-in-Chief, judging the obstacle to be insurmountable, gave a gesture and ordered a retreat.'

Smith sensed that this was Bonaparte's final attempt, for almost half his army was out of action, either killed, wounded, or suffering from heat-exhaustion or the plague that had begun to infect it at El Arish. He wrote again, 'General, I am acquainted with the dispositions that for some days past you have been making to raise the siege; the preparations in hand to carry off your wounded ... do you credit.' Then he returned to psychological warfare to recall the prophesy he himself had made when his prisoner in Paris. 'Could you have thought that a poor prisoner in the Temple prison ... could have compelled you in the midst of the sands of Syria to raise the siege of a miserable, almost defenceless, town? Such events, you must admit, exceed all human calculations ... Asia is not a theatre made for your glory. This letter is a little revenge that I give myself.'

Stung with humiliation, Bonaparte ordered his guns to shift their targets from the walls to the city beyond to take what revenge he could. Retreat was now the only option but he could not bring himself to ask Smith for permission, let alone help, to evacuate his wounded by sea. In a final conference, he asked his senior officers for their own opinions and Kléber replied, 'General, I liken the town of Acre to a piece of cloth. When I go to the merchant to buy it, I ask to feel it; I look at it, I touch it and, if I find it too dear, I leave it.'

The French would now leave Acre, Bonaparte's dreams in ashes, and, on 20 May, they could be seen forming columns and marching south towards Egypt. Commodore Smith returned to his ship and wrote to Nelson, his immediate superior, 'My Lord, the Providence of almighty God has been wonderfully manifest in the defeat and precipitate retreat of the French army; the means we had of opposing its gigantic efforts against us being totally inadequate of themselves to the production of such a result ... The plain of Nazareth has been the boundary of Bonaparte's extraordinary career.'

Nelson at once changed his opinion of Smith, realising that he had not only completed his own achievement at the Battle of the Nile but, with only two ships of the line, had achieved a victory to be measured in terms of the grandest grand strategy. Six years later, he was to invite Smith to command his inshore squadron off Cadiz, the invitation arriving too late because the Battle of Trafalgar had been fought before he could take it up; a week after the victory his friend, Captain John Wright, who had, like Smith before him, been taken prisoner while running agents into France, was murdered in the Temple prison but on whose orders remains unknown. General Bonaparte was to remain haunted by Smith and, when, as the former Emperor Napoleon, he was staring at the South Atlantic horizon from exile on St Helena, he was to say of him, 'That man cheated me of my destiny.'

BIBLIOGRAPHY

Manuscript sources
A small archive of Smith papers are at the National Maritime Museum and references can also be found in the Admiralty, War Office and Foreign Office collections at the Public Record Office.

Published sources
John Barrow, *The Life and Correspondence of Admiral Sir Sidney Smith*, 2 vols (London 1848)

General Alexandre Berthier, *The French Expedition into Syria* (London 1799)

J Christopher Herold, *Bonaparte in Egypt* (London 1963)

The Hon. Edward Howard, *Memoirs of Sir Sidney Smith* (London 1849)

William James, *The Naval History of Great Britain*, 5 vols (London 1822-4)

G S Parsons, *Nelsonian Reminiscences* (London 1905)

Tom Pocock, *A Thirst for Glory: The Life of Admiral Sir Sidney Smith* (London 1996)

Lord Russell, *Knight of the Sword: The Life and Letters of Admiral Sir William Sidney Smith* (London 1964)

Peter Shankland, *Beware of Heroes: Admiral Sir Sidney Smith against Napoleon* (London 1975)

Elizabeth Sparrow, *Secret Service: British Agents in France 1792-1815* (London 1999)

CHAPTER 2

'Science and Labour'. The Naval Contribution to Operations Ashore in the Great Wars with France 1793-1815
by Michael Duffy

Throughout British history the State has maintained only a small military strike force. Fear of the political dangers of a large standing army after the experience of the 'Roundheads' and the rule of the Major-Generals in the 1650s, together with the availability of an alternative naval means for the defence of the British Isles, has meant that Britain has never been able to produce an army to match Continental opponents at the start of any war. In 1789 it had 40,000 troops at home and scattered in garrisons across its far-flung empire, at a time when France had 170,000. While Britain could expand its field army during war, rising to 130,000 in 1803 and to 250,000 in 1813-14, France expanded its army to over 600,000. Moreover, existing imperial commitments and the restricted availability of shipping for transport meant that a normal large-sized expedition was confined to 10-15,000 troops as a first lift, and many expeditions were smaller, at around the 5000 level. Even at their biggest, on shores opposite to the home islands from whence they could be easiest sustained, the British regular armies with Wellington in the Peninsula or at Walcheren in 1809 were no larger than 40-45,000 men. In these circumstances governments and army commanders alike readily looked to supply manpower needs of the army ashore by assistance from a navy expanded from 20,000 men in 1792 to over 142,000 in 1810.

With complements of 600 men for the workhorse 74-gun ships of the line, 220 for 32-gun frigates, and 125 for 16-gun sloops, the naval squadrons which accompanied expeditionary forces had both manpower and artillery available to assist in shore operations, particularly if there was no local enemy squadron to fight. Their marines were a trained reinforcement to the troops of the line, and indeed, early in the Great War with France at Toulon in 1793 and in Corsica in 1794, were sometimes line regiments which had been turned over to the fleet to act as marines and enable its more rapid mobilisation. When General Sir Ralph Abercromby could land only 13,400 infantry in Egypt in 1801, Admiral Lord Keith promised him a battalion of 500 marines from his fleet.[1] Seamen were also employed as substitute infantry, but they had clear limitations to their performance in this role. Such service was not part of their formal training. On at least some long-distance overseas expeditions, careful commanders had the foresight to exercise companies for shore duty during the voyage, as did Admiral Sir John Jervis for the West Indian expedition of 1793-4. When they reached Carlisle Bay, Barbados, they were further landed and trained in the use of small arms and pikes.[2] It was a water-borne naval assault on the seaward defences that decided the siege of Fort Royal, Martinique, in March 1794. The storming of Fort Fleur d'Épée on Guadeloupe in April revealed one problem of such joint assaults, when red-coated light-infantrymen mistook a blue-jacketed sailor hauling down the French colours for a Frenchman and bayoneted him. At the assault on the Fourneille redoubt on Corsica in February 1794, the naval contingent followed the redcoats with entrenching tools.[3]

Moreover, seamen were frequently called upon for such assistance in emergency circumstances in which they had not received infantry training. Consequently while they excelled in actions comparable to their sea-service, such as storming or defending fortifications, they were unsuited to field operations as infantry. As Captain Crawford RN later reminisced:

> Few men, if any, are to be preferred to sailors at a rush or an assault, when headlong impetuosity and daring courage are required; but take them out of their ships, and marshal them on shore, and they will be found restless and unsteady, and particularly impatient of inactivity.[4]

They had no march-discipline. Of 300 seamen who set out on a four-mile march through difficult terrain for a night attack on Point-à-Pitre, Guadeloupe, on 1 July 1794, only thirty could be immediately mustered when called to go into action in support of the light infantry at 4.00am next morning. Nor did they have formation-discipline. When a force of 350 seamen and 250 marines landed in an operation to capture a French convoy and its escorts at Palamos on the north-eastern coast of Spain in 1810, it quickly cleared the 150-strong French garrison from the port to a neighbouring hill and formed in ranks at the foot of the hill to protect the removal of the convoy by the boats of the squadron. The seamen then, however, began to straggle from the ranks, 'first in ones and twos, and then in greater numbers' into the town, whereupon the French commander, reinforced, counter-attacked the diminished line and drove them into their boats with a loss of nearly a third of the landing force killed, wounded and prisoners.[5]

Raids such as that at Palamos represent perhaps the most common naval shore operation of the period - a landward extension of the Navy's traditional cutting-out operations against merchantmen or isolated warships sheltering in a protected harbour. Usually the landing force was sent to take out a covering shore battery and encountered a few poorly-trained and easily frightened-off local militia rather than the larger numbers of disciplined regulars at Palamos. Sometimes the Navy was drawn into a more extensive shore commitment because the superior mobility of its patrolling warships enabled them to discover and reinforce threatened coastal strongpoints far more quickly than the army. On such occasions, whether combating French-inspired insurrection in the Caribbean or supporting Spanish insurgents against the French along the Catalan coast, reinforcement of the local defenders by marines and seamen, as well as covering fire for shore defences from the warship's guns, could make a major difference. Lord Cochrane's account of his defence of Rosas in Catalonia in 1808 remains a classic description of what naval manpower and ingenuity could contribute to such resistance.[6] Naval expertise with explosives could also be put to good account. Cochrane delayed the French advance on Barcelona in 1808 by landing parties of seamen from the frigate *Imperieuse* to blow down overhanging rocks and destroy bridges along the coastal road.[7]

On major expeditions the first contribution of the Navy was to provide fire-support from the guns of the escorting squadron for a contested landing. While the heavy guns of the ships of the line and frigates would be employed to take on shore batteries, sloops, bomb-vessels and gunboats were brought in close to sweep the beaches, before ships' boats and flat-bottomed landing craft pushed for the shore. Such a bombardment might include Congreve rockets – the Navy was using ship-to-shore rockets from as early as 1805 when it launched them at the invasion barges assembled at Boulogne. With ships' launches equipped with carronades, this fire-support could be brought right up to the shoreline.[8]

Once ashore, there was an immediate need to seize a fortified port or harbour as a safe supply base and to eliminate the principle enemy strongpoint. In this type of operation the Navy had a particular role which was made the more necessary by the army's inability (for reasons of precious shipping space) to transport large numbers of draught horses. While 20,000 infantry could be sent to Hanover on 30,000 tons of shipping in 1805, 2000 cavalry required 16,000 tons and 1500 artillerymen and their horses 10,000 tons.[9] For longer distances the problem was even more acute: the Egyptian expedition landed 630 artillerymen with only 173 horses in 1801.[10] Moreover, sometimes horses were unable to cope with the difficult terrain frequently encountered. On some expeditions up to half of ships' companies were consequently allocated to logistical support, including haulage, of the troops ashore. To support the 16,000-strong expeditionary force in Egypt in 1801, Lord Keith allocated 820 seamen as boats' crews and reliefs, and 545 as work parties ashore. These amounted to 40 per cent of the complements of five of his seven ships of the line (the other two blockaded Alexandria harbour), in addition to the 500-strong marine contingent he supplied. Within weeks over two-thirds of his crews were sucked into the shore operation.[11] Usually the main naval task ashore was to manhandle the essential heavy artillery. As another contemporary participant, Captain Edward Brenton RN, later recalled:

> In all conjoint expeditions of the army and navy the landing and transporting of cannon is performed by the seamen, after which the artillery officers mount the guns and complete the batteries.[12]

Frequently the accompanying squadron was required to provide the heavy guns needed, either in their entirety or more usually to supplement the army's own siege train. For the siege of Fort Royal, Martinique, in 1794, Sir John Jervis's crews pulled up seventy heavy cannon and their ammunition.[13] On occasion, in default of sufficient artillerymen to operate the available heavy firepower, they also had to provide seamen to serve the guns. This latter requirement was one in which seamen gunners did need close supervision by Royal Artillery officers, for they were trained to fire off broadsides as quickly as possible, which was not what was required in siege warfare. In the latter, ammunition could not be quickly brought up by powder-monkeys from the ship's magazine, but had to be hauled to the batteries under great difficulty over long supply lines, and the need was for sustained, accurate, deliberate shooting to bring down curtain walls. At the siege of Fort Bourbon, Martinique, in March 1794, the naval battery shot away all its ammunition on the first day of the bombardment![14]

In the event, the main surprise weapon that the Navy brought to combined operations ashore was less its manpower or its firepower, than its expertise at haulage – something for which its crews were fully trained! This gave the attackers the ability to get their guns to places thought largely inaccessible by defenders used to more conventional military capabilities in siege warfare. As Captain Brenton commented on the capture of the outer defences of San Fiorenzo, Corsica, which led to fall of that town in February 1794: 'The mountains which overlooked this post were deemed by many to be inaccessible, and probably few but Englishmen would have attempted to place guns in such a situation.'[15] The capture of the port was necessary as the base for the conquest of Corsica. It was defended by a redoubt at Fourneille which was exposed to fire from a steep, rocky height between 600 and 700 yards away. The army experts, Major Koehler of the Royal Engineers and Colonel John Moore, believed that if a couple of 18-pounder guns could be mounted there

Sailors from the Mediterranean Fleet land their guns in Mortella Bay, on the west coast of Corsica, in 1794. The terrain looks easy, but General Dundas said 'it was childish stuff to talk of getting cannon there'. In the background is the famous Mortella tower, the model for many similar towers erected a few years later around the south and east coasts of Britain. (National Maritime Museum, London: Neg No B1894)

then no one could live in the redoubt, and they turned to the Navy for help. Moore recorded in his diary: 'It was resolved to make the trial, and by force of tackle joined to the exertions of the sailors from the men of war, two 18-pounders and one 8-inch howitzer were dragged up a steep rock and mounted in the course of two days.'[16] The incredulous French garrison shortly surrendered. After the town fell, the diplomat Sir Gilbert Elliot described what had happened to his wife.

> I went the other day to see the road by which they carried cannon to the top of a high hill, in order to attack the French battery on the heights of Fornalli. General Dundas, and indeed many other people, said it was childish stuff to talk of getting cannon there – it actually seems impossible. But Captain Cook of the Navy, with 200 seamen, carried up four 18-pounders and two mortars, and opened the battery in two days; if this had not been done, we should not have taken San

Fiorenzo. The distance about a mile, the ground very steep and rough, considerably steeper than the green face of the craigs [the Minto Crags] leading to the castle from the new strip near the mill, and it is infinitely rougher with rocks and underwood. They fastened great straps round the rocks, and then fastened to the straps the largest and most powerful purchases or pulleys and tackle that are used on board a man-of-war. The cannon were placed on a sledge at one end of the tackle, the men walked down hill with the other end of the tackle. The surprise of our friends the Corsicans and our enemies the French was equal on this occasion. The battery played four days on the French redoubt on the heights of Fornalli before it was stormed; during this time Captain Cook and the seamen and several officers and soldiers slept in holes in the rocks.[17]

In his victory despatch, General Dundas paid full tribute to the Navy's efforts: 'In four days by the most surprising exertions of science and labour, they placed four 18-pounders, a large howitzer and a 10-in mortar, on ground elevated 700 ft above the level of the sea, and where every difficulty of ascent and surface opposed their undertaking.'[18]

The difficulties were considered even greater at the subsequent siege of Bastia, when Nelson supervised the naval support with 250 seamen alongside 1200 troops, but again the work was performed in erecting batteries in the most advantageous situations.[19] The journal entries in Nelson's *Dispatches and Letters* give a good indication of the tasks on which his seamen were employed. Landing on 4 April 1794, the seamen and carpenters spent the first night cutting down trees to form an *abatis*, and also clearing the ground by which the French could easiest approach the British camp. From the 4th to the 10th 'all the Seamen were employed making batteries and roads, and in getting up guns, mortars, platforms, and ammunition; works of great labour for so small a number of men, but which was performed with an activity seldom exceeded.' The bombardment was begun on the 11th with two 13in and two 10in mortars, an 8in howitzer, five 24-pounders, two 18-pounder carronades, three 12-pounders and a 4-pounder field piece. From the 13th until the 21st they were employed in getting up guns, mortars, shells, shot, powder, and platforms, and in making batteries as well as a breast-work to cover a hundred men in

Captain William Hoste: general, admiral, governor, engineer and complete 'jack of all trades'.
(National Maritime Museum, London: Neg No A5051)

case of attack. On 27 April a battery was begun on a ridge close to the town for two 18-pounder carronades and a 12-pounder. 'The labour of getting up guns to this battery was a work of the greatest difficulty, and which never, in my opinion, would have been accomplished by any other than British seamen.' While building another between the 3rd and 7th May, the seamen 'always slept on the battery with their pikes and cutlasses' in anticipation of threatened enemy attack. On 19 May the French garrison sought surrender terms. Nelson claimed victory for what 'truly, ... has been a Naval Expedition: our Boats prevented anything from getting in by Sea, and our Sailors hauling up great guns, and then fighting them on shore.'[20]

The topography was just as difficult in the assault on the main French strongpoint, the Morne Fortune, on St Lucia in the West Indies in 1796, where Admiral Christian supplied an initial 300 seamen to support General Abercromby's 13,000 troops. As the attack bogged down, he provided a further 500. Captain Lasalle de Louisenthal of the German mercenary regiment, Loewenstein's Chasseurs, described what happened: 'Up to then, nothing had happened which allowed us to encircle the Morne Fortune or to attack it completely. We had just taken the hill of Jonas which is only separated from the Morne Fortune by a flat ridge.' It was decided to make the attack from this high point. 'To put cannons in place it was necessary to raise them to a great height. It was necessary then to bring munitions, shells and balls, after that howitzers and mortars. All this on a man's back. This absolutely impossible labour was carried out by the English sailors. They compelled admiration. The naval officers encouraged them by promising them that they would have the right to be the first to raise the British colours.' The batteries opened fire on 16 May and the fortress fell on the 25th.[21]

Perhaps the most extraordinary example of this facility of the Navy to get guns to places where no-one expected them took place at the end of 1813 in the Adriatic. On this occasion the naval squadron, commanded by Captain William Hoste RN of the frigate *Bacchante*, had only a company of British soldiers with them, and was operating in support of rebel Pandoors and Montenegrans against the French garrisons along the coast of Dalmatia. On this occasion, too, the Navy not only provided the shore firepower but also directed and manned the bombardment themselves. In December 1813 Hoste reconnoitred Cattaro (Kotor). The topography of the Dalmatian mainland was not dissimilar to that he had encountered as captain's servant with his patron Nelson in Corsica in 1794. Hoste described himself as 'sent ... here to take a very strong place without the means of doing it',[22] but he improvised from his Corsican experience. Cattaro was overlooked by the adjacent Mount Theodore, and Hoste decided to form a battery on its summit of two long 18-pounders and two 11in mortars, for which purpose on 14 December he landed 54 officers and men with the guns, stores, pulleys and tackle. From the summit it would be possible to lob shot and shells into a town protected at sea-level by 30-foot thick walls. The French garrison commander, General Gauthier, was confident that the height and precipitous and rugged nature of the mountain were so difficult that relief would reach him before a battery could be erected there and oblige him to surrender.

On the first day one gun was raised 400 yards up the mountain and another 440 yards next day. The task was immensely difficult since the surface boulders proved too loose to support the purchase-strops, so that grooves had to be cut in the solid rock outcrop to provide purchase. This however threatened to slow the whole operation, so on the 16th the gun was hauled up by means of a kedge anchor, placed in position and then buried in heaps of the abundant boulders scattered around. On that day it was raised another 300 yards. Personally superintended and encouraged by Hoste, constantly wet from driving wind and torrential rain, and with their shoes torn to pieces by the rocky soil, the seamen finally got their first gun on the summit on 20 December, while other work-parties were constantly employed in carrying up shot, shell, powder casks, and filling sand-bags to form batteries. By the 25th the battery of two 18-pounders and two 11in mortars on Mount Theodore were ready to open fire, along with a 12-pounder carronade and a mortar to the north-west of Cattaro, a 12-pounder carronade to the south-east, and rockets on Mount St Elvies. For the next ten days the town was bombarded, with still more guns being brought up from the frigates and brought

Early 'cruise missiles': rocket boats as proposed by Colonel Congreve and used against the Boulogne flotilla in 1805. Naval brigades would carry these weapons and their launch tubes far inland. (National Maritime Museum, London: Neg No B3735)

into action. With fire raining on him from places above which had been thought inaccessible and consequently against which no protection had been built, the French general was seen 'conveying the powder himself from a magazine, which was not bomb-proof, for fear of rockets'. On 4 January Gauthier asked for a cease-fire and on the 6th surrendered with his surviving 297-strong garrison, complaining of Hoste's 'most unmilitary way of proceeding.'[23] From the landing of the guns to their re-embarkation and Hoste's departure for his next target took exactly five weeks. 'Thus', commented Hoste's chaplain, 'was performed, to the astonishment of friends and foes, a labour deemed impracticable by the French general, and with the loss of only one seaman.'[24]

From Cattaro, Hoste proceeded to the immensely strong fortress-port of Ragusa (Dubrovnik) which was surrounded by Austrian and renegade Croat troops who were short of heavy artillery. Arriving on 19 January, he again looked for commanding heights on which to place batteries, finally determining to place two mortars to the north of the city and two 18-pounders up on the 1200-foot high Mount Sergius to the south-east. Since the French Fort Imperial commanded the direct route to his intended battery, he was obliged to get

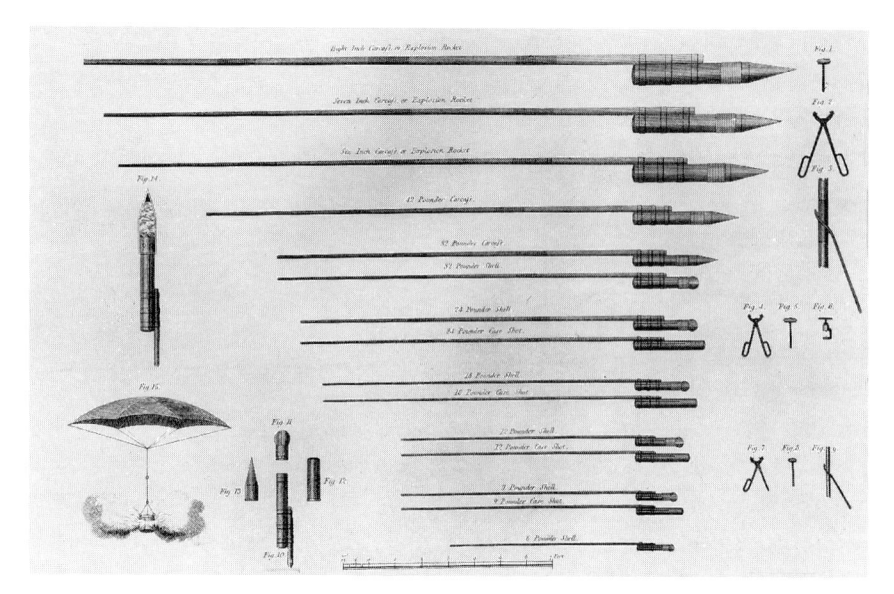

Congreve rockets: the range of weapons proposed by Colonel Congreve. (National Maritime Museum, London: Neg No B3737)

his cannon into place via a circuitous six-mile route round the back of the mountain, for two miles of which he took advantage of an aqueduct which supplied the city with water: this he cut and drained and then used its precarious eight-foot wide course as a road. The first 18-pounder was landed on 21 January and the two guns were in place and ready to open fire on the 27th, when the demoralised French offered to capitulate after the first few ranging shots. Every shot from Hoste's battery would bring down houses, while they were unable to reply. One hundred and fifty-one cannon and 360 troops, provisioned for six weeks, were surrendered for the naval loss of one seaman killed and two badly wounded. Hoste, a naval captain who described himself in these operations as 'general, admiral, governor, engineer, and complete jack of all trades',[25] received an English baronetcy and the Austrian Order of Maria Theresa for his exploits.

What the Navy could supply to shore operations therefore was mobility to and along coasts by ship, and mobility on shore by means of the haulage 'science and labour' of its seamen. In this way it was responsible for much of the heavy firepower of overseas expeditions, both by shore bombardment from sea and by the ability of its seamen to take heavy artillery where no-one else could, and then use it. The Navy further supplied much of the shore logistics for expeditionary armies until they acquired their own store bases and transport. The Navy was used to shore raiding and ready to provide infantry manpower to an expeditionary force when necessary (which was frequently the case), though in this it was much more effective at close-quarters fighting, especially in storming or defending fortified positions, rather than in field manoeuvres. Was there also a psychological contribution to shore operations? All army observers commented on the energy and enthusiasm of the sailors engaged in shore operations. The novelty of acting beyond their element may have contributed to some of the enthusiasm, but the energy perhaps betokens a more active work discipline on a warship than in an army regiment. In operations ashore, as Crawford commented, sailors were impatient of inactivity. When undertaken by an energetic captain such as Cochrane or Hoste, or pressed by an energetic Admiral such as Lord Hood on Corsica in 1794, this could lead to unexpectedly greater results than the normal military mind might have contemplated. However, impetuosity could also lead to disaster. Hood engaged the army in a hopeless defence of Toulon in 1793, and even Nelson came to grief in his assault on Tenerife in 1797. But even in defeat the Navy was only occasionally unable to get the army off again. The evacuation of an entire army and its equipment in a hurry was the most difficult task of all that the Navy had to perform. The loss of most of an émigré force at Quiberon Bay in 1795 was its worst disaster, and a Guards brigade surrendered when rough seas prevented its withdrawal after a raid on Ostend in 1798, while capitulations were arranged at Tenerife in 1797, the Helder in Holland in 1799 and at Buenos Ayres in 1807 (all permitted the British forces to leave unmolested in return for concessions).[26] Yet at Toulon in 1793, Puerto Rico in 1797, and Corunna in 1809 the Navy was spectacularly successful in achieving evacuations with the enemy in close proximity, and in southern Italy twice in 1806, in Egypt in 1807, and at Walcheren in 1809 the Navy brought off the army when required. Therein, perhaps, was the ultimate confidence-giving boost to expeditionary operations ashore.

NOTES

1. Lord J Dunfermline, *Lt Gen Sir Ralph Abercromby ...A Memoir* (Edinburgh 1861), p273.
2. M Duffy, *Soldiers, Sugar and Seapower. The British Expeditions to the West Indies and the War against Revolutionary France* (Oxford 1987), p61.
3. Duffy, *Soldiers, Sugar and Seapower*, pp86, 94; Sir J F Maurice (ed), *The Diary of Sir John Moore* (London 1904), Vol 1, p59.
4. Captain A Crawford RN, *Reminiscences of a Naval Officer* (1851, new ed. London 1999), p213.
5. Duffy, *Soldiers, Sugar and Seapower*, p123; Crawford, *Reminiscences*, pp212-14.
6. Duffy, *Soldiers, Sugar and Seapower*, pp141, 302; Thomas, Earl of Dundonald, *The Autobiography of a Seaman* (London 1908), pp147-86. See also Codrington's account of his operations along the Catalan coast in 1810-12 in Lady Bourchier (ed), *Memoir of the Life of Admiral Sir Edward Codrington* (London 1873), Vol 1, pp185-307.
7. Dundonald, *Autobiography*, pp144-7. Sometimes the expertise went awry. Captain Hoste lost his marine lieutenant who blew himself up by firing the train instead of the port-fire when demolishing a watch-tower on the Dalmatian Coast in 1813: Lady Harriet Hoste (ed), *Memoirs and Letters of Sir William Hoste* (London 1833), Vol 2, p213.
8. W E May, *The Boats of Men of War* (London 1974, repr. 1999), pp113-15. For an excellent account of one contested landing see P Mackesy, *British Victory in Egypt, 1801* (London 1995), Ch.6.
9. C D Hall, *British Strategy in the Napoleonic War 1803-1815* (Manchester 1992), p46.
10. Dunfermline, *Abercromby ...A Memoir*, p273
11. Mackesy, *British Victory in Egypt*, pp46, 80-1.
12. E P Brenton, *The Naval History of Great Britain* (London 1837) Vol 1, p304.
13. Mackesy, *British Victory in Egypt*, p46.
14. Duffy, *Soldiers, Sugar and Seapower*, p83.
15. Brenton, *Naval History*, Vol 1, p304.
16. Maurice (ed), *Diary of Moore*, Vol 1, p57.
17. Countess of Minto (ed), *Life and Letters of Sir Gilbert Elliot, First Earl of Minto from 1751 to 1806* (London 1874), Vol 2, pp235-6.
18. Brenton, *Naval History*, Vol 1, p304.
19. Maurice (ed), *Diary of Moore*, Vol 1, p306.
20. Sir N H Nicholas (ed), *The Dispatches and Letters of Vice Admiral Lord Viscount Nelson* (London 1845), Vol 1, pp380, 382-3, 390, 397.
21. G Debien (ed), *Aventures de guerre aux Antilles (1795-1805)* (Paris 1980), pp17-19; Duffy, *Soldiers, Sugar and Seapower*, pp229-35.
22. H Hoste (ed), *Memoirs of Hoste,* Vol 2, p220. What follows is based upon Hoste's letters and the journal of his chaplain in these *Memoirs*, Vol 2, pp200-49 and T Pocock, *Remember Nelson. The Life of Captain Sir William Hoste* (London 1977), Ch 9-10.
23. *Memoirs of Hoste*, Vol 2, pp248-9.
24. *Memoirs of Hoste*, Vol 2, p227.
25. *Memoirs of Hoste*, Vol 2, p221.
26. At Tenerife for a promise not to molest the town or any of the Canary Islands, at the Helder in exchange for 8000 French P.O.W.s in Britain, and at Buenos Ayres in return for the evacuation of the entire La Plata region.

CHAPTER 3

Nelson Ashore, 1780–97
by Colin White

On 13 March 1795, the British Mediterranean Fleet, under Vice-Admiral William Hotham, encountered the French Toulon fleet in the Gulf of Genoa. The French avoided action and, in shifting, uncertain winds, Hotham ordered a general chase, thus allowing his faster ships to draw clear of their consorts and attack the rearmost enemy ships. The first battleship into action was the light and handy 64-gun HMS *Agamemnon*. In the confusion of retreat, one of the large French ships, the 80-gun *Ça Ira*, had collided with one of her consorts, losing her fore and main topmasts. Dropping astern of the fleet, she found herself harried by the much smaller *Agamemnon* whose captain skilfully placed his ship across the Frenchman's stern and poured in a series of murderous close-range broadsides. The French fleet turned to defend their comrade and Hotham, still too far off with the rest of the fleet to help the *Agamemnon,* was forced to order her to withdraw. However, the following day the battle was rejoined and this time the *Ça Ira* was captured, along with the *Censeur*, which tried to help her.[1]

The captain who handled his ship so skilfully in the first action was Horatio Nelson. He was one of the senior captains in the Royal Navy and already recognised as a rising star after his distinguished service in the Mediterranean since the beginning of the war two years earlier. Yet, remarkably, this was the first full-scale fleet action in which he had ever taken part. Indeed, at that time, he was best known as an expert in joint operations.

Nelson saw a great deal of active service ashore – service that left distinctive marks on his body. In 1802, during the brief period of peace following the Treaty of Amiens, he jotted down a list of his main wounds;

His eye in Corsica
His belly off Cape St Vincent
His arm at Teneriffe [sic]
His head in Egypt.

and then added ruefully, 'Tolerable for one war'.[2] It was indeed a 'tolerable' list – one that no other senior officer could match. And significantly two of the four wounds – and arguably the most disabling ones – had been received while fighting on land.

Nicaragua 1780

Nelson's first shore campaign was in 1780 when, just 21 and a newly promoted Post Captain, he commanded the naval contingent in a campaign in Central America. The American War of Independence was at its height and Spain had entered the war on the French side. An expedition was sent up the San Juan River to attack Spanish possessions in Nicaragua from the rear. Originally, Nelson's role was simply escort duty but, when the small expeditionary force attempted to land at the mouth of the San Juan, it quickly became apparent that the military forces had no experience of boatwork. Nelson therefore volunteered to accompany them with two of his ship's boats and fifty sailors.

In the end, however, he did not confine himself to manning the boats. When the first Spanish outpost was encountered, he personally led a frontal assault with his sailors, while the soldiers attacked it in the rear: 'I boarded, if I may be allowed the expression, an outpost of the enemy', he later wrote in his autobiographical *Sketch of My Life*.[3] And when the expedition eventually reached its chief objective, El Castillo de la Imaculada Concepcíon, guarding the approaches to Nicaragua, he constructed a battery using the small cannon from his boats. Although the castle was captured, the British force was decimated by dysentery and malaria and the expedition came to a floundering halt. But Nelson's drive and professional skill had been noted and reported back to London. It was a small but significant first step on his rise to fame.[4]

Corsica 1794

Nelson's most notable services ashore occurred in Corsica in 1794. Throughout the Great War with France, Britain sought to establish a secure naval base to support her fleet in the Mediterranean. In 1793, the French naval arsenal of Toulon had been handed over to Britain and her allies by French Royalists but it was soon recaptured by the revolutionaries – among them a young artillery officer Napoleon Bonaparte.

An anti-French uprising in Corsica, led by Pasquale Paoli, offered another opportunity for a British strategic foothold and Nelson was sent in the *Agamemnon* to command the naval part of the assault on the key town and port of Bastia. Once again, he could not resist becoming involved in the land operations. He landed some of his ship's guns and, with his sailors, manhandled them across rough terrain to positions commanding the town's defences.

Once Bastia had fallen, Nelson repeated the same feat on the other side of the island at the even more strongly fortified town of Calvi. Here, twenty 6-pounder guns were landed in a convenient inlet some three and half miles from the town and a special road was constructed, along which all the guns and supplies were dragged. Batteries were then constructed within range of the French defender's guns. It was in one of those batteries, on 12 July, that Nelson was hit in the face by a shower of gravel thrown up by a French cannonball and lost the sight of his right eye.[5]

Nelson was disappointed when his deeds were only briefly mentioned in the official dispatches reporting the capture of Corsica. But although public acclaim eluded him, his leading role in the capture of the island had brought him to the attention of some important men. Chief among them was the new Viceroy of Corsica, Sir Gilbert Elliot. Having watched the campaign at close quarters, he had been able to compare the way in which the Army and the Navy approached warfare and he wrote to his wife, 'I like the sea better. The character of the profession is more manly. They are full of life and action while on shore it is all lounge and still life.'[6]

Miniature of Captain Horatio Nelson, painted in Leghorn in 1794. His wife's favourite picture, it gives a good impression of his appearance before wounds and suffering transformed him. (National Maritime Museum, London: Neg No D9180)

This 'life and action' was never better shown than in two very similar operations in which the two men collaborated in 1796. Both show Nelson's mastery of the art of joint operations and both are striking demonstrations of the ubiquity of seapower.

Elba and Capraia 1796

In July 1796, a detachment of General Bonaparte's victorious Army of Italy arrived in Livorno (Leghorn) then part of the independent Grand Duchy of Tuscany. Elliot and his advisors believed that the French presence on the nearby coast posed a major threat to the British in Corsica. Almost on the route from Leghorn to Corsica lay the Tuscan island of Elba, with its excellent harbour at Porto Ferraio and Elliot realised that the French might capture it, as a base for full-scale operations against Corsica. He therefore determined on a pre-emptive strike.

By this time, Nelson had been appointed Commodore by the new Commander-in-Chief Sir John Jervis and ordered to do all in his power to hamper the French advance in Italy. He had been operating with a small squadron in the waters off Leghorn and the surrounding coast and had begun a close blockade of Leghorn itself. Jervis was away off Toulon with the main fleet but when Elliot proposed the capture of Elba, Nelson at once agreed to help, believing that this lay within the remit of his orders.

A detachment of troops, under the command of Major John Duncan, was sent in convoy to Porto Ferraio and there Nelson met them in the 74-gun HMS *Captain* with the frigate HMS *Inconstant* and the sloop HMS *Peterel*. After a quick conference, Nelson and Duncan decided to land the troops about a mile to the westward of the town, covered by the *Peterel*, on the night of 9 July. They marched on the town, arriving in front of its main gate at about dawn. Meanwhile, Nelson with his two other ships appeared off the port and took up positions close to the fortifications, ready to fire on them if required.

Duncan then presented the Governor of the town with a letter from Elliot asking him to allow the troops to take possession of the

Nelson wounded at Calvi on 14 July 1794, where he lost the sight in his right eye when hit in the face by stones and fragments thrown up by a French shell hitting an earthwork. (Royal Naval Museum)

town and promising in return that Elba would be regarded as still under the government of the Grand Duke of Tuscany and that the British would withdraw, and the place be restored, when peace returned. After asking for time to consult with the chief inhabitants, the Governor agreed to the terms and the island was surrendered to Nelson and Duncan without bloodshed. As Nelson reported to Jervis 'The harmony and good understanding between the Army and Navy employed on this occasion, will I trust be a further proof of what may be effected by the hearty co-operation of the two services.' [7]

Less than two months later that 'hearty co-operation' was used again with equally decisive and bloodless effect. By early September, the French advance was threatening another independent Italian state, the Republic of Genoa. Until then, Genoa had been friendly to the British and a valuable source of provisions for Jervis's fleet. But now, pressure from the French had forced the Genoese to act in a hostile manner. A drove of cattle was waiting there to be transported to the British fleet – a much-needed supply of fresh meat – and news came that their passage had been prevented. Arriving off the port, and finding that the British minister was absent Nelson sent a polite, formal note to the Doge, expressing a hope that 'there is some mistake in the matter'. But the French were there before him and had set up their batteries. After a few days of tense stand-off, the *Captain* was fired on and the Commodore was brusquely informed that all the ports of the Republic were now closed to British ships.

Nelson immediately cast about for the most effective way to make the Genoese aware of the power of the British fleet. Just to the north-east of Corsica lay the small Genoese-held island of Capraia: a thorn in the side of the British, since it acted as a safe haven for French privateers. Nelson now decided to seize the island and so he hurried to Bastia to consult with Sir Gilbert Elliot.

Elliot agreed on the need to act decisively and quickly and so on 15 September he gave Nelson orders to attack and capture the island. He also persuaded Lieutenant General de Burgh to give Nelson some 300 troops from the 51st and 69th Regiments to assist with the capture, under the command of Major James Logan. The troops were hurriedly embarked in the *Captain* and HMS *Gorgon* and sailed from

The capture of Elba, July 1796. Nelson's HMS *Captain* (centre) flying his commodore's pendant, lies off the citadel of Porto Ferraio. (National Maritime Museum, London: Neg No PY2433)

Bastia less than 24 hours after Nelson's arrival. With them went the brig, HMS *Vanneau* and a cutter, HMS *Rose* and they were joined the following day by another frigate, *La Minerve* under Captain George Cockburn, one of Nelson's special protégés.

Despite this speedy start, the squadron took two days to reach the island because of 'excessive calm weather' but Nelson and Logan made good use of the time to plan their attack in more detail. The captains of the other vessels were summoned on board the *Captain* for a conference at which it emerged that Lieutenant Gourly, commanding the *Vanneau*, knew Capraia well. He told Nelson that there was a landing place on the north side of the island close to a hill commanding the main town. It was decided that troops and guns would be landed at this point to take the town in the rear, while the rest of the squadron made a show of force in front of the town itself.

The plan worked smoothly. On 17 September, 200 troops were safely landed from the *Rose* and *Vanneau* at the appointed place and a party of seamen from the *Captain,* under the command of her second lieutenant, James Spicer, landed some cannon, which they manhandled easily up the hill and erected a battery on top of it, thus threatening the town with plunging fire. Four privateer vessels in the port attempted to escape but were prevented by Gourly in the *Vanneau* who took his little ship right into the harbour mouth and remained there until Cockburn came up in *La Minerve* to support him.

Minerve had also brought Nelson and Logan to the scene and at first light on the morning of the 18th, they sent in their summons to island authorities. Carefully drawn up by Viceroy Elliot, these offered the same terms as had been given to Elba: all local officials would retain their offices, local laws and religion would be preserved and all private property would be protected. The Padri del Commune tried to buy time by asking permission to seek orders from Genoa but received in reply only a brusque, more threatening, letter from the British commanders, giving them just one more hour to agree to terms. With a strong force of warships off their port and a small but professional body of troops in their rear, backed by a battery of guns aimed at their houses, the Padri duly surrendered.

It had been another textbook combined operation: 'I do not believe the two services ever more cordially united than on the present occasion,' Nelson later reported to Elliot.[8] Capraia fell into the hands of the British without any bloodshed on either side, barely a week after the *Captain* had been fired upon in Genoa Roads. Retribution had been swift and ruthlessly efficient.

It is interesting to note that the Capraia operation, like the capture of Elba, was conducted without any consultation with Jervis. Speed was essential if the attack was to have maximum impact on the Genoese and so, with Elliot's support, Nelson was prepared to make the decision to attack himself, without wasting time trying to contact his admiral. Earlier, in February, he had told his wife that Jervis, 'seems at

The Mole at Santa Cruz, where the majority of British casualties were suffered on the night of 24 July 1797. (Royal Naval Museum)

present to consider me as an assistant more than a subordinate for I am acting without orders',[9] and his actions at Capraia show that he trusted Jervis to support him when he acted on his own initiative. That trust was amply rewarded for, when he forwarded a copy of Nelson's official report on the Capraia operation to the Admiralty, Jervis commented that it 'reflects the highest honour on his skill, judgement and enterprize'.[10]

Santa Cruz de Tenerife 1797

The origins of the operation

Almost exactly a year later, that trust between the admiral and his gifted subordinate bore rich fruit when Nelson played a key role in

Jervis's remarkable defeat of a superior Spanish fleet at the Battle of Cape St Vincent. Acting once again 'as an assistant more than a subordinate', Nelson seized the opportunity offered by his commander's boldness and tactical skill and, in a move similar to his handling of the *Agamemnon* in the Gulf of Genoa, threw his ship into action against the whole Spanish fleet. This time, however, he was fully supported instead of being ordered to withdraw and four Spanish ships were captured – two of them by a boarding party led by Nelson himself.[11] Instead of sailing north as planned to support an invasion of England, the Spanish withdrew in confusion into Cadiz where the British blockaded them. Nelson, by now a Rear-Admiral, was given command of the inshore squadron with orders to annoy the Spanish and force them to emerge for another fight. But, as the weeks dragged by, there was no sign of movement from the Spanish. Successive attacks by bomb-vessels and flotillas of boats led only to a strengthening of the Spanish defences and, by mid-July, Jervis realised that his tactics were not working and recalled Nelson and his squadron.

By then, another plan for striking at Spain had emerged. In March, a rumour had reached the British fleet that two rich Spanish treasure ships were sheltering at the port of Santa Cruz, in the island of Tenerife in the Spanish Canaries, and two frigates, HMS *Terpsichore* and *Dido* had been sent to reconnoitre. They had cut out one of the ships but the other, apparently by far the most valuable, remained under the shelter of the Santa Cruz forts. And so the idea of a full-scale attack on Santa Cruz de Tenerife began to be considered.

Santa Cruz, or Tenerife as it is usually called, occupies a key place in the Nelson mythology. It was, after all, his most spectacular defeat, matched only by his bloody reverse at Boulogne in August 1801. It very nearly cost him his life and it did cost him his arm. None of the other wounds he suffered in action were immediately apparent - but the empty arm sleeve was almost a stigmata, a potent reminder of his failure that he carried with him everywhere. His biographers have tended to see the operation in isolation and so, in the past, it has been generally misunderstood. In particular, it has given rise to the notion that he was not particularly successful on land.[12] But, as we have seen, in the years leading up to Tenerife he had in fact proved a very successful exponent of the art of combined operations. So why was Tenerife such a disaster?

Until recently, our knowledge of the battle was very limited, based almost entirely on Nelson's own account and the official reports of those who fought with him. However, a most revealing 'unofficial' account by Nelson's flag captain, Ralph Miller, has been discovered that has thrown fascinating new light on the events.[13] At the same time extensive research in the Spanish sources, and a series of scholarly Spanish publications to mark the bicentenary in 1997, have enabled us, for really the first time, to see the battle from the Spanish point of view and, indeed, to discover how tantalisingly close Nelson and his men came to succeeding.[14] As a result, we now understand the battle very much better than before and so can explain more satisfactorily why Nelson was defeated.

The plan

On 12 April 1797, Nelson wrote to Jervis with a plan for an attack on Santa Cruz. Essentially, he proposed to use the same methods that had already proved so successful in Elba and Capraia – but on a much larger scale. He envisaged a landing by some 4000 troops who would seize command of heights dominating the town, while a squadron of battleships moved into a position from which they could bombard. Once these forces were in place, a demand would be sent in for the surrender of the treasure ships' cargoes. 'My plan,' he urged, 'could not fail of success, would immortalise the undertakers, ruin Spain and has every prospect of raising our Country to a higher pitch of wealth than she ever yet attained.'[15]

However, it was not until mid-June that Jervis felt ready to consider putting the plan into operation. By then, the two men knew that they would not be able to count on any help from the Army. General de Burgh at Elba had disappointed them by refusing to allow his troops to be used and a similar request to General O'Hara, Governor of Gibraltar, was also turned down. But this did not deter Nelson: on 7 June he wrote again suggesting that all that was needed was an extra force of Royal Marines. 'Under General Troubridge ashore, and myself afloat, I am confident of success.'[16] Unknowing, he had taken his first step towards disaster: the attack that had originally been conceived as a large-scale combined operation, involving a significant body of trained soldiers, had now become a much smaller, and purely naval, affair.

Despite this disappointment, Jervis began to look at the Tenerife plan more closely. Not only would it result in the loss to Spain of a costly cargo but it would also demonstrate that none of her colonies were safe from British attack, thus, Jervis hoped, increasing the growing internal opposition to the war with Britain. It was, in short, to be a classic use of seapower to bring political and economic pressure to bear on an opponent. Intelligence from the island appeared to suggest that, although Santa Cruz was strongly fortified, a well-planned full-scale attack had every chance of succeeding. And in Nelson, Jervis had a commander with a unique experience of this sort of operation, who had demonstrated that he possessed exactly the right combination of ruthless decisiveness, and meticulous planning ability that brought success.

So eventually, on 14 July, Jervis issued orders to Nelson 'for taking possession of the Town of Santa Cruz by a sudden and vigorous assault'. He gave him a strong force: three 74-gun ships, the *Theseus*, *Culloden* and *Zealous*, three frigates, the *Seahorse*, *Emerald* and *Terpsichore*, the cutter *Fox* and a small mortar-boat called *Terror*. The ships were probably chosen as much for their captains as for the force they offered. For Jervis was giving Nelson the stars of his fleet: Ralph Miller, Thomas Troubridge, Sam Hood, Thomas Waller, Richard Bowen and Thomas Fremantle. He also gave him his blessing but added a phrase which suggested that, even at this stage, the operation was regarded as especially difficult: 'God bless and prosper you. I am sure you will deserve success. To mortals is not given the power of commanding it.'[17]

Santa Cruz lies in a broad semi-circular bay at the north-east tip of Tenerife. In 1797, the town was confined within a sheltered valley, with low ground immediately to its rear, and flat open ground to the south-west. To the north-east, it was protected by the sheer sides of jagged volcanic hills and could be approached only along a narrow

Seapower Ashore

coastal strip. The town was strongly defended by a series of well-armed forts. These ran along the shore in a six-mile line from the north east: sixteen individual fortifications in all, mounting a total of 84 guns and linked by a rough, dry-stone wall, running along the line of the beach. They ranged in size from the large Castillo de San Cristóbal guarding the centre of the town itself, a star-shaped sixteenth century castle mounting 10 guns, to small open-backed 3- or 4-gun batteries, placed at regular intervals along the beach wall.

In overall command was the Commandant General of the Canary Islands, Don Antonio Gutiérrez, a distinguished regular soldier. He had 387 gunners in the forts, only half the number required to man all his guns. In addition, he had just 400 professional soldiers. In time of crisis the General could also call upon five regiments of militia, although these naturally took some time to assemble, which meant the island was very vulnerable to a sudden and determined attack. In the end, the militia call-up worked well. Over 700 men rallied to the colours and fought extremely courageously, even though most of them were armed only with sickles or sticks. Nonetheless, even at the height of the battle, Gutiérrez had only 1669 men under his command.[18]

Having left Jervis's fleet early on 15 June, Nelson's squadron made its way to Tenerife at a brisk pace propelled by moderate breezes from the north. Once again, as in the Elba and Capraia operations, he used the interlude of the voyage to consult fully with his colleagues. The captains were regularly summoned to the *Theseus* and they discussed freely and openly the various options before them. In the event, the tactics they decided to employ were strikingly similar to those which had been so successful in Caparia the previous September. While Santa Cruz appeared to be strongly fortified, earlier reconnaissances had suggested that there was a weak link in the defences: one of the outlying forts, the Castillo de Paso Alto, which lay about a mile to the northeast of the town at a point where the sheer volcanic hills of Tenerife plunged precipitously into the sea. Nelson and his captains decided that if they could gain possession of the castle, Santa Cruz's weakly-defended north-eastern flank would then lie exposed and the town could be threatened with bombardment. The land forces would be supported by the ships of the line, which would take up a position from which they could also bombard the town. At this point, Nelson would send ashore an ultimatum demanding the surrender of the treasure ship and her cargo in return for sparing the inhabitants of Tenerife from 'the horrors of war'. The wording of this ultimatum was similar to the document prepared, with Sir Gilbert Elliot's, assistance for the attack on Capraia: so similar, indeed, that seems likely that Nelson was working from a copy of the earlier document. Clearly, the experience he had gained in 1796 was being put to very good use.[19]

Having decided on their initial objective, the actual method of capturing the castle had then to be debated. They considered two possibilities: to land further up the coast to the north-east, gain possession of the heights behind the castle and then call on it to surrender; or to land on a weakly-defended stretch of beach to the south-west of the castle and then turn and attack it directly. In the end, the second idea was adopted and detailed planning began.

It was decided that the frigates would go on ahead, taking with them all the available boats and a landing force of seamen and Royal Marines, the latter including an extra detachment supplied by ships of the main fleet. They would then approach Tenerife under the cover of darkness and land their forces on the appointed spot at dawn. The hope was that, by this means, the castle would be surprised and captured before the Spanish had time to reinforce it.

Once again, Nelson's characteristic attention to detail manifested itself. Already, before leaving the fleet, he had ordered the construction of special, light scaling ladders, platforms for 18-pounder guns and a 'slay' for dragging cannon, similar to the ones he had employed in Corsica. Now, he issued a set of 'regulations' for the attack: boats were to be kept together by towing one another, thus ensuring they got on shore at the same moment. A Captain was to be posted on the beach to make sure that the boats turned around quickly and made their way back to the ships to collect reinforcements and supplies. Iron ramrods were to be specially made for the muskets, to replace the standard-issue wooden ones which tended to break in the heat of action. Finally, in order further to dishearten the enemy, as many of the sailors as possible were to be dressed in spare Marines' red uniform coats, so as to give the impression that the landing force was made up of regular soldiers.

Most of these details were published by Nicolas in 1847 and so have featured in earlier narratives of the operation. However, Ralph Miller's recently-discovered account, gives some fascinating new information about how the landing force was actually organised:

> The whole 740 seamen were divided into three companies ... each having a Master at Arms, or Ship's Corporal, a Boatswain's mate, and Quarter Master or Gunner's mate, an Armourer with a cold chisel, a hammer, spikes for guns, and a crow, a carpenter with a short broad axe, a heavy mall and two iron wedges, a Midshipman or mate and a Lieutenant to command it ... These men were exercised twice a day, and tried with ball at target.[20]

If success had depended on good planning alone, the Tenerife operation should have been a foregone conclusion.

The first two attacks: 22 July

On the morning of 21 July, the squadron lay to and, while the admiral and his captains had their last conference, the landing parties were assembled in the frigates, a total of about 900 men. The complicated transfer took most of the day but eventually, at about 4.00pm, the heavily-laden frigates parted company towing all the extra boats behind them.

Giving the frigates about three hours start, Nelson then made his own way to Tenerife with the ships of the line, arriving in sight of the Santa Cruz at about 4.30am on 22 July. There, instead of a landing in full progress, he found the boats still more than a mile from their objective. Adverse winds and currents had slowed the boats' progress to such an extent that the element of surprise had been lost and, even as Nelson watched, three shots were fired in the town, showing that his ships had been spotted. Within moments, Gutiérrez had been alerted to the danger and had begun to take counter-measures.

Briefly, the attack hung in the balance. The Spanish reinforcements would take time to reach their positions and so there was still a chance that the British could establish a foothold if they pushed on quickly. If Nelson had been leading the first attack in person, this is probably what would have happened: instead, at the first signs of Spanish activity, Troubridge ordered his boats to return to the shelter of the frigates and then rowed out to the *Theseus* to consult with Nelson. The whole momentum of the British attack was lost.

On board the *Theseus* Nelson and his colleagues now revived the other option they had considered earlier – to occupy the heights above the fort and then storm it from the rear. A convenient landing beach was available close to the frigates and from there it appeared a relatively easy climb to the ridge above the fort. Nelson gave his assent to the plan and between about 10 and 10.30 in the morning, the boats left the frigates for a second time, again under Troubridge's command. In the meantime, the ships of the line tried to create a diversion by attacking the fort but were unable to get within range because of light winds and contrary currents.

But even this second attempt met with failure. Having toiled at their oars in the baking sun, and struggled up the heights, the British found there was a deep valley between them and the castle which was their objective. And there, firmly entrenched behind a rough wall on the opposite ridge, were the Spanish defenders, the Regiment of the Militia of La Laguna, who had even managed to carry four field pieces on their shoulders up the steep hillside. General Gutiérrez's hastily-assembled forces had reached their posts in time.

By now Troubridge's men were 'much fatigued and in want of refreshment' as his own log put it. Worst of all was the heat. The islanders were used to the climate and, in any case, behind their lines, women and children were carrying food and water up to their menfolk, but the British had very little water. Eventually, Troubridge accepted defeat and ordered a retreat, which was carried out in reasonable order. First went the sick and those suffering from heat exhaustion, then the main force beat to arms, to give the Spanish the impression they were about to attack, and began to move off in companies, with the Marines bringing up the rear in case of a counterattack. By ten o'clock that night, the whole force had been re-embarked in the frigates, worn out and in an extremely bad temper.

Nelson was very frustrated. His natural instinct was to lead from the front and now he had been forced to witness from a distance the failure of two assaults under his overall direction. Nonetheless, by any reasonable standard, he had done all he could to carry out his orders: winds, and other natural obstacles beyond his control, were mainly responsible for his failure and he would therefore have been perfectly justified in sailing away without making any further attempt. Instead, within 24 hours he was not only leading a third attack in person but was also making it in the most hazardous manner possible – a direct, frontal assault on the centre of the town itself.

Various attempts have been made to explain this decision. Nelson himself said in his letter to a friend '… My pride suffered …' and so it has been suggested that he was acting more out of a sense of wounded personal honour than of cool evaluation. There is also an idea that he was simply over-confident – believing after his remarkable exploits at Cape St Vincent that he was a match for any Spaniard. However, Miller's account has revealed that the decision to make the second attack was not arrived at by Nelson in isolation; but was in fact urged on him by his captains at a full council of war. It was also based on information from an informer who told the British that the Spanish had only 300 regular troops and that they were in a state of great alarm and confusion.[21] It is one of the ironies of this extraordinary event that the first part of the information was actually very close to the truth.

In the light of this news, Nelson now proposed to aim his blow on the central citadel itself, relying on being able to land sufficient men to overwhelm the defences. Once again, his seamen and marines were to land from the squadron's boats, with a reserve of some 200 men carried in the cutter *Fox*. The men were divided into six divisions: five each under Captains Troubridge, Miller, Waller, Hood and Thompson and the sixth under Nelson's personal command with Captains Fremantle and Bowen 'to regulate the attack'. All were to land on the town mole, and then storm the citadel which stood at its landward end. In other words, Nelson was concentrating all his available forces for a knockout blow on Gutiérrez's headquarters, in the hope of paralysing the Spanish defences by eliminating their command centre.

The night attack: 24/25 July

At about 10.30 on the night of 24 July, the squadron's boats, laden once more with men, began to rendezvous around HMS *Zealous*, where they were formed into their six divisions and roped together. Then, with their oars muffled, they began the two-mile row to the mole, accompanied by the cutter *Fox*, with the reserves on board. 'It was a star light, yet not a clear night', says Miller, 'with little wind and a swell that became considerable as we approached the shore'.[22] As a result the little flotilla managed to get closer to the objective without being discovered than they had dared hope. But eventually the boats were spotted by a lookout in the battery on the molehead and others in the vessels lying nearby. The alarm bell rang and the whole of the Santa Cruz front burst into flame as the guns roared out. Immediately, with a concerted cheer, the boats cast off their connecting ropes and each made their own way to the mole. But in the darkness and confusion, only five – mostly those of Nelson's division – found it.

First ashore was Bowen, with a party of about 50 men. Landing on the beach just to the north of the mole, they managed to establish a foothold on the molehead itself, capturing the battery and spiking its seven guns. They then regrouped, ready to storm and capture the landward defences of the mole, but by now the strength of those defences was becoming all too apparent. The whole length of the mole was being swept by gunfire from the citadel, supported by musketry from nearby houses. Now a second and larger British wave arrived on the beach. Fremantle leapt out of his barge and began running to the mole, his men close behind them. The barge was a large boat, so it took some time to empty. Nelson had reached the middle and was in the act of drawing his sword, prior to leaping down onto the beach, when he suddenly felt a sharp blow to his elbow and his whole arm went limp. A musket ball had entered just above the joint, shattering the bone and severing a major artery. It was a very dangerous, and potentially mortal, wound.

Luckily for Nelson his stepson, Josiah Nisbet was at his side. In the light of the nearby gun flashes, he saw his stepfather stagger and heard the words, 'I am shot through the elbow' as the admiral collapsed into

Nelson was hit in the right arm before he was able to get ashore at Santa Cruz. His stepson Josiah Nesbit managed to stop the bleeding and he was taken to HMS *Theseus*. Despite what this picture shows, his arm was not actually amputated until he had returned to the ship. (Royal Naval Museum)

the bottom of the boat. The blood was pumping fast from the wound and so Nisbet found the place where it was broken, grasped hard with one hand to stop the flow and used a couple of neckerchiefs to tied up the wound. He then gathered a scratch crew together, refloated the heavy barge which was firmly aground on the beach, and set off through a hail of Spanish fire for the ships. When they arrived at the *Theseus,* willing hands tried to help Nelson on board. 'Let me alone', came the reply, 'I have yet my legs left and one arm'.[23] The amputation was performed almost at once, without anaesthetic.

Meanwhile, the rest of the force that had reached the beach by the mole was pinned down by the Spanish fire. Fremantle and his men tried to join up with Bowen on the mole but before they could do so, Fremantle and Thompson were seriously wounded and Bowen killed by successive blasts from the guns. Thus, within about ten minutes, the Spanish had succeeded in knocking out all the British leaders on the mole. The mole itself, and the adjoining beach, were so narrow that a few well-aimed guns, loaded with canister, could easily pin down the small force that had actually managed to land. Most of the rest of the landing force had been swept by the strong current past the mole towards the southern part of the town where some of the boats gave up the attempt altogether, daunted by the fierceness of the fire and the heavy swell which was pounding the rocks. But some actually managed to get ashore.

Troubridge and his division fetched up just a few yards south of the citadel, together with some of the *Emerald*'s division under Waller. Their boats were either swamped by the breakers, or stove in on the rocks and all their powder was soaked; but they nonetheless charged with bayonets and pikes and drove away the defenders, who were all inexperienced militiamen. They then ran for cover into the nearest street and eventually, emerged into the town's main square. Their ammunition was wet and they had lost their scaling ladders when their boats were wrecked on the rocks. All they could do therefore was wait in the hope that Nelson and his division would gain control of the mole and then come and join them. The long moments went by and then, suddenly, they were spotted from the citadel and fired upon, so they took shelter in a convenient warehouse.

Miller, in the *Theseus*'s pinnace, supported by Captain Oldfield of the Royal Marines in her launch, landed in a small gully. The boats grounded in the heavy surf about thirty yards from the shore and began to fill with water, so they were forced to wade to the beach, with the water chest-high under fire from a nearby battery which they charged with pikes and bayonets and captured. At this point Captain Sam Hood joined them with another group. Miller and Hood tried to rally their men for an attack on the citadel but they found that, by now, morale was very low. Most of their powder was wet and some of them had actually lost their arms in the struggle to get ashore; moreover they had already suffered heavy casualties and so, says Miller frankly, 'as a body [they] behaved indifferently through the night'.[24] The few Royal Marines present seemed prepared to advance but, despite all Miller's efforts, and those of his officers, the sailors could not be persuaded to make what was obviously a desperate attack.

The British were now in a serious predicament. Their planned concerted attack on a single point had disintegrated into a series of uncoordinated landings on a broad front and there were now three separate British groups ashore, none of which was in touch with the others. It was still pitch dark and they were now confronted with a confusing maze of narrow, winding streets filled with the dark forms of Spanish soldiers. A series of scrappy, bewildering skirmishes broke out in which the defenders – with their local knowledge and plentiful supplies of ammunition – had the advantage.

But the Spanish, too, were in trouble. As we have seen Gutiérrez had only 400 trained soldiers at his disposal and they were far too thinly stretched. Gradually, rumours of the successful British landings began to spread among the inexperienced militiamen and, as such rumours do, they quickly became exaggerated until it was being said that over 2000 men had got ashore. The defenders in the northern defences began to melt away. Even Gutiérrez himself, cut off in his command centre at San Cristobal, was unsure of what was going on and sent out some of his officers to discover the true situation.[25] Recent research has also established that Nelson, by then recovering from his operation in the *Theseus*, received information that led him to believe that Troubridge had succeeded.[26] So it would seem that for perhaps about an hour around three in the morning, the issue swung in the balance and victory could have gone to either side.

In the end, it was the British who broke first. Unable to persuade their men to attack the citadel, Hood and Miller now tried to reach the agreed rendezvous in the main square. They blundered about in the dark, meeting first some more British who had just landed and then another party of Spaniards, who melted away into the nearby dark alleyways. Finally, they ended up outside the Convent of Santo Domingo with the Spanish closing in behind them. Somehow, a message had got through to Troubridge that the other party had landed and so, realising his position in the square was hopeless, he retreated towards his colleagues and finally succeeded in joining up with them outside the Convent, which they seized and barricaded themselves inside.

Troubridge and his fellow captains now realised that their position was very serious. Although by concentrating they had managed to gather together some 300 men, they did not have enough ammunition to fight a serious action with the ever-increasing forces that were now surrounding them. So, instead, they tried a bluff. Captain Oldfield was sent with a flag of truce with a threat to burn the town, unless the treasure ship was surrendered. He was admitted with due ceremony to the citadel but Gutiérrez now realised just how small and helpless the landing force actually was and so he refused to negotiate.

At last, the British accepted defeat and Captain Hood went to the citadel to negotiate a surrender. Gutiérrez could afford to be generous and he agreed to allow his opponents to leave with full military honours, even keeping their arms. In return, Hood promised that his forces and the ships of the squadron 'shall not molest the Town in any manner ... or any of the Islands of the Canaries.' Troubridge ratified these terms and, by 7.00am on 25 July, the hostilities were finally over.

With colours flying, the British marched down from the convent to the main square, where all the available Spanish troops had been drawn up in orderly lines. Gutiérrez had decided to make an impressive show of strength, in the hope of deterring the British from making any further attacks. His men were also busily spreading the rumour that there were 8000 troops on the island – a figure not unnaturally seized on first by Troubridge, and then by Nelson, as an explanation for their humiliating defeat. Both quoted this figure in their reports and, as a result, it has featured in most British accounts of the battle since. But the Spanish sources are quite clear on this point: Gutiérrez had at his disposal only the 1669 men mentioned earlier. The figure of 8000 was the parting propaganda shot of a wily opponent. Meanwhile, the wounded were being re-embarked and the body of Captain Bowen was buried at sea to the accompaniment of gun salutes and with colours at half-mast. The final British casualty list was disproportionately high: 153 killed, drowned or missing and over 100 wounded out of a force of just over 1000.

Nelson failed at Santa Cruz for three key reasons. First, he was undoubtedly unlucky with the hostile terrain and weather conditions – although it is arguable that he should have known about them and taken them into consideration in his planning. Second, it was a purely naval affair, rather than the large-scale combined operation that had originally been planned. As Miller's very frank account now makes clear, the sailors were obviously out of their depth and disoriented in the confused street-fighting of the night of 24/25 July, while the few Royal Marines remained steady and prepared to fight. In such circumstances, it is just possible that the presence of a disciplined body of trained soldiers could have tipped the delicate balance in favour of the British. Finally – and decisively – Nelson and his men were matched with opponents of their own calibre. The defenders of Santa Cruz may not have been very numerous but they were skilled and courageous, with the great advantage of local knowledge, and General Don Antonio Gutiérrez was an experienced professional soldier, who was not easily cowed. Against such opponents, the sort of bluff and bluster that had won the day in Elba and at Capraia, was not likely to succeed.

The attack on Tenerife was the last time Nelson personally took part in fighting on land. The loss of his arm meant that he was no longer able to manage the athletic feats and the hand-to-hand fighting such operations required. But he always remained alert to the possibilities of amphibious warfare – the ability to 'crush the Enemy at home'[27] as he once put it – and sailors under his command continued to fight ashore in amphibious campaigns. Of course his abiding reputation rests principally on his skills as a fleet commander and the remarkable string of sea victories which he either assisted at, or masterminded himself. But his record of service ashore is a striking reminder that, even in the age of great sea battles such as the Nile and Trafalgar, the Royal Navy was an amphibious force.

Bibliography and Sources

The source for the official accounts of all the operations described here is the authoritative *Letters and Despatches of Lord Nelson* by Sir Nicholas Harris Nicolas (1844-6). Although it is now known that there are many gaps and flaws in this great work, it remains the best source available for Nelson's official correspondence.

The best biography for an analysis of Nelson as a naval commander is still the two-volume *Life of Nelson* by A T Mahan (1897). The best modern biography is *Horatio Nelson* by Tom Pocock (1987 – and recently published in paperback).

There has, however, been much new research, especially into the St Vincent and Tenerife battles as a result of the renewed interest caused by the bicentenary of both events. Most of these new insights were gathered into my book *1797: Nelson's Year of Destiny* (1998). For an excellent résumé, in English, of the new Spanish insights on Tenerife, see Agustin Guimera, *Nelson and Tenerife* (published by The 1805 Club, 1999).

The key new British document is the account of Tenerife written by Ralph Miller to his wife. Edited by Kirstie Buckland, it has now been published as a booklet, *The Miller Papers*, by The 1805 Club (1999).

Notes

1 For the best account of this action, with diagrams, see A T Mahan, *The Life of Nelson* (London 1897), Vol I, pp 163-71.
2 T J Pettigrew, *Life of Lord Nelson* (London 1849), Vol II, p 243.

3 J S Clarke and J M'Arthur, *The Life of Nelson* (London 1809), Vol I, p34.
4 For the best account of this action see T Pocock, *Horatio Nelson* (London 1987), pp32-46.
5 The best modern account of this campaign is T Pocock, *Nelson in Corsica* (published by the 1805 Club in 1994).
6 Countess of Minto, *Life and Letters of Sir Gilbert Elliot* (London 1874), Vol I.
7 Sir Nicholas Harris Nicolas, *The Dispatches and Letters of Lord Nelson* (London 1844-6), Vol I, p209. This account of the Elba operation has been reconstructed from the letters and dispatches printed by Nicolas.
8 Ibid, p275. Again Nicolas is the main source of information for this operation.
9 G Naish, *Nelson's Letters to His Wife* (London 1958), p284.
10 Nicolas, *op.cit.* p271.
11 For the most up to date account of the battle, based on the latest Spanish and British research, see C White, *1797: Nelson's Year of Destiny* (Stroud 1998).
12 See, for example, O Warner, *A Portrait of Lord Nelson* (London 1958), p123.
13 Kirstie Buckland (ed), *The Miller Papers* (published by The 1805 Club, 1999).
14 See especially, Luis Cola Benítez, *La Historia del 25 de Julio de 1797*. English readers will find all the new Spanish material admirably distilled in a monograph by Agustín Guimera, *Nelson and Tenerife* (published by The 1805 Club, 1999).
15 Nicolas, *op.cit*, p379.
16 Ibid, p393.
17 Ibid, p413.
18 Until recently, all English accounts of the operation have said there were 8000 troops on the island – a figure taken from Nelson's dispatches. But the Spanish sources are quite clear that the numbers given here are the correct ones. The figure of 8000 was deliberately spread about by the Spanish to deter future attacks. See Benitez, p43.
19 For a comparison of the two ultimata, see White, *op. cit*, p10.
20 Buckland, *op. cit.*
21 See Buckland, *op. cit.* and White, *op. cit.* pp112-114.
22 Buckland, *op. cit.*
23 Lady Harriet Hoste, *Memoirs and Letters of Captain Sir William Hoste* (London 1833), Vol I, p73.
24 Buckland, *op. cit.*
25 Guimera, *op cit.* p19.
26 In 1989, a copy of the ultimatum was discovered, signed by Nelson *with his left hand*. This means it can only have been signed *after* the amputation of his arm - which suggests strongly that news must have reached the *Theseus* that Troubridge had succeeded in getting ashore. For a fuller discussion of this new discovery see White, *op. cit.* p106.
27 Nicolas, *op. cit.*, Vol IV, p457.

CHAPTER 4

'Within Cannon Shot of Deep Water': The Syrian Campaign of 1840
by Andrew Lambert

The Syrian campaign of 1840 provides an important case study in role of naval power projection in the pursuit of national aims. At various times it required deterrence, power projection and coalition operations, liaison with local and national regimes and intervention in local politics rendered complex by deep-rooted religious and ethnic tensions. At the same time it had to be co-ordinated with operations in two other areas, China and Afghanistan, and the prospect of war in North America. The campaign demonstrated that in the mid-nineteenth century Britain was a unique global power. Her maritime strategic posture, built on combination of economic primacy, fiscal strength, naval forces, and global basing enabled her to project power across the world in a way that no other power, or combination of powers, could contemplate.

The Crisis of 1839-40

The Syrian crisis ended a long-running power struggle within the Ottoman Empire, which arose out of the troubled relationship between Turkey and her provincial governor in Egypt after the Napoleonic invasion. In 1805 Mehemet Ali, an Albanian officer, became viceroy of Egypt, and attempted to create a modern, independent state.[1] By contrast his nominal suzerain, the Ottoman Sultan Mahmud II, found it very difficult to begin the reform process, and Turkey slipped behind the other major military powers.[2] This weakness was cruelly revealed when the Turks failed to suppress the Greek Insurrection of 1821, and had to call on Egypt for aid. Mehemet sent a fleet and an army, but the fleet was destroyed at Navarino in 1827, along with part of the army. Dissatisfied with his reward for service in Greece, and anxious to expand his resource base, Mehemet Ali rebuilt his forces and in 1831 advanced into Ottoman-controlled Syria. The following year his son, Ibrahim Pasha, defeated the Turkish army at Koniya and conquered the province. Ibrahim advanced into Anatolia, and the Sultan turned to Britain and France for help. France supported Mehemet, as a potential ally. Britain, while committed to Turkey, had no forces to spare in 1832-3, over-stretched by crises in Belgium and Portugal. In desperation the Sultan accepted a temporary Russian occupation of Istanbul, which deterred the Egyptians. In return the Sultan awarded the Russians privileges under the Treaty of Unkiar Skelessi which appeared to run counter to British interests.

Stung by this defeat, the Foreign Secretary Lord Palmerston worked to reduce Russian influence at Istanbul, and prevent clashes between Egypt and Turkey. He believed Turkey could be transformed into a modern, effective state, and under the Treaty of Balta-Liman of 1837 exchanged free access to Turkish markets for political support and military aid.[3] The commercial policies favoured British trade, and also undermined the economic base of Egyptian development, forcing Mehemet Ali to act, or be subsumed back into the generality of the Ottoman Empire.

The Sultan was desperate to recover Syria, and so, long before British support could improve his military situation, he prepared for war. Recognising the threat posed by the Balta-Liman agreement Mehemet declared himself independent of Turkey in 1838, and the Sultan acted, but at Nezib in June 1839 Ibrahim routed another Turkish army. The Sultan died before news of the disaster reached Istanbul, but worse was to follow. The Turkish fleet deserted to Alexandria, joining the Egyptian force in a combined squadron of fifteen battleships, more than double the size of the British Mediterranean Fleet.

Having committed British policy to uphold Turkey as a buffer against Russian expansion, and opened her markets, Palmerston recognised that British strategic and commercial interests required

Mehemet Ali to be reduced to proper subordination, through the eviction of Egyptian forces from Syria. He hoped this could be achieved before the other powers intervened. The only forces on the spot to carry out this policy was the Mediterranean Fleet under Vice-Admiral Sir Robert Stopford (1767-1849) and the remnants of the Turkish forces. Initially the British and French fleets had assembled at Besika Bay, just outside the Dardanelles, to support Turkey against Russia. Palmerston hoped for French co-operation, but soon discovered that Russia favoured his policy, while France was vehemently opposed to coercing Mehemet Ali. The strategic situation was further complicated by the fact that French fleet was larger and better manned than the British.

The British Fleet, Stopford and Napier

Stopford's fleet was largely composed of old, relatively small ships. His flagship, the 104-gun three-decker *Princess Charlotte*, was a copy of the *Victory*, and most of the other battleships were wartime 74s. The only modern units were the 84-gun *Powerful*, *Thunderer* and *Asia*. There were several small frigates and corvettes, and four steamers, all carried weak peacetime complements. Only later in the crisis, too late for active service, did more powerful ships arrive.

Stopford, then 72, had seen much service in the French wars, but unfortunately he was out of sympathy with the government, and particularly Palmerston, on two key issues. His caution and anxiety to follow orders irritated the Foreign Secretary, who looked for some initiative. Furthermore as a Tory serving under a Whig ministry, he could not be trusted with politically sensitive information. His second-in-command, the energetic and resourceful Commodore Charles Napier (1786-1860) was altogether different. Advanced liberal politics and wide experience of amphibious and coastal operations made him ideal. He was also in regular private correspondence with the First Lord of the Admiralty, Lord Minto, and with Palmerston, who held him in high regard after his service in the Portuguese Civil War of 1833, which had solved a major diplomatic problem without British intervention.[4] The officers

Once a dashing frigate captain at the Glorious First of June and Cornwallis's Retreat, Sir Robert Stopford, now 72, had become more cautious. (National Maritime Museum, London: BHC 3041)

of the squadron were a mixture of Whigs and Tories, many of the latter being Stopford's relatives, including two sons, and three nephews.

The Campaign of 1840

In April 1840 Stopford was instructed to protect Istanbul from an Egyptian attack, then two months later a minor revolt broke out in Beirut, which was quickly suppressed. In July Britain, Russia,

Austria and Prussia signed the Treaty of London, to protect Turkey and reduce Mehemet Ali to his old position as a vassal of the Sultan. France refused to sign, reflecting her unwillingness to coerce Mehemet Ali. Stopford was instructed to cut the sea communications between Egypt and Syria, the only route for men and stores, and to support the insurrection with arms and Turkish troops. These operations would be carried out short of war, which left them under Palmerston's control. Had war been declared responsibility would have passed to Secretary of State for War and the Colonies, Lord John Russell, who lacked Palmerston's ability and did not share his aims.

Palmerston hoped the Egyptians would bow to *force majeure*, leaving Syria without a fight. The position of France remained critical, for if she intervened the Syrian campaign would become irrelevant. Under Chief Minister Thiers French policy was threatening, and war seemed likely.[5] However, British intelligence reports made it clear that France could not match British naval mobilisation, and by October she had run out of ships. Without a fleet at least equal to the Royal Navy the aggressive diplomacy of Thiers lacked weight, while Prussia and Austria were actively preparing for war on the Rhine. Alarmed by this twin danger, King Louis Phillipe replaced Thiers with a conservative and pacific ministry in mid-October. Yet if Palmerston and Minto had been certain France would not act, their colleagues, and Stopford, had been less sanguine. In a divided Cabinet Palmerston had to rely on his brother-in-law Lord Melbourne, the Prime Minister and Minto, an old friend. If his policy had been compromised at any stage he may well have been removed. The risks he ran were high, both at home and abroad.

To avoid complications with France Palmerston wanted to move quickly. The pace of the campaign would be dictated by two overriding considerations; seasonal gales hit the eastern Mediterranean in November and December, forcing sailing fleets to suspend active operations on the coast. If operations had not been completed by then France would have another chance to challenge British policy. Consequently when Stopford hesitated to blockade

Alexandria or seize Egyptian shipping, he earned a strong rebuke from Palmerston, who called him, somewhat unfairly, 'a superannuated twaddler ... quite unfit for the mixed political and naval duties he had to perform'.[6] Stopford's hesitation ensured that Napier, directed by Palmerston's private letters, would be the driving force of the campaign.

In August Stopford sent Napier to Beirut, where he attempted to raise a revolt, without success. He then proceeded to Alexandria, and after going ashore to meet Mehemet Ali left two ships of the line, the *Asia* and *Implacable*, to blockade the Turco-Egyptian fleet. This squadron remained on station throughout the campaign, and because only one ship at a time could leave Alexandria harbour it imprisoned Mehemet's fleet. In September Stopford was joined by a small squadron of Austrian ships, a Turkish battleship commanded by Captain Baldwin Walker RN, seconded to the Ottoman fleet, and 5000 Turkish soldiers. The troops, with Napier temporarily in command, landed north of Beirut to arm the local insurgents. Meanwhile the fleet cleared the Egyptians from the smaller forts along the coast. These small triumphs proved vital for Palmerston. It deflated the opposition in Cabinet, and bolstered his diplomacy. He immediately wrote to the ambassador in Paris: 'Napier for ever! Pray tell the King and Thiers that they have lost the game, and that it would be unwise now to make a brawl about it'.[7]

Shortly afterwards Napier and Walker led a small force that bombarded and stormed Sidon on 26 September. Back ashore Napier's army of British and Austrian marines, rocket troops and Turkish soldiers went into battle with Ibrahim Pasha at Boharsef in the mountains west of Beirut on 10 October, gaining one of the Royal Navy's most interesting victories. The defeat of the hitherto invincible Ibrahim by the despised Turks influenced the subsequent collapse of Egyptian morale. In combination with naval pressure, essentially the complete cutting of his supply links with Egypt, Boharsef forced Ibrahim to evacuate Beirut.[8] The last remaining position in Egyptian hands was Acre, the most powerful fortress on the coast, which Mehemet Ali wanted to keep as a jumping-off point for a future reconquest. Recognising the power of the fortress

Stopford hesitated to attack, but Palmerston's unequivocal orders arrived at the end of October.

The Bombardment of Acre

On 29 October Stopford and the senior military officer, Sir Charles Smith, agreed a plan of action. The White Mountain pass north of Acre would be occupied by 2000 Turkish troops, while another 3000 would embark with the fleet to storm the fortress. Stopford and the senior captains discussed Acre aboard the *Princess Charlotte* on the 30th, and despite Stopford's reservations about the French fleet, agreed to attack. The combined fleet arrived off Acre late on 2 November, where the shoals had been surveyed by the frigate captains Edward Boxer, *Pique*, and Henry Codrington, *Talbot*. Their work had been facilitated by the Muslim festival of Ramadan which required the faithful to fast throughout the day. As darkness fell the Egyptians were too busy eating to notice the surveying parties. In the morning their Polish adviser mistook the surveying buoys for moorings, and instructed the gunners to lay their pieces on them. Codrington described the position as follows:

> The walls of Acre are built on a rocky shelf, partly some feet above, and partly level with the water's edge, and surrounded by a prolongation of that shelf on a ledge in the water. The walls rose up nearly perpendicularly; to a height, I think, of between thirty and forty feet ... it was an irregular line of battery ... mostly (I speak now of the southern face) of open batteries; they were armed with long guns, 18 pounders and 24 pounders ... I think I saw 32 pounders. ... They were almost all very efficient guns, and had been but recently cast. The supply of ammunition ... was dangerously superabundant; for on going round the batteries *next d*ay, I saw to the left of each gun, round shot, double headed shot, *live* shell in abundance, and *heaps of full cartridges*.[9]

At 5.30pm the Captains assembled in Stopford's cabin, and elected to tow the fleet into action the following morning, although the shortage of steamships would require each steamer to make two journeys. The fleet would engage the two sea faces of Acre, the larger battleships and the modern frigate *Pique* on the western face, where their heavy guns would be effective, the smaller ships, armed for short

The driving spirit behind the campaign was Commodore Charles Napier, seen here in heroic pose at the storming of Sidon. (National Maritime Museum, London: BHC 2875)

range action to the south, close to the walls. Walker's flagship, the Turkish 74, was placed directly opposite the small water gate, supported by the 74s *Edinburgh* and *Hastings*. Their role was to batter a practicable breach in the wall, through which the troops could storm the city. In addition the Austrian frigates *Medea* and *Guerriere* with the corvette *Lipsia* joined the British line.[10] The plan was based on Napier's capture of Sidon. Napier requested the post of honour for the *Powerful*, but it was decided that two small battleships would be more effective than one large one in the restricted space available. The role of Napier's western division was, apart from providing enfilading fire onto the southern walls, entirely diversionary.

Early on November 3 the plan of attack was changed, as the wind had shifted, and the fleet would now sail into action. The steamers would remain underway, firing shells into the city from the angle between the two sailing formations. Stopford shifted his flag into the *Phoenix* so that he could control the action, becoming the first British Admiral to command a fleet action from a steam warship. The fleet got underway at 11.00am. In view of the light onshore breeze Napier, in the *Powerful*, led his division to the north before running down for the western face of the fortress from 1.00pm. At 2.30pm the *Powerful* anchored by the head and stern 800-900 yards out, before opening fire. She continued firing until 5.45pm, receiving considerable damage aloft, but few hits in the hull. The gunners ashore had laid their pieces to hit the navigational marks, which were laid over the shoals, and then filled in their embrasures with sandbags. When the squadron anchored considerably closer to the walls it was too late. The mistake proved to be fatal, for smoke drifting in on the faint breeze quickly obscured the target, while the rapidity and precision of British fire gave the Egyptians no opportunity to correct their error.

It had been intended that Napier's squadron would anchor in succession from the north, each ship passing on the disengaged side of those already in action, to occupy the entire western face of the fortress down to the juncture of the two seaward faces. However, the orders on this issue were not clear. In the event when the *Powerful* came to her squadron anchored astern, leaving a large gap at the head of the line. At 2.50pm both Napier and Stopford signalled the *Revenge*,

The bombardment of Acre - the southern attack. Walther's Turkish flagship is the centre while the steamers in the foreground prepare to fire their shell guns. (National Maritime Museum, London: Neg No 7019)

78, Captain Waldegrave, to fill the position. Waldegrave, furious at being kept in reserve for the attack, moved ahead of the *Powerful*, anchoring at 3.30pm. This incident caused a major dispute between Napier and Stopford, which came close to a Court Martial. By the time Stopford signaled the cease fire, at 5.50pm, only one or two guns on the sea face were still firing, and they were quickly silenced by the *Princess Charlotte*. This side of the attack had exceeded even the most sanguine expectations, but it did not, of itself, lead to the fall of the city.

The southern attack also went in on the sea breeze, the smaller ships had very little in the way of instructions, they supported the battleships, knocking out Egyptian guns to prepare the way for an assault. The ships anchored shortly before 2.00pm, 500-600 yards out. At this range the carronades of the older and smaller ships like Codrington's *Talbot* were still effective. Once again the Egyptian guns were aiming too high, once again they had no chance to rectify their error. Midshipman Montagu Burrows of the *Edinburgh* recorded:

> The very first broadsides were murderous, and the smoke soon enveloped the whole of them, as there was very little wind. It is also an historical fact that for guns of that period, in wooden ships, something like perfection had been attained. Officers and men had been thoroughly trained under the newest system; and all matters connected with gunnery worked with the regularity of clocks.[11]

Aboard the *Edinburgh* four men were killed and seven wounded when a single shot struck an upper deck carronade, the only shot to strike the hull, as opposed to the rigging. Gradually the Egyptian guns were disabled by direct hits, by the destruction of the stone walls and by killing the gunners. Only one obstinate piece behind sandbags continued to fire at the *Talbot* until the end, and remained undamaged the following morning. Operating at the angle between the western and southern lines the steamers fired shells from their upper-deck pivot guns.

At 4.20pm there was a flash of light in the south-eastern section of the city, followed by a catastrophic detonation and shockwave. A shell, variously attributed to the steamer *Gorgon* or the *Benbow*, had penetrated the main magazine. In the explosion 1100 men, more than one-quarter of the garrison, were killed. Many sailors were temporarily deafened. All firing, ashore and afloat, ceased for a few minutes, and when the shore batteries did resume their fire was weak and quickly fell away to almost nothing. This allowed the naval gunners to concentrate on those pieces that were still firing. The drill of HMS *Excellent*, instilled into a peacetime fleet by trained seamen gunners and professional officers proved irresistible. By 5.00pm the southern division had ceased firing. Burrows, later an *Excellent* man, commented:

> Many of the guns were dismounted and shattered by our shot, gun-carriages in shivers, embrasures driven in. Great credit is therefore due

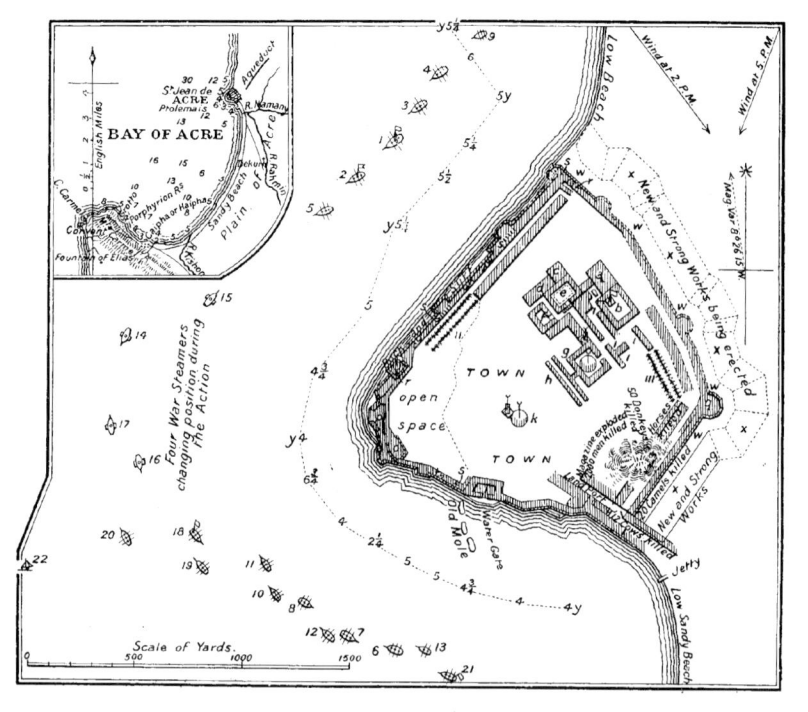

The Bombardment of Acre, 3 November 1840. (From William Laird Clowes, *History of the Royal Navy*, Vol VI)

Key:
1. *Princess Charlotte*
2. *Powerful*
3. *Thunderer*
4. *Bellerophon*
5. *Revenge*
6. *Benbow*
7. *Edinburgh*
8. *Castor*
9. *Pique*
10. *Carysfort*
11. *Talbot*
12. *Hazard*
13. *Wasp*
14. *Gorgon*
15. *Phoenix*
16. *Stromboli*
17. *Vesuvius*
18. *Medea* (Aust.)
19. *Gurriera* (Aust.)
20. *Lipsia* (Aust.)
21. Turkish 84 (flag)
22. Turkish cutter

to the defence. It is questionable whether any troops would have done better in standing to their guns, though doubtless many would have fired better while there.[12]

Stopford signalled the western division to cease fire at approximately 5.50pm, although some ships had already done so for lack of targets. Later the heavy ships of the western division moved into deep water, some having to be towed, being badly cut-up aloft. Preparations were made to assault the city the following day. However, during the night the Egyptians evacuated the city. Walker quietly sent

'Within Cannon Shot of Deep Water'

The moment of truth – the main magazine detonates in the centre of Acre. The western division, with the *Revenge* at the head of the line, is engaging the sea face. The southern attack can be seen to the right. (National Maritime Museum, London: Neg No C682)

his troops ashore, followed by British and Austrian marines. By daybreak Acre was in allied hands, although there would be further casualties when another magazine detonated. The fleet suffered only 18 killed and 41 wounded, which, together with the loss of a few spars, some rope and the expenditure of over 48,000 rounds made this one of the cheapest of the Royal Navy's major victories.

Napier's Convention

After Acre Stopford sent Napier to command the blockade of Alexandria. Privately informed by Palmerston of the terms he desired, Napier settled the crisis with Mehemet Ali. They signed a convention on 25 November; in return for hereditary rule in Egypt Mehemet would evacuate Syria and restore the Turkish fleet. While Napier had no authority to sign the convention, and was in breach of his duty to Stopford in acting alone, Palmerston approved the measure. Once Turkey awarded Mehemet a hereditary pashalic, the crisis was settled. Condemned by many as insubordinate and self-promoting, Napier's action was seen in a very different light after 2 December, when a severe gale wrecked the *Zebra*, dismasted the *Pique* and placed many other ships in danger. Napier had been well aware of the danger, and had acted accordingly. Once reduced to a proper subordination Egypt ceased to be a problem until the 1880s, and then it would be her weakness, not her ambition, that involved the great powers.

Acre is rightly considered to be an outstanding example of naval power projection, from the completeness of the victory, the immediacy of the results and the skillful handling of the campaign by Palmerston and Napier. It should be recalled that the Egyptian army that was forced out of Syria began the campaign close to 70,000 strong. It returned to Egypt across the Sinai desert as a disorganised, demoralised rabble. In 1840 the Royal Navy upheld the integrity of an ally, disciplined a rebellious and troublesome vassal, disabused France of her dreams of maritime equality and enabled Palmerston to replace Russian influence at Istanbul with the Four, later Five Power Straits Convention of 1841 that neutralised the Turkish straits. The triumph belonged to Palmerston, and to the fleet. Palmerston himself was in no doubt of its value. Acre was:

> an event of immense political importance as regards the interests of England not only in connection with the Turkish Question, but in relation to every other question which we may have to discuss with other powers. Every country that has towns within cannon shot of deep water will remember the operations of the British Fleet on the Coast of Syria in September, October and November 1840, whenever such country has any differences with us.[13]

The British Fleet at Acre.

Vice-Admiral Sir Robert Stoptford

Ship		No of guns	Commander
Princess Charlotte		104	Captain Robert Fanshawe
Powerful		84	Commodore Charles Napier
Thunderer		84	Captain Maurice Berkeley
Bellerophon		80	Captain Charles Austen
Revenge		78	Captain William Waldegrave
Benbow		72	Captain Houston Stewart
Edinburgh		72	Captain William Henderson
Pique		36	Captain Edward Boxer
Castor		38	Captain Edward Collier
Carysfort		26	Captain Henry Martin
Talbot		28	Captain Henry Codrington
Hazard	Sloop	18	Commander Charles Elliot
Wasp	Brig	16	Commander George Mansel
Gorgon	Steam	6	Captain William H. Henderson
Phoenix	Steam	6	Commander Robert Stopford, carrying the Flag of – Vice-Admiral Stopford.
Stromboli	Steam	6	Commander Woodford J Williams
Vesuvius	Steam	6	Commander Thomas Henderson
Turkish		74	Rear-Admiral Baldwin Walker (Captain RN)

Austrian

Medea	Frigate	60	Rear-Admiral Bandiera
Guerriere	Frigate	48	The Archduke Frederick
Lipsia	Corvette	20	

Defences of the Fortress of Acre.

After the battle British officers counted 121 guns mounted on the walls, 42 not mounted and 20 mortars. In addition there were 97 bronze field guns and a large store of small arms, ammunition and military supplies.

BIBLIOGRAPHY

Manuscript Sources:

Admiralty Papers, Public Record Office including Ship and Admiral's Log Books, Official Correspondence.

Austen, Codrington, Minto, Napier and Stopford Papers National Maritime Museum

Palmerston Papers, Southampton University Library

Martin and Napier Papers British Library

Secondary Sources

F E Bailey, *British Policy and the Turkish Reform Movement, 1826-1853* (London 1942)

C Bartlett, *Great Britain and Seapower 1815-1853* (Oxford 1963)

Lady Bourchier, *Letters of Sir Henry Codrington* (London 1880)

K Bourne, *Palmerston* (London 1982)

M Burrows, *Autobiography of Montagu Burrows* (London 1908)

J P T Bury and R Tombs, *Thiers 1797-1877* (London 1986)

J Hattendorf, 'The Bombardment of Acre, 1840' *Les empires en guerre et paix 1793-1860*. (Paris 1990)

Admiral Sir John Hay, *Lines from My Log Book* (London 1892)

A Lambert, *The Last Sailing Battlefleet: Maintaining Naval Mastery 1815-1850* (London 1991)

A Marsot, *Egypt in the Reign of Muhammad Ali* (Cambridge 1984)

Maj.Gen. E Napier, *Memoirs and Correspondence of Admiral Sir Charles Napier* (London 1862)

A Pearsall, 'The Bombardment of Acre, November 3, 1840', *Sefunium* 1967-68 (The Maritime Museum, Haifa)

K S Salbi, *The Modern History of Lebanon* (Connecticut 1965)

P W Schroeder, *The Transformation of European Politics, 1763-1848* (Oxford 1994)

S J Shaw, *History of the Ottoman Empire and Modern Turkey* (Cambridge Mass. 1976)

L Sondhaus, *The Habsburgs and the Sea* (Purdue, Indiana 1990)

H Temperley, *England and the Near East: The Crimea* (London 1936)

Sir C Webster, *The Foreign Policy of Palmerston* (London 1951)

Notes

1 A Marsot, *Egypt in the Reign of Muhammad Ali* (Cambridge 1984).
2 S J Shaw, *History of the Ottoman Empire and Modern Turkey* (Cambridge Mass. 1976).
3 F E Bailey, *British Policy and the Turkish Reform Movement, 1826-1853* (London 1942).
4 Maj.Gen. E Napier, *Memoirs and Correspondence of Admiral Sir Charles Napier* (London 1862). Major Napier served in Syria with his step-father, making his account particularly useful.
5 J P T Bury and R Tombs, *Thiers 1797-1877* (London 1986), pp63-79.
6 Palmerston to Minto 30 Aug 1840. Sir C Webster, *The Foreign Policy of Palmerston* (London 1951), p703.
7 K Bourne, *Palmerston: The Early Years 1784-1841* (London 1982), p606.
8 H Temperley, *England and the Near East: The Crimea* (London 1936), pp120-7.
9 Lady Bourchier, *Letters of Sir Henry Codrington* (London 1880), p488.
10 L Sondhaus, *The Habsburgs and the Sea* (Purdue, Indiana 1990), pp102-4.
11 M Burrows, *Autobiography of Montagu Burrows* (London 1908), p128.
12 Ibid, p127.
13 Palmerston to Minto 17 Nov 1840: Minto Papers, National Maritime Museum, ELL/118.

CHAPTER 5

Under the Heel of Britannia: The Bombardment of Sweaborg 9-11 August 1855[1]

by Andrew Lambert

After the final defeat of Napoleon the Royal Navy was unchallenged as the dominant naval force. However, it did not rest on its laurels, and devoted much attention to the problem of carrying naval power from the sea to the shore. The main target would be rival naval arsenals, and especially the fleets that skulked inside them, unwilling to risk battle at sea. By the 1850s naval power projection was the right arm of a global empire. This chapter will examine the most important naval power projection operation of the century, the attack on Sweaborg between 9 and 11 August 1855, when large parts of the arsenal, and the shipping it supported, were destroyed by long-range bombardment.

The origins of the attack can be traced back to concerns rather closer to Britain. The introduction of steam shipping in the early nineteenth century gave the long-running Anglo-French rivalry a new direction. After 1840 the French developed a steam fleet, and completed a major new base at Cherbourg, on the Cotentin peninsula, pointing directly at southern Britain.[2] To counter the threat of steam-powered raids, or even an invasion, the Royal Navy developed the ships, weapons and forward bases for large-scale offensive operations against Cherbourg. In the event of war they planned to build steam gunboats and rocket craft for a sustained long-range bombardment, to be followed up, if possible, by battleships. The object was to destroy the ability of the arsenal to support any hostile shipping.[3] However, naval policy remained focused on maintaining sea control with a superior fleet of capital ships. With the limited funds available no new flotilla craft were produced. They would be built when required. By 1852-3 Anglo-French relations had reached a crisis, with the new Imperial regime of Napoleon III challenging British naval mastery. This resulted in a naval arms race.

The Crimean War and the Baltic Campaign of 1854

However, in mid-1853 Anglo-French tension was suddenly replaced by a crisis over Turkey, in which the two rivals found themselves on the same side, in opposition to the Russians, who were threatening to overthrow, or seriously weaken, the Ottoman Empire. Although war did not break out until March 1854, active planning for the 'Crimean' war began nine months earlier.[4] While the French expressed little interest in the Baltic the British considered it a vital strategic theatre, initially to keep the Russians within the Danish Narrows, and then to blockade Russia, cripple her economy and use the lure of Finland to bring Sweden into the coalition. The Swedish army and coastal flotilla would make up for British weakness in both areas, and provide much needed local expertise. Unfortunately for the British the Swedish King, Oscar I, was too astute to enter into a limited war with Russia, and the allies, who were not ready for an unlimited struggle, could not guarantee Sweden's post-war security.

The British Baltic campaign of 1854, which began with high hopes that a pre-emptive strike on the Russian warships at Reval would secure Swedish support, faltered when the harbour proved to be empty. Sweden remained neutral. The theatre commander Vice-Admiral Sir Charles Napier had requested troops, mortar vessels and coastal craft. The First Lord of the Admiralty, Sir James Graham, had also been advised to prepare them by the last surviving senior officer of the British Baltic campaigns of 1809 to 1814, Admiral of the Fleet Sir Thomas Byam Martin, but the lure of a rapid 'decisive' attack on Sevastopol persuaded Graham to forego such costly efforts. Consequently the campaign was restricted to a thorough blockade until the French sent a fleet, and later 10,000 troops, who arrived in late July. The troops were landed on the Åland Islands, where the

Russian fortress of Bomarsund was quickly invested, bombarded and taken.[5] Recognising that isolated positions were indefensible against such forces the allies could move by sea the Russians abandoned the works at Hango when the fleet approached. However, the allies were now thinking about Sweaborg.[6] Napier and the French Admiral Parseval Deschenes recognised that with the forces to hand they could not make a serious attack. The French army, stricken with cholera, went home, while the allied flotilla comprised a few old packet boats and one new gun vessel. Critically there were no mortars. This weak, ramshackle flotilla had no power to harm Sweaborg, while an attack by battleships would have been beaten off with severe losses.

Widespread public disappointment at the inconclusive end to the season led Graham to ridicule Napier's repeated calls for mortars.[7] In July Lord Dudley Stuart argued in the House of Commons that mortars should be provided, but Graham left it to the First Sea Lord, Admiral Sir Maurice Berkeley, to ridicule his approach.[8] The failure to provide this key weapons system for littoral power-projection was part of a wider failure to prepare for war. Graham was widely criticised for placing the needs of economy above those of war-fighting. Here he was reflecting the policy of William Ewart Gladstone, the doctrinaire Chancellor of the Exchequer, who argued that the war should be funded from current revenue.[9]

The fortress of Sweaborg had been begun by the Swedes in 1748. It lay on a series of seven islands to the south-east of Helsingfors, covering the deep-water approached to the city. It combined the roles of sea fortress and naval arsenal, being the base of the Swedish coastal flotilla. The seaward face of the fortress presented a series of granite casemate forts, linked by masonry walls with guns mounted *en barbette*, reinforced by new earthworks erected in 1854-5. The islands were linked by bridges. In the years following the surrender of the fortress to the Russians in 1809, and the cession of Finland to the Tsar, little work had been done on the base, the fortifications or the dockyard. Even the emergency of 1854 did little to improve matters; by the end of the year there were hardly any shell-firing guns in place, few new batteries and little understanding of the inshore navigation.[10] Although by mid-1855 the fortress and the supporting works around Helsingfors mounted nearly 2000 guns on a seaward facing arc more than five miles long, with 800 alone on Sweaborg, the great majority were old fashioned, short-ranged 24-pounder cannon firing solid shot. The fortress had a garrison of 8-9000 men. The military strength of the position was reinforced by the shallow, rocky navigation of the seaward approaches. Although less formidable than Cronstadt, which covered the sea approaches to St Petersburg, Sweaborg was a major fortress. It could not be attacked by heavy ships alone, and there were no deep water positions close inshore, from which battleships might overwhelm the defenders by sheer weight of metal. Nor could steam ships bypass the defences, as they had at Bomarsund, and any attack by troops would be thwarted by the presence of a large Russian army. Only the long-range flotilla attack, developed to destroy Cherbourg, could damage the arsenal without having to subdue the batteries.[11]

When Graham realised that Sevastopol would not be taken quickly by a combined operation, as he had planned, he ordered a coast assault flotilla for the 1855 Baltic campaign. The main vessels were five armoured batteries, five blockships (old 74-gun battleships fitted with small engines), twenty mortar vessels and twenty steam gunboats.[12] Despite his admission that the 1854 campaign had been crippled by the lack of flotilla craft, he dismissed Napier as a scapegoat for the failure of the campaign to meet wildly exaggerated public expectations. His initial plans also called for a significant body of British troops to be sent to the Baltic in 1855, but the debacle in the Crimea ensured that they were diverted to meet more pressing needs. Consequently the British fleet returned to the Baltic in March 1855 with an incomplete flotilla, no troops, and only the promise that a French force would arrive later. The new Commander-in-Chief, Rear-Admiral Sir Richard Saunders Dundas (1802-61), had been selected by Graham for his caution, his long experience at the Admiralty and his malleability. He could be relied upon to do as he was told, and would not do anything rash. The only problem would be in persuading him to do anything!

Rear-Admiral Richard Saunders Dundas – a cautious officer, he commanded the bombardment of Sweaborg, but the main inspiration came from the Fleet Surveying Officer, Captain Bartholomew Sulivan. (National Maritime Museum, London: PAD4703)

The plans prepared for the 1855 campaign were derived from consultations with the Fleet Surveying Officer, Captain Bartholomew Sulivan. Sulivan had worked closely with Napier, charting the key areas of the coast and planning operations. His work had outflanked the defences at Bomarsund. He advised Graham that Sweaborg should be attacked by a flotilla, with a force of heavy ships in reserve, in case the opportunity arose to complete the task at close quarters. He stressed that Cronstadt was the more important target, but Graham ignored this advice. He was only interested in Sweaborg, which Napier's failure to attack had been the central to his case.[13] Shortly after Dundas had been appointed and the plans prepared Graham resigned. His successor, Sir Charles Wood, had no time to reconsider the campaign, relying on advice from his predecessor throughout the year. When the troops were diverted to the Crimea, Wood resigned himself to a blockade. Once the fleet reached the Baltic he became more optimistic, hoping coastal operations would divert Russian troops from the Crimea.

The 1855 Campaign

In mid-May Sulivan took Dundas close in to inspect the works at Sweaborg, where he noted additional batteries. At the end of the month Dundas took his fleet up to Cronstadt, the main Russian naval base, and the maritime bastion of St Petersburg. Sulivan advised him that with an adequate flotilla it would be possible to attack Cronstadt, but there were few flotilla craft with the fleet, and he did not expect many more. The pessimistic Dundas was more concerned with the rumours that the Russians had created a powerful steam flotilla of their own, to supplement their oared gunboats.[14] To keep the Russians busy Dundas spread his forces along both shores of the Gulf of Finland, to harass shipping, attack communications and investigate anchorages. He encountered further problems when the allied fleet (the small French detachment had finally arrived), returned to Cronstadt the following month. The Russians had laid a large number of primitive contact mines (known as 'infernal devices'). Fortunately these were too small to damage a ship, and often failed to function, but they did cause concern. At least fifty of them were dragged up with grapnels in the world's first sustained mine counter-measures operation, and both British Admirals were wounded during ill-advised attempts to pioneer bomb disposal. Lacking the flotilla to attack Cronstadt Dundas, in concert with the French commander Admiral Penaud, decided to attack Sweaborg.[15] They considered that the dockyard, and the gunboats it housed, posed a significant threat to their theatre strategy, which relied on dispersed forces to achieve the maximum impact and the most complete blockade. The allies could not commit themselves to large operations in the Gulf of Finland, let alone a full-scale attack on Cronstadt, while fresh coastal forces remained in their rear at Sweaborg.

While Dundas inspected Cronstadt his coastal forces were assembling at Nargen, the island anchorage off Reval. Rear-Admiral Baynes reached Nargen on 27 June with four blockships, mortar vessels and the remaining gunboats. The blockships were well manned but still required some fitting-out, and the other vessels were equally ill-finished. Dundas had turned down the armoured batteries, which were sent to join their French sisters in the Black Sea. At the Admiralty Sir Charles Wood was resigned to a blockade, reporting that no-one in London expected more.[16] The blockading cruisers were proving effective, stopping all maritime activity, destroying forts and government buildings, yet Dundas gloomily anticipated the Russians would attempt to drive off his ships with steam gunboats before the season ended.

Dundas returned to Nargen, leaving Admiral Baynes in command off Cronstadt and spread his battleships and cruisers along the Gulf.[17] Privately he told Wood that having seen Russian guns range out to 4500 yards at Cronstadt, the extreme range of his principal weapon, the 13in sea service mortar, he feared the mortar vessels would go into action under fire. When the mortar expert attached to the flagship, Captain Nugent RE, referred to an eight-day bombardment, Dundas feared a counterattack and decided the heavy ships should not take part.[18] Wood had told him that as Sweaborg was the only suitable target for the mortar vessels they could then be sent home after the attack. The First Lord had considered sending spare mortars but had decided against it.[19]

When Dundas and Penaud arrived at Nargen on 16 July the Allied force was incomplete; there were few mortar shells, while a French floating battery crew arrived only to find that their vessel had been sent to the Crimea. However, the mortars were tested on the 17th.[20] Dundas realised the fleet was desperate for action, yet he found little encouragement when the two admirals inspected Sweaborg from

HMS *Merlin* on the 19th.[21] He considered abandoning the attempt, but Sulivan persuaded him to persevere.[22] Several new works had been built in commanding positions that threatened the operation:

> In short it seems impossible to take up positions anywhere in which mortars would be out of range of heavy guns, but still here are the mortars and here will be the shells when *Calcutta* and *Aeolus* arrive and they may be here this week.

The two Admirals saw little prospect of doing any real damage; 'the wish to do something must be the principal inducement'.[23] Dundas found further cause for alarm when Admiral Penaud sent two ships into the Gulf of Riga without consulting him.[24] By the end of July the allied forces at Nargen comprised four blockships, one French and fourteen British gunboats, and fifteen British and five French mortar vessels. The ammunition had arrived, and the French were expecting more flotilla craft.[25] In the face of 800 guns, and the largely uncharted natural defences of the islands, the two Admirals agreed to bombard with mortars, but a 'serious attack' was impossible.[26] Privately Dundas told his brother that he planned to attack with mortars to burn the arsenal but expressed his concern that the weather might break, and anticipated problems 'keeping the Frenchman in hand'.[27]

At home no-one appreciated quite how cautious Dundas had become. The Queen shared Wood's view that Cronstadt was the place to take risks, not realising Dundas had no intention of taking any risks.[28] Sulivan blamed this lack of resolve on the Admiral's friend and Captain of the Fleet, Commodore the Hon. Frederick Pelham.[29] Wood became alarmed when he realised Dundas was only attacking 'because' he had the mortars, being more concerned to plan a grand attack across the northern barrier at Cronstadt for 1856.[30] Anxiously waiting for news Wood did not anticipate any worthwhile result, although he sent more ammunition.[31]

Mortars and Mortar Vessels

The principle weapons for the bombardment would be heavy 13in sea service mortars, mounted in purpose-built mortar vessels. The

French used relatively large craft, carrying two 12in mortars. The British mortar vessels were small single-masted craft, based on dockyard lighters, and far removed from the large sea-going bomb vessels of the Napoleonic era. They had been developed from the *Drake* and *Sinbad*, two old dockyard lighters converted into mortar vessels in late 1854.[32] Both took part in the attack:

	Sinbad (Mortar Vessel No 2)	*Pickle* (Mortar Vessel No 22)
Length:	60ft 1in	70ft
Beam:	20ft 9in	23ft 4in
Draught of Water:	5ft	8ft 6in
Displacement:	105 tons	155 tons

Armament: 1 x 13 inch sea service mortar: weight 5 tons
Stowage: 446 shells, 30 cases of 1lb shot for close-range fire, 40 carcasses, (incendiary projectiles) and 1 ton of powder.
Crew: 1 midshipman or senior petty officer and 16 seamen to navigate the vessel.
1 Royal Marine Artillery officer and 9 NCOs and gunners to fight the mortar.

These simple, cheaply-built craft could only be used by navies with a complete command of the sea. They had no means of self-defence, relying on larger vessels to tow them in difficult weather, to place them for attacks, to support and supply their crews and withdraw them once the bombardment had finished. In peacetime they were quickly cast aside. However, the mortar vessel was the key to effective naval operations against the shore, as they had been since their introduction in the late seventeenth century. Only mortars could provide the range, accuracy and firepower to destroy large shore installations, without risking the battlefleet in a role for which it was not designed.

Although the Royal Navy had not used mortars operationally since the 1820s, and had not built any new bomb vessels for twenty-five years, the theory and practice of mortar bombardments was well understood. The Royal Marine Artillery (RMA) had been formed in 1804 specifically to serve these weapons. However, in early 1831 the Reform Ministry of Earl Grey had abolished the Bomb Service, cancelled the construction of new bomb vessels and halved the number of men in the RMA. Believing the shell gun would replace the less flexible mortar, and anxious for economies, the First Lord of the Admiralty, Sir James Graham, had not hesitated to act, ignoring the advice of senior naval officers and gunnery experts.[33] The fact that he had abolished the service two decades before may well explain Sir James Graham's reluctance to see it re-established in 1854.

The 13in sea service mortar was a massive iron casting some 5ft 3in long weighing 101 cwt. Mounted on a heavy wooden bed, they were installed on top of a strong structure, designed to absorb the shock of repeated firing. They fired explosive shells and incendiary carcasses, shells filled with a mixture of turpentine, tallow, oil, sulphur, saltpetre, resin and antimony, intended to be inextinguishable. The leading British authority on naval gunnery, General Sir Howard Douglas, had written extensively about the British experience with mortars during the Revolutionary and Napoleonic wars. He also printed range tables and advice on targeting. Unlike the younger naval officers who were running the gunnery training ship HMS *Excellent*, Douglas was a mortar enthusiast. He complained that the weapon had been prematurely abandoned in favour of shell-firing artillery mounted on board steam warships. He considered this ill-advised, as the mortar, mounted in cheaply-built lighters, was 'the most valuable piece of ordnance' for the bombardment of arsenals. In 1854 he had written:

> Bomb shells, fired at considerable angles of elevation, should be used, in order that the momentum acquired in their descent may be sufficient to penetrate magazines or casemates down to the foundations, and there exploding, set fire to the buildings and create havoc and disorder among troops, or should they fall on ships, either pierce through and sink them, or, by exploding, blow them up ... .
>
> A range of 4,000 yards, or about 1fi miles, is quite adequate to the bombardment of any arsenal, with its magazines, barracks, dock-yards and basins: these could scarcely be missed at every discharge, and a few

13 inch shells would suffice to crush the buildings and destroy the shipping.[34]

A bomb ship may, without much exposure, do great damage to an extensive fortress or arsenal, which, being a large object, ought to be struck at every discharge at upwards of 4,000 yards, whilst she is a mere speck on the sea at that great distance.[35]

When fired from a fixed base on shore 50 per cent of the shells would fall within a 50-yard square at maximum range. From a floating platform the accuracy would be significantly reduced, although the weather off Sweaborg was calm, and there were no reports of any problems caused by the sea state. The 200lb shells containing a 7lb gunpowder burster were propelled by 18lb of powder. Fired at an angle of 45 degrees mortars relied on a parabolic arc to achieve accuracy. The shells were fitted with a simple fuse, cut to length to explode either over, or inside, the target. After dark the fuses could be followed as the shells slowly climbed into the sky, and began their descent toward the target, enabling the gunners to correct their aim. At a range of 3300 yards each shell had a time in flight of 27 seconds. Once the line had been settled the range could be adjusted by altering the powder charge, or moving the vessel.[36]

Douglas's textbook ensured that when called upon to revive this old weapon Captain Nugent RE, Captain Wemyss and the RMA officers and NCOs under his command had access to the experience of their predecessors.[37] Wemyss had to train his men to serve weapons long abandoned. He also developed the practice of rapid fire, which went against all previous practice, which had called for slow and steady fire.[38] Sulivan was a willing and effective coadjutor, having the local knowledge, navigational and surveying skills required to place the mortar vessels.

Preparations

While the fleet had been up at Cronstadt, Captain Astley Cooper-Key in the small steam frigate *Amphion* had been watching Sweaborg for two months. He lay close in, observing work on the batteries, interrupted the supply of stone to the fortress, and went in at night to sound the approaches.[39] He passed this information to his friend Sulivan, the acknowledged expert on inshore navigation. Arriving off Sweaborg on 2 August with several captains and masters on board *Merlin*, Sulivan noted new batteries, while the populace of Helsingfors were evacuating the city. That night he swept the approaches for 'infernal devices' and electric cables, using light grapnels, but found none. He spent the following days marking the shoals and laying down buoys for the fleet and the flotilla. Captain Wemyss, who accompanied Sulivan, prepared a plan of attack, based on the information provided by Sulivan, and the force at his disposal. Returning to Nargen on the 5th Wemyss submitted the plan to Dundas and Penaud, who approved.[40] That afternoon the gunboats had been towed across to Sweaborg by the *Hasting*, *Cornwallis* and *Amphion*.[41] The gunboats selected for the bombardment had already been fitted with an extra heavy gun, either a 68-pounder 95 cwt, or a 10in 84 cwt shell gun, from the heavy ships lying at Nargen. They also received drafts of officers and men to fight the guns.[42]

When Dundas arrived off Sweaborg with the fleet on the afternoon of 6 August, Sulivan piloted the big ships into a secure anchorage at Melko Roads. The mortar vessels were towed across from Reval by the frigates, *Euryalus*, *Arrogant*, *Vulture* and *Magicienne*. While at Nargen they had been painted lead grey, to disguise their already small profile. *Edinburgh* and *Geyser* towed the ammunition ships *Calcutta* and *Aeolus*. Penaud arrived later that evening. The cruisers were spread along the coast. Although the weather was far from ideal, Dundas now anticipated causing significant damage to part of the island of Vargon.[43] From the flagship the town of Helsingfors was in plain sight, with a large force of troops visible on the hills beyond, while crowds of sightseers occupied the slope between the town and the beach. West of the city a large hoarding could be seen above an official building, carrying the words 'Lunatic Asylum', a claim few believed.[44] Noting the extensive development of batteries commanding the intricate seaward approaches the two admirals restricted themselves to a mortar bombardment of the arsenal. Dundas then ordered a further search for mines, which was conducted by boats from *Duke of Wellington*, *Exmouth*, *Pembroke*, *Arrogant* and

Euryalus. A few were fished up near Grohara.[45] This suggests the Russian claim to have laid over 900 mines was somewhat exaggerated.

With the approaches still imperfectly charted Sulivan had to place all ships and mortar vessels, especially the four frigates detailed to support the flotilla. Despite this, several gunboats ran aground. The battleships and large transports were anchored in Melko roads, some 5000 yards from the fortress. As the bombardment would rely entirely on Sulivan's surveying plans and placement of the ships, most presumed Sulivan would direct the operation, but Dundas ordered Pelham, the Captain of the Fleet, to take charge, with Captain Ramsay of the *Euryalus* as senior officer of the flotilla, and Lieutenant Augustus Hobart of the *Duke of Wellington* commanding the mortar vessels. This arrangement restricted Sulivan to a subordinate role.

On the morning of the 7th Sulivan anchored the mortar vessels. He placed them in a segment of a circle, with the five French craft in the centre, equidistant from Svarto and Vargon, the objects of the attack. The British mortar vessels were divided into three divisions, commanded by Captains Wemyss, Lawrence and Schomberg RMA. The gunboats would keep under way, circling ahead of the mortar vessels, laying down suppressive fire and diverting the Russian gunners from the real threat. Four frigates would be anchored 300 yards behind the mortar vessels to provide support, ammunition and relief crews.[46] The paddle steamers, *Dragon, Vulture, Magicienne* and *Geyser* were each ordered to fit up a paddle-box boat to carry wounded men from the mortar vessels.[47]

The flotilla deployed comprised sixteen gunboats and sixteen mortar vessels from Britain, with five mortar vessels and six gunboats from France. As the French had fewer craft Dundas agreed to them landing five 10in mortars on Abraham Holm. Sulivan had originally proposed placing British mortars on the islands, but Dundas had rejected this as too risky and none were sent. The only battleships present were the two British flagships, three new blockships, all three French battleships and the *Edinburgh*, commanded by the gunnery expert Captain Richard Hewlett. With so few heavy ships it was obvious to the Russians that there would be no serious attack. Sulivan placed the mortars 600 yards back from their firing positions, which were 3000 yards from the nearest batteries, with long cables so they could haul up into range. At Pelham's prompting Dundas insisted they be a further 300 yards back. After consulting Captain Wemyss of the Royal Marine Artillery, Sulivan reluctantly concurred. They recognised that the increased range would hamper attempts to reach the more distant parts of the arsenal.[48] Pelham then urged Dundas to move the supporting frigates *Euryalus*, *Magicienne*, *Vulture* and *Dragon* 400 yards further back.[49] However, when given orders to this effect Sulivan went aboard the ships and swung them on their anchors. Subsequently he refused to move the mortar vessels again.

Going aboard the mortar vessels late on the 7th Sulivan found they were anchored on too short a cable to haul up into range. He then postponed the attack for a day, on his own authority, and ordered the vessels back to their original moorings.[50] Both Dundas's dispatch and the report in *The Times* attributed the delay to the French building their mortar battery.[51] During the 8th additional cables and anchors were sent to the mortar vessels, while the gunboats landed their boats, spare gear and unnecessary fittings on the island of Oterhall.[52] That day the Russian Imperial Standard was seen flying over the arsenal, revealing the presence of Grand Duke Constantine, the Tsar's brother and Navy Minister.

The Bombardment

On the night of the 8th Sulivan was summoned to the mortar vessels, which he found were stationary, with their crews asleep, when they should have been hauling up into range. Once again he blamed Pelham, who seems to have assumed that Sulivan would carry out the work, even though he was not in command. Ramsay sent his boats away on the same task at 1.00am. Dundas went on board *Merlin* at 4.30am, to be close to the action, and to the man who gave the whole enterprise spirit and direction.[53] After waiting for the French mortar vessels and the battery on Abraham Holm the attack finally commenced at 7.25am on the 9th, long after dawn. Wemyss fired the first shell from HMS *Pickle*, and the other mortar vessels then opened fire. Although the gunboats *Pelter*, *Starling* and *Thistle* joined the

The night attack. Rocket boats, with their prominent frames and launch tubes, fire on Sweaborg. (National Maritime Museum, London: Neg No 58/433)

action almost immediately, firing on magazines and other targets, some gunboats did not open fire for an hour.[54] The wind was very light, no more than Force 1, and variable, shifting from the north in the morning, round to the south-southeast in the afternoon.[55] Target selection had been settled by Sulivan and Wemyss, using major landmarks for line, and relying on accurate ranging for effect. When the first bombs landed squarely on target Sulivan, greatly relieved after six days of unrelenting effort, was observed dancing on the paddle box of the *Merlin*. Wemyss had decided to throw as many shells as possible in a short time, to build up a body of flames and prevent effective fire-fighting. During the first hour *Growler*'s mortar, cast in 1813, fired over thirty rounds, an unprecedented feat which the new mortars could not match. On board the mortar vessels the RMA crews stuffed their ears with cotton and pulled the flaps of their woollen caps down over their ears to reduce the damage to their hearing.[56] Even so they came out of action deafened, and did not recover their hearing for days.[57]

The Russians responded with a heavy fire from almost every gun, mortar and rocket that would bear. However, this storm of shot and shell, which reached out to the mortar vessels, and even came close to the flagship, did very little harm. A few gunboats were hit by splinters, and one or two men wounded. After an hour the Russians reduced their fire, using only a handful of long-range guns and mortars that could reach out to the mortar vessels. They were distracted by the gunboats, which kept under way and developed a powerful counter-battery fire from their heavy guns. *Magpie*, having been given her targets by the Admiral, spent the morning, 'cruising round and round inside Oterhall, firing upon Sweaborg'.[58] *Stork* and *Snapper*, armed with Lancaster guns and directed by Captain Hewlett, together with some of the mortar vessels, attacked the three-decker *Rossiya*. She had been moored in an enfilading position between Bak Holmen and Gustafsvard to block the main channel into the harbour, and mounted a long-range gun. During the first day she was hit by at least twenty mortar shells and two from the Lancaster guns, suffering 100 killed and wounded and severe structural damage. She was withdrawn during the night and moored behind the church on East Svarto. Five more gunboats, led by Commander Preedy of the flagship on board the *Starling*, engaged the batteries at the western end of the fortress. The remainder operated to the east, under the direction of the Captains of the frigates moored astern of the mortar vessels. Occasionally over-enthusiastic lieutenants ran their gunboats onto the hazards clearly marked by Sulivan, who was not impressed, but none suffered any serious damage. *Magpie* had to tow *Snap* off a rock at 2.00pm.

Dundas added a diversionary attack to the Sulivan/Wemyss plan, although without troops these were hardly convincing. Late on the 8th he ordered Captain George Wellesley, of the blockship *Cornwallis*, to take *Hastings* and *Amphion*, and engage the batteries on Stora

Miolo at Sandhamn, six miles to the east of Sweaborg. Wellesley had already surveyed the anchorage.[59] The ships went into action shortly after 8.00am, keeping under way using steam and headsails to manoeuvre into favourable firing positions and avoid return fire. *Amphion* closed to within 2000 yards of the batteries, and had her mainyard nearly shot through, in addition to lesser damage and a number of men wounded. *Cornwallis* was hit nineteen times, and suffered some casualties, but *Hastings* was more circumspect, engaging at 2500 yards. At that range the Russian shells burst short, although shot passed over the ship. At 10.00am four row gunboats engaged the ships from a position between Starholm and Eckhom, their shot fell 50 yards short. They were driven off by *Hastings*'s after 10in gun.[60] At 10.35am the three ships steamed out and anchored. *Amphion* had fired 550 rounds of 10in and 8in shell and 32-pounder shot. *Cornwallis* fired 250 rounds and *Hastings* 374 rounds.[61] The British suffered fourteen wounded and some damage to their ships, the Russians had one gun dismounted. Sulivan criticised the attack, which he believed exposed ships to damage for no purpose.[62]

Early on the 9th, before the attack began, Captain Yelverton of the *Arrogant* had been detached to the west of the archipelago with *Cossack* and *Cruiser* to watch the movement of Russian troops and gunboats. After briefly getting aground at 7.00am *Arrogant* anchored off the island of Drumsio at 7.30. Yelverton 'observed a large body of enemy troops passing across an opening in the woods, and from thence take up their positions behind earthen breastworks the whole length of the island'. At 10.30am the three ships opened fire with shot and shell, dislodging the troops, who were observed to be retreating in all directions by 11.30am. Firing ceased at 1.00pm and the ships rejoined the flagship in the late afternoon. *Arrogant* took up her station off Drumsio the following day, but there were no more targets.[63]

By 10.00am large fires had taken hold of the buildings on Vargon, where two large explosions were observed at 10.25am. Shortly after noon a far larger explosion occurred on Vargon or Gustafsvard, followed by a succession of at least twenty detonations, over a period of several minutes, culminating in the destruction of a large new

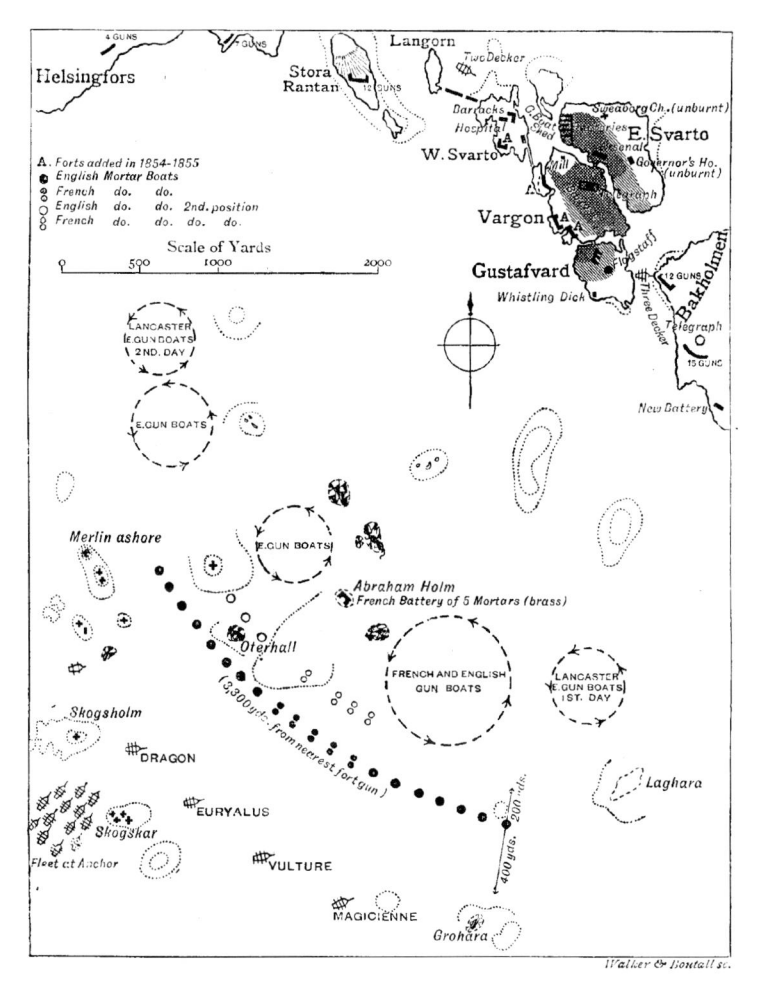

The Bombardment of Sweaborg, 1855. The shaded areas show the extent of the fires caused by the bombardment. (From William Laird Clowes, *History of the Royal Navy*, Vol VI)

earthwork battery on Gustafsvard, which was transformed from a neat green mound of turf into a shapeless heap of stones, earth and smashed timber. Greatly pleased by their handiwork, the British crews manned the rigging and gave three rousing cheers, at which point the crowd of spectators outside Helsingfors fled in all directions.[64] The results of five hours rapid fire had been much as Wemyss predicted. After the war a Russian officer admitted that the sheer volume of fire had defeated all plans for fire-fighting.[65] Dundas observed that Russian fire slackened significantly after mid-day, allowing the gunboats to come closer, where they could target the shore defences and buildings. However, the British had little cause to celebrate; their mortars were defective, some boats already hauling out of action for repairs to the suspension gear, while the rate of fire had to be reduced to preserve the barrels.[66] At 3.30pm the citadel in the centre of Vargon was seen to be on fire.

At 6.30pm Dundas recalled the gunboats as they risked running aground after dark. They withdrew to the fleet, where they replenished their ammunition, food and water. During the night several large ships were detailed to fill cartridges for the mortar vessels and gunboats.[67] HMS *Badger* went alongside the flagship, which hoisted out and replaced a damaged 8in gun.[68] The gunboats were replaced by twenty boats from the fleet, commanded by Captain Caldwell of the *Duke of Wellington*. The boats kept up a heavy fire of 24-pounder Congreve rockets for three hours, from 10.15pm, adding to the conflagration that was being fanned by a northeast wind. Nine boats from *Amphion*, *Cornwallis* and *Hastings* attacked a Russian frigate anchored between Kingsholm and Sandhamn, without success.[69] Two men from the *Hastings* and four from *Euryalus* were injured when rockets exploded in the firing tube. More were hurt when an uncovered rocket was set off and went through the bow of a boat belonging to *Vulture*. The rocket boats continued firing until 2.30am. During the night the mortars reduced their rate of fire, and some hauled out of action for repairs.

The Second Day

As most of the buildings on Vargon and Svarto had been destroyed, Sulivan advised Dundas to warp four mortar vessels 400 yards closer before they resumed firing the next morning. Two French vessels also moved in. The mortars resumed firing at 4.15am. Even so, defective barrels prevented the British weapons from reaching the more distant parts of the arsenal, while the smaller French pieces simply could not make the range. This anxiety about the limited range of the mortars brought the gunboats into consideration. At

The view from the bow of a British gunboat as Sweaborg's main magazine explodes. Helsingfors Town Hall is on the left, the battleship *Rossia* on the right with mortar boats in the foreground. (National Maritime Museum, London: Neg No 8084)

5.00am Captain Hewlett visited several gunboats, ordering them to shift their fire from the batteries to the gunboat sheds and the dockyard buildings.[70] Others, like *Stork*, spent the morning 'engaging forts that fired on us'.[71]

When the mortars resumed full-scale firing on the 10th they were once again warmly received, the Russians having used the brief respite of the night to increase elevation of their guns. The batteries, being well in advance of the buildings, were largely unaffected by the attack on the arsenal. The Russian fire was still reaching the gunboats and occasionally the mortar vessels, but without causing any significant damage. The conflagration within the arsenal continued throughout the 10th, starting to the north of Vargon, and finally reaching the gunboat sheds and storehouses on East Svarto. These were full of tar, pitch and timber and burnt furiously, Dundas noting, 'A large fire among the buildings and gunboat sheds on East Svarto.' The oared flotilla was consumed in the flames. In addition the barracks and storehouses on Vargon were also on fire. The failure of the mortars prevented the attack from reaching West Svarto. In the afternoon the remaining mortars were moved in, and smaller charges were used to keep the bombardment going. During the day the wind varied between Force 1 and Force 3, veering between the southeast and east-southeast.[72]

At 8.30pm *Merlin*, with Dundas on board, had stuck fast on a rock while steaming slowly along the line of mortar vessels.[73] Despite blowing down her boilers, shifting stores unloading ammunition and having the assistance of several vessels she could not be moved. The gunboat *Badger* was soon in the same predicament. Both were within extreme range of the shore batteries, although neither was targeted. At 9.00pm the gunboats ceased firing and pulled back to replenish ammunition and stores. At this time Captain Ramsay noted; 'The whole of the interior of the fortress on fire'.[74] At 10.00pm a division of rocket boats opened fire supported by a second division at 11.00pm. The Russians returned fire from Gustavsard and Rantan. In addition the mortar vessels sustained a slow fire throughout the night. The north and west sides of East Svarto were consumed by flames. Commodore Pelham reported: 'Flames on shore very bright, and fires burning fiercely'.[75] The rocket boats retired at 2.30am on the 11th. Thereafter the Russians did not fire.

During the 10th *Havoc*'s mortar burst, half of the barrel flying over the bow, the other half striking the stanchions on the forecastle. Fortunately, no-one was injured. The shattered stump of the barrel demonstrated what was happening. A small hollow, no bigger than a walnut shell, had gradually formed in the powder chamber of the mortar. This hollow was increased with every discharge, and eventually opened a flaw in the metal, creating a longitudinal split which allowed the mortar to burst.[76] When the factory ship *Volcano* arrived on the morning of the 10th she took up a position near the mortar vessels.[77] This allowed the Inspector of Machinery, Mr Ward, and his artificers to repair the damaged mortar barrels by pouring molten zinc into the hollows and cracks that were appearing. *Beacon's* weapon was repaired six times, each repair allowing a further burst of up to thirty rounds. It would have been preferable to replace the damaged barrels, but Sir Charles Wood had decided against sending any spares. Two more barrels burst as the mortars kept up a steady fire during the night of the 10th. The French 12in weapons stood a powder charge of 22lb, while the British 13in were ruined by 18lb. At 3.00am on the 11th Wemyss called on Sulivan and advised him that nearly all the remaining mortars were dangerous, and could fail at any moment. Sulivan advised him to cease firing and consult the Admiral. The mortars were supported by the rocket boats, which operated in two divisions under Caldwell and Captain Seymour of the *Pembroke*, allowing the fire to be sustained for much of the short period of darkness. Another premature rocket detonation injured a man belonging to *Vulture*. During the night three more mortars failed, without causing serious injury. By this stage only four weapons remained serviceable. At 3.45am the cease fire was signalled, and the mortar vessels began to haul back out of range. The French mortar battery continued firing for some time.[78]

During the early morning of the 11th Dundas spent several hours searching for Penaud, to discuss ending the bombardment. Eventually a midshipman aboard the *Tourville* revealed that the Admiral had taken his gunboats to attack the Russian two-decker battleship *Hezekiel* lying between Langhorn and West Svarto. This wild project came to a sudden end when the gunboats ran aground. In the glare from the burning arsenal they made excellent targets. Penaud considered abandoning them, but they floated off before dawn. Dundas wanted to cease fire at dawn, from lack of targets in range and the dangerous condition of his remaining mortars, and a shaken Penaud was happy to agree.[79] By this time the Russian fire had effectively ceased, although many batteries were capable of firing if the allies had moved in closer. *Merlin* finally floated off at 1.30pm on the 11th.

The attack had been a great success. The arsenal was ruined and the allies had not suffered a single fatal casualty. Dundas and Penaud sent telegrams and their despatches that evening aboard the aviso *Pelican*. The following day they went inshore aboard the small steamer *Lightning* to observe the damage. That night one of the British spectators joined the action, albeit unwittingly. The Reverend Hughes' yacht, the *Wee Pet*, went in too close and was greeted with a hail of shot and shell, although the foolhardy cleric escaped without damage, his predicament being seen from *Euryalus*. Captain Ramsay noted 'Observe the Russian Forts open fire on a madman cruising inshore in a cutter, sent cutter to her'.[80] The arsenal continued to burn long after the cease fire – the heart of Vargon was still blazing furiously after midnight on the 12th.

Withdrawal and Reflection

In public Dundas was sparing of praise, although he did tell Sulivan 'everyone in the fleet knows our success is due to you'.[81] This was correct: Sulivan was responsible for everything of value in the 1855 campaign, while Dundas's contribution was caution. The attack had exceeded the expectations of all, except Sulivan and Wemyss, both in the damage inflicted (fully three-quarters of the arsenal was ruined), and the absence of fatal casualties. Before publishing Dundas's dispatch the Board removed all references to the failure of the mortars. Penaud, once he had recovered his nerve, alarmed Dundas by proposing all manner of wild schemes, including a direct attack on the Man-of-War Harbour, and bombarding Helsingfors. Sulivan had anticipated this, reporting the city had been evacuated and prepared for fire-fighting. Fortunately humanity and the lack of mortars made it impossible.[82] Early on the 13th the fleet and flotilla weighed anchor and proceeded across the Gulf to Nargen, arriving before noon. Later that month Penaud reported that the Russians had lost eighteen ships destroyed in the basins, 2000 killed and massive damage to the arsenal. After the war the Russians admitted that six battleships, two frigates and a corvette had been destroyed with around 250 killed and wounded, but they were less forthcoming about the damage to the base.[83]

The bombardment of Sweaborg made the best use of the available light forces, achieving a useful result at very small cost. As Cooper-Key observed 'the entire works within the fortress, except the large buildings, were destroyed. These are the works which the fortress was built to protect ... we left Sweaborg in ruins'.[84] *The Times* correspondent was ecstatic: 'the blow ... will be severely felt by Russia. It shakes her confidence in her stone walls, and makes her tremble for every town along her coasts'.[85] Sweaborg was not only an effective operation of war, it was also a timely boost to British morale. From the Black Sea Admiral Sir Edmund Lyons reported that the news 'delights us all'.[86] Wood was pleased with the success: 'I confess I did not expect so much ... I do not know that I could have wished for anything better ... injuring your enemy most seriously at little cost to yourself'.[87] The man who had appointed Dundas to the command, Sir James Graham, congratulated him in a letter that revealed the underlying reason for his selection. 'The prudence and success of your arrangements are signal and fully justify the confidence which has been reposed in you.'[88]

Although Dundas announced the success of the attack in a telegram of the 11th, news of the mortar failure did not reach London for another nine days. Returning to Nargen early on the 13th Dundas prepared the mortar vessels to return to Britain. They left on the 17th and 18th, escorted by three cruisers. Once clear of the Gulf they proceeded independently to Elsinore where a cruiser and a transport would assist them past the Skaw. Unaware of this the Admiralty ordered the steam battleship *Sans Pareil* to load eight new mortar barrels, while two steamers would carry the ammunition. The following day the battleship was ordered to land her lower deck guns and embark sixteen mortars. Wood was now determined Dundas should not lose an opportunity for lack of material. Where he had previously looked for no more than a blockade, Sweaborg encouraged him to call for another bombardment. On the 24th Dundas was telegraphed to keep his mortar vessels and await the *Sans Pareil*: Dundas reported their departure, claiming that even with new barrels they would only be a nuisance, and protested at the dispatch of new barrels. He also claimed the mortar beds were defective, when in truth they were still quite sound. Fortunately for Dundas, Wood was more concerned to prepare for an attack on Cronstadt in 1856 than pick a quarrel.[89]

The bombardment of Sweaborg was the last and largest use of mortars by the Royal Navy. With the development of rifled artillery they fell out of favour, despite playing a critical role in the capture of Sevastopol, and enjoying considerable success during the American Civil War.[90] During the bombardment of Sevastopol the British used land pattern 8in and 10in mortars, and both the lighter land service and the heavy sea service 13in mortars. Between early April and the 9 September 1855 the 13in weapons alone fired 40,000 shells, 2500 of them on one day. During this time only one old land service barrel burst, despite firing up 3000 rounds each.[91] The heavy shells had largely destroyed the city, and were particularly effective in demolishing the deep, supposedly bomb-proof shelters that the Russians used to keep large infantry reserves close to the front line.

At Sweaborg the mortar performed well as an engine of destruction; 3141 shells were fired, using 100 tons of powder to deliver 1000 tons of shells. The French fired 2828 shells. *Havoc's* weapon was used only ninety-four times, *Growler's* 355. However, nine of the sixteen barrels fired less than 200 rounds, while only two managed more than 300. Eleven barrels were repaired, some more than once. *Growler's* was not repaired, indicating the approximate service life of a well-made mortar. The failure of the others reflected poor casting and boring. Captain Roberts' suspension gear, which allowed the barrel to train, rather than being fixed to the base, was given a combat trial; *Growler* used the system to achieve the highest rate of fire, the equipment in *Surly* and *Drake* broke during the first day, while *Havoc's* barrel failed after ninety-four rounds. Although Roberts' system was an advance, Wemyss observed that it would make changing barrels more difficult. Several of the vessels built for the 1856 campaign were fitted on Roberts' plan. Sulivan and Wemyss decided mortars should be expendable stores, to be replaced from stock.[92]

The gunboats had also performed well at Sweaborg. *Magpie* reported firing 534 rounds over the two days, 360 shells and 174 roundshot from her 10in and 68-pounder guns.[93] The similarly armed *Pelter* fired 270 rounds.[94] However, their organisation left something to be desired. In 1855 each gunboat had been attached to a larger ship, but with the flotilla being increased from 20 to 200 for 1856 a new system was required. The flotilla would be divided into four squadrons, each commanded by a senior Captain, operating from a part armed steam battleship, which would serve as a depot, magazine and base for the small craft.[95]

After the attack on Sweaborg the British watched Cronstadt, pushing their forces up to the head of the Gulf and preparing for a full-scale attack the following season. *Edinburgh* and *Amphion* were left to watch the coast around Sweaborg. Local newspapers indicated the Russians were attempting to play down the significance of the bombardment, the Finns tended to the other extreme.[96] No sooner had Dundas persuaded Wood to recall the mortars than Penaud produced long-range rockets to attack Reval. Fortunately specific orders arrived, restricting their use to Cronstadt.[97]

After Dundas's speculation that inferior metal had caused the mortar failure, Prime Minister Palmerston called for the old Russian guns at Bomarsund to be recovered and recast. More logical enquiries were made for supplies of Swedish ore and mortars.[98] To ensure the failure of 1855 would not be repeated in 1856 the Board of Ordnance was instructed to order 200 13in mortars for 1856, while additional mortar vessels and iron-hulled floats were built, providing 100 bombardment platforms.[99] Proposals for rifled mortars to fire at longer range, were considered, along with a more scientific enquiry into the most suitable metals.[100] Lord Palmerston's enthusiasm had already secured an order for two 36in mortars, designed by Robert Mallet to fire 2500lb shells, although these would not be ready in time for the early stages of the 1856 campaign.[101] To support the mortar fleet in 1856 the 90-gun sailing battleships *London* and *Rodney* were prepared as depot ships. They would be able to replace mortar barrels and beds, supply shells and provide engineering support.[102]

Sulivan had little to do after Sweaborg. He left the Baltic in late October, depressed by petty attacks on defenceless targets. Back in Britain his enthusiasm was rekindled by discussions of the 1856 campaign, and these took on a new urgency when reports arrived of the successful layered bombardment of Kinburn by the allied Black Sea Fleets on 17 October. This operation, using armoured batteries, mortar vessels, gunboats, battleships and troops had destroyed a large Russian fortress, and captured the garrison.[103] On 6 November Wood and Sulivan agreed that floating batteries would be an important element for the Cronstadt attack. After meeting the French Marshal Canrobert at Kiel on 30 November Dundas realised the French wanted to land a large army in the Baltic during 1856, but remained convinced the Russians could hold Cronstadt.[104] In the long term he was frightened by Russian steam gunboats, calling for more of his own, long-range guns and mortars, and twelve First Class steam battleships.

The lessons of the attack were clear to both British and Russians. The flotilla had demonstrated the tactics required to assault sea forts, and the way to Cronstadt was open. The essential differences between Sweaborg and Cronstadt lay in the object and scale of the attack. At Sweaborg the intention was to destroy the arsenal, workshops and support facilities, so it was not necessary to deal with the batteries. The 1855 attack ruined Sweaborg as a base for ships and gunboats, and destroyed many of the ships and boats in the arsenal. However, as Sulivan had always known, and Dundas, Wood, Palmerston and the Queen now acknowledged, Sweaborg was not vital to Russia. Helsingfors was open to attack and Finland could be more easily invaded anywhere else; closing with the batteries would have been futile and costly. By contrast the batteries at Cronstadt covered the deep water passage to St Petersburg. They would have to be silenced to open the Russian capital and fleet to attack.

To destroy Cronstadt the fleet would have to engage several massive granite casemate fortresses, requiring a sustained mortar bombardment, followed by concentrated close range broadsides. Sulivan was confident the enlarged flotilla and armoured force prepared for 1856 could have forced the barrier to the north of the island, bombarded the arsenal, and engaged the fortresses in detail exploiting the limited firepower of the circular forts.[105] The fall of Cronstadt would open the Russian capital to attack, inflicting a tremendous blow on the prestige of the Russian state. The forces available in 1855, even with the floating batteries and the full French complement, were inadequate to attempt Cronstadt. Anything less than a decisive attack would be worse than useless, pointing out weaknesses and giving the Russians a winter to remedy them.

While British activity in the Baltic during 1855 produced no decisive results it fulfilled several important roles. Primarily it created strategic problems for the Russians, forcing them to keep a large army, estimated at 300,000 men, spread along the coast. Second, the minor operations provided a regular display of British moral ascendancy which could only discourage the enemy. Finally, the way to Cronstadt was examined and new lessons learned at Sweaborg; the defects revealed could be rectified before the next season. The attack also convinced the Russians that Cronstadt was vulnerable. The new tactics for littoral power projection operations dovetailed nicely with the diplomatic and strategic developments of late 1855. All pointed to the Baltic becoming the decisive theatre in 1856. Ultimately the new strategy served its purpose by providing the military muscle to back British efforts in the diplomatic end game of the war. It persuaded Russia to accept the allied terms. In 1854 and 1855 the ability of the fleet to attack Russia was limited by severe shortages of flotilla craft, weapons and troops. Despite that, the Baltic campaigns crippled the Russian economy, forced her to expand a major part of her human and material war effort defending her northern coasts. For a campaign of which so little was expected in March, the results were significant. 1856 promised much more.

After the Peace of Paris was signed on 30 March the British organised a Grand Fleet Review for St George's Day, 1856. The Baltic Fleet for 1856 was paraded around the anchorage, culminating in a mock gunboat attack on Southsea Castle. The object was to impress the representatives of the assembled allied, neutral and ex-enemy powers with the strength of British power projection forces.[106] As *The Times* observed:

> A new system of naval warfare had been created ... We have now the means of waging really offensive war, not only against fleets, but harbours, fortresses and rivers, not merely of blockading but of

invading, and carrying the warfare of the sea to the very heart of the land.[107]

British strategic thinking developed to counter the specific threat posed by a French steam fleet based at Cherbourg in the 1840s had matured into a flexible instrument for war-fighting or deterrence, one that could be applied against any power with maritime interests. Wemyss considered:

> Vertical fire from the sea has now been greatly developed and will be made great use of by the power that commands the sea in a future war. May that power still be our own country![108]

Sir Howard Douglas remained convinced that mortars, reinforced by rifled artillery, were the key to maritime operations. Steam fleets with enough mortars and rifled cannon could destroy any base and the fleet it contained with relative impunity.[109] Although 1855 was the only occasion on which the British attacked Sweaborg, they did anticipate repeating the process on three more occasions before the end of the century. In 1863, 1878 and 1885 crises over Poland, Turkey and Afghanistan led the Admiralty to consider the possibilities. On all three occasions they turned to Sulivan for advice. In 1878 Cooper-Key was destined to command the Baltic Fleet, in 1885 he was First Sea Lord.[110] The Russian government responded to this threat with programmes to upgrade the fixed and mobile defences of Sweaborg, Cronstadt and the Gulf of Finland.[111] The British Empire had been secured by the global reach and deterrent threat of such operations for almost a century, and the most compelling evidence for the success of that strategy is written in stone, not only at Sweaborg, but also at Cronstadt, Cherbourg, Toulon, Brest, New York, Boston, Charleston, Wilhelmshaven and Kiel. Between the Battle of Trafalgar and the First World War every great power with a significant sea coast had good cause to fear the power of the Royal Navy. The bombardment of Sweaborg was the most complete demonstration of that power, although it was little more than a warm-up for the full-scale attack planned for Cronstadt.

APPENDIX ONE:

Order Dates for Mortar Vessels

October 1854	2 (*Drake and Sinbad*) converted from lighters
	10 new vessels ordered.
November-December 1854	44 vessels ordered.
November 1855	50 mortar floats ordered.

APPENDIX TWO:

The Allied Fleet at Sweaborg

Duke of Wellington	131 guns		Flag of Rear-Admiral Sir R S Dundas
Exmouth	91 guns		Flag of Rear-Admiral Sir M Seymour
Amphion	40 guns	Frigate	Captain A Cooper-Key
Arrogant	49 guns	Frigate	Captain. H Yelverton
Euryalus	51 guns	Frigate	Captain G. Ramsay
Cornwallis	60 guns	Blockship	Captain G Wellesley
Edinburgh	60 guns	Blockship	Captain R. S. Hewlett
Hastings	60 guns	Blockship	Captain R. C. Caffin
Pembroke	60 guns	Blockship	Captain G H Seymour

Cruisers:
Dragon		Captain W H Stewart
Magicienne		Captain N Vansittart
Cruiser		Commander G H Douglas
Cossack		Captain E H Fanshawe
Vulture		Captain F H H Glasse

Smaller Support Craft
Merlin	Survey Vessel	Captain B J Sulivan, Fleet Surveying Officer
		Commander R Dew

Geyser
Locust
Lightning

Volcano Floating Factory (arrived on 10th)

Belleisle	Hospital Ship
Princess Alice	Transport
Calcutta	Sailing Ammunition Transport
Aeolus	Sailing Ammunition Transport

Mortar Vessels

Beacon, Blazer, Carron, Drake, Grappler, Growler, Havock, Manly, Mastiff, Pickle, Porpoise, Prompt, Redbreast, Rocket, Sinbad, Surly.

Gunboats

Badger, Biter, Dapper, Gleaner, Lark, Magpie, Pelter, Pincher, Redwing, Skylark, Snap, Snapper, Starling, Stork, Thistle, Weasle.

FRENCH SQUADRON

Tourville	91 guns	Rear-Admiral Penaud
Austerlitz	91 guns	
Duquense	91 guns	

Avisos

Aigle

Pelican

Tonnere

Mortar Vessels (each armed with two 12in Mortars)

Tocsin, Fournaise, Trombe, Torche, Bombe

Gunboats

Four armed with two guns

Aigrette, Avalanche, Dragonne, Fuliminante

Two armed with one gun

Tempete, Tourmente

NOTES

1 This chapter uses the place names adopted by the British in 1854-5. The title refers to the Baltic Campaign medal issued in 1856, in which Sweaborg in placed in this position. This chapter is based on a paper originally delivered at Suomenlinna (the modern name of the fortress, literally Finnish Castle), on 14 August 1998, as part of a programme of events designed to celebrate the 250th anniversary of the foundation of the fortress. The author is indebted to all those individuals ands organisations who made it possible for him to explain to modern day Finns why the British attacked a Swedish fortress, occupied by Russians, on the outskirts of their capital city.

2 M Battesti, *La Marine de Napoleon III*, 2 vols (Paris 1997), Vol. II, pp564-72.

3 A D Lambert, 'The Cherbourg Strategy' Unpub. Paper delivered in 1995.
4 A D Lambert, *The Crimean War: British Grand Strategy against Russia 1853-1856* (Manchester 1990), pp28-36
5 A D Lambert, 'Åland, Bomarsund and Anglo-Russian Relations. 1815-1856' in C Ericsson and K Montin (eds), *I Vedlast Over Skiftet Och Alands Hav* (Abo 1993); B Greenhill and A Giffard, *The British Assault on Finland 1854-1855: A Forgotten Naval War* (London 1988).
6 Napier's archive contains numerous plans and drawings of Sweaborg. PRO MFQ 37/1&2.
7 G B Earp, *Sir Charles Napier's Campaign in the Baltic* (London 1857), pp264, 530.
8 J C Hoseason, *Remarks on the late war with Russia, together with plans for the attack on Cronstadt, Sweaborg and Helsingfors* (London 1857), pp3-4.
9 Ibid, p32.
10 Greenhill and Gifffard, pp325-9.
11 O af. Hallstrom, *Suomelinna/Sweaborg* (Espoo 1988); E Fraser and L G Carr Laughton, *The Royal Marine Artillery 1804-1923* (London 1930), Vol I, p441.
12 Lambert, *Crimean War*, pp197-9.
13 Ibid, pp200-1; H N Sulivan, *Life and Letters of Admiral Sir B.J. Sulivan* (London 1896); D Bonner-Smith (ed), *The Russian War; Baltic 1855*. London Navy Records Society 1944. (henceforth NRS). This volume reproduces the Cabinet Confidential Print of Correspondence between the C-in-C and the Admiralty. Sulivan's Memorandum is printed at pp382-98.
14 Lambert, *Crimean War*, pp274-5.
15 Dundas to his sister Jane Dundas 2 Jul 1855. Scottish Record Office, General Documents (henceforth GD) GD 51/8/4 f142.
16 Dundas to Admiralty 27 Jun and 9. & 16 Jul 1855 no. 242, 247: Public Record Office Admiralty (henceforth ADM) ADM 1/5647; Dundas to Wood 2 Jul 1855: British Library Additional Manuscripts (henceforth Add). 49,533 f86-90 Wood to Dundas 3 Jul 1855: Add. 49,563 f40.
17 Dundas to Wood 9 Jul 1855: Add. 49,533 f97-104.
18 Dundas's conversation with Cooper-Key reported in Key's letter of 3 Jul 1855: P Colomb, *Memoirs of Sir A Cooper-Key* (London 1898), p259.
19 Wood to Dundas 10, 17, & 24 Jul 1855: Add. 49,563 f53, 64, 73.
20 W G Don, *Reminiscences of the Baltic Fleet of 1855* (Brechin 1894), p83.
21 Dundas to Wood 17 Jul 1855: Add. 49,533 f106-110; J P Baxter, *The Introduction of the Ironclad Warship* (Cambridge Mass. 1933), p82.
22 Sulivan, p275.
23 Ibid.
24 Dundas to Admiralty 24 Jul. rec. 6 Aug 1855 no. 307: ADM 1/5647.
25 Dundas to Admiralty 30, 31 Jul 1855 no. 335, 337, ibid.
26 Dundas to Wood 31 Jul & 6 Aug 1855: Add. 49,533 f122-3, 129.
27 Dundas to Viscount Melville 31 Jul 1855: GD51/8/7/63 f17x.
28 The Queen to Wood 4 Aug 1855: Borthwick Institute, York, Halifax Papers (henceforth Halifax) A4/73.
29 Sulivan, pp274-5.
30 Wood to Dundas 7 Aug 1855: Add. 49,563 f100.
31 Wood to Dundas 14 Aug 1855: Add. 49,563 f114.
32 C Ware, *The Bomb Vessel: Shore Bombardment Ships of the Age of Sail* (London 1994), pp.68-75; D K Brown, *Before the Ironclad: The Development of Ship Design, Armament and Propulsion in the Royal Navy, 1815-1860* (London 1990), pp154-6.
33 Fraser, pp330-69; Ware, pp54-76
34 Sir H Douglas, *A Treatise on Naval Gunnery* (4th edn. London 1855), pp174-6.
35 Ibid, p355.
36 Ibid, p594.
37 Fraser and Laughton, Vol 1, Ch 1.
38 Wemyss to Sulivan 7 Jan 1857: Sulivan, p342.
39 Colomb, pp256-9.
40 Fraser and Laughton, p441. 41 Ibid, pp442-3.
41 Ibid, pp442-3.
42 Logs of HMS *Magpie, Pelter, Stork*.

43 Dundas to Admiralty 6 rec. 13 Aug 1855 no. 358 ADM 1/5648. Dundas to Wood 6 Aug 1855: Add. 49533 f.129.
44 Don, p90.
45 Dundas to Admiralty 13 rec. 27 Aug 1855 no. 367: ADM 1/5647.
46 Sulivan, pp320-1.
47 Commodore Pelhams' Journal, 6 Aug 1855: ADM 50/339.
48 Sulivan, p275.
49 Ibid, pp322-3.
50 Ibid, p324.
51 Report dated 9 Aug 1855 in A Lambert and S Badsey, *The War Correspondents: The Crimean War*. (Gloucester 1994), pp298-300.
52 Log of HMS *Duke of Wellington* 8 Aug 1855: ADM 53/5587.
Log of HMS *Magpie* 8 Aug 1855: ADM 53/5313.
53 Log of HMS *Merlin* 4.30 am 9 Aug 1855 ADM 53/5129.
54 Log of HMS *Magpie* 8.25 am 9 Aug 1855: ADM 53/5313. Log of HMS *Pelter* 9 Aug 1855: ADM 53/5286.
55 Log of HMS *Duke of Wellington* 9 Aug 1855. As the flagship was not under fire, or under way, her officers had a better opportunity to record the weather than ships in action, whose recording of wind and sea states are quite inconsistent. ADM 53/5587
56 Fraser, p443.
57 Don, p98.
58 Log of HMS *Magpie* 9 Aug 1855: ADM 53/5313.
59 Log of HMS *Cornwallis* 7 Aug 1855: ADM 53/5211.
60 Log of HMS *Hastings* 9 Aug 1855: ADM 53/4939.
61 Ibid & Log of HMS *Amphion* 9 Aug 1855: ADM 53/5500.
62 Dundas to Admiralty 13 Aug 1855 no. 367: ADM 1/5647.
63 Log of HMS *Arrogant* 9-10 Aug 1855: ADM 53/5534.
64 Don, p97.
65 Fraser, p446.
66 Log of HMS *Euryalus* 9 Aug 1855 gives details of the movement of the mortar vessels: ADM 53/5597.
67 Commodore Pelham's Journal 10 Aug 1855: ADM 50/339.
68 Log of HMS *Duke of Wellington* 9 Aug 1855: ADM 53/5587.
69 Log of HMS *Hastings* 9-10 Aug 1855: ADM 53/4939.
70 Log of HMS *Magpie* 5.30 am 10 Aug 1855: ADM 53/5313.
71 Log of HMS *Stork* 10 Aug 1855: ADM 53/5372.
72 Log of HMS *Duke of Wellington* 10 Aug 1855: ADM 53/5587.
73 Log of HMS *Merlin* 8.30 pm 10 Aug 1855: ADM 53/5130.
74 Log of HMS *Euryalus* 9.30 pm 10 Aug 1855: ADM 53/5597.
75 Commodore Pelham's Journal 10 Aug 1855: ADM 50/339.
76 Fraser, p448.
77 Log of HMS *Volcano* 10 Aug 1855: ADM 53/4980. D Evans, 'The Royal Navy and the Development of Mobile Logistics, 1851-1894', *The Mariner's Mirror*, Vol. 83 (1997), pp318-27.
78 Log of HMS *Euryalus* 3.45 am. 11 Aug 1855: ADM 53/5597.
79 Dundas to Wood 21 Aug 1855: Add. 49,533 f137-40.
80 Log of HMS *Euryalus* 8.45 pm 12 Aug 1855: ADM 53/5597.
81 Colomb, p261: Sulivan, p338.
82 Sulivan, p337.
83 Battesti, *La Marine de Napoleon III*, Vol 1, p132, citing Penaud's dispatches of 11, 14 & 28 August 1855 and C L Bazancourt, *L'éxpedition de Crimée: La Marine Français dans la Mer Noire et la Baltique* 2 vols (Paris 1858), p373; Greenhill and Giffard, pp332-6.
84 Colomb, p260.
85 Report of 11 Aug 1855 in Lambert and Badsey, pp300-2.
86 Lyons to Wood, 18 Aug 1855: Add. 49,536 f36.
87 Wood to Dundas 21 Aug 1855: Add. 49,564 f2.
88 Graham to Dundas 23 Aug 1855: GD 51/1008/43 authors' italics.
89 Admiral to Sheerness Dockyard 20 Aug 1855: ADM 2/1570; Admiral to Board of Ordnance 20, 21.8.1855: ADM 2/2681; Wood to Dundas 21, 28 Aug 1855: Add. 49,564 f2, 11; Admiralty

to Consuls at Kiel, Elsinore and Dantzig 21, 24, 27 Aug 1855: NRS pp. 240-1; Dundas to Admiralty 27 Aug 1855 no. 421: ADM 1/5647; Dundas to Wood 28, 29 Aug 1855: Add. 49,533 f142-8; Deptford Dockyard to Surveyor 8 Oct 1855: ADM 87/55 f5430.
90 Lambert, *Crimean War*, pp241-8. The success of these operations, and those at Kinburn convinced Lieutenant David Dixon Porter USN to recommend mortar vessels be used in the attack on New Orleans. See C G Hearn, *The Capture of New Orleans, 1862* (Baton Rouge 1995), pp98-100 etc.
91 Capt W E Reilly, RA, *Artillery Operations conducted by the Royal Artillery and Royal Naval Brigade before Sevastopol in 1854* (London 1859), pp218-23.
92 The 13in sea service mortar in the Royal Armouries collection was cast in 1856 at Low Moor Foundry. It weighs 104 cwt 2lb and 14oz.
93 Log of HMS *Magpie* 10 Aug 1855: ADM 53/5313.
94 Log of HMS *Pelter* 9-11 Aug 1855: ADM 53/5286.
95 Wood to Captain Henry Keppel 30 Nov 1855: Add. 49,565 f18; Admiralty to Medical Director 24 Jan 1856: ADM 1/5648 enclosing Hewlett to Dundas 7 Sep 1855.
96 Dundas to Admiralty 10 rec., 17 Sep 1855 no. 494: ADM 1/5648 enclosing Hewlett to Dundas 7 Sep 1855.
97 F H Winter, *The First Golden Age of Rocketry* (Washington 1990), pp111-12.
98 Wood to Palmerston 21 Sep 1855: Bdlds. GC/WO f58; Dundas to Wood 25 Sep & 14, 23 Oct 1855: Add. 49,533 f162, 171-4; Dundas to Admiralty 3, 8 rec. 15 Oct 1855 no. 573, 582: ADM 1/5648.
99 Admiralty to Board of Ordnance 13 & 29 Sep 1855: ADM 2/1681 pp313, 453; Admiralty to Surveyor 18 Oct 1855: ADM 87/55 f5646; Admiralty to War Department 3 Nov 1855: ADM 2/1682 p15.
100 Admiralty to Ordnance 11, 18 Oct 1855, to War Department 22 Dec 1855: ADM 2/1681 pp390, 406: ADM 2/1692 p189; Admiralty to War Department 31 Oct 1855: ADM 2/1682 pp2-3.
101 Palmerston to General Sir Hugh Ross 1 May 1855: Add. 48,579 f11. See O F G Hogg, *The Royal Arsenal: Its Background, Origin and Subsequent History* 2 vols (Oxford 1963), Vol II, pp756-60 for an account of this weapon. Further trials were conducted when Palmerston returned to office in 1859.
102 Admiralty to War Department 19 Jan 1856: ADM 2 p/309.
103 Lambert, pp254-63.
104 Wood to Dundas 1318, 26 Nov 1855: Add. 49,5656 f2, 17; Dundas to Admiralty 6, 15, 20 Nov 1855 & 10 Dec1855 no. 676, 686, 697, 759: ADM 1/5649; Dundas to Wood 15, 28 Nov 1855: Add. 49,534 f4, 9-12, 14-6.
105 Sulivan, pp273-4, 367, 404-10.
106 Lambert, pp335-7.
107 *The Times* Editorial of 24 Apr 1856: Lambert & Badsey, pp304-5.
108 Wemyss to Sulivan 7 Jan 1857: Sulivan, p342.
109 Sir H Douglas, *Observations on Modern Systems of Fortification* (London 1859), p191.
110 A D Lambert, ' "Part of a Long Line of Circumvallation to confine the future expansion of Russia": Great Britain and the Baltic 1809-1890' in G Rystad, K-R Bohme, and W M Carlgren (eds), *In Quest of Trade and Security: The Baltic in Power Politics, 1500-1890* (Lund 1994), pp297-334, esp. pp321-30.
111 Hallstrom, pp21-2; Fuller, W. *Strategy and Power in Russia, 1600-1914* (New York 1992), pp279, 286-9, 330-5.

CHAPTER 6

March into India:
The Relief of Lucknow 1857-59
by Richard Brooks

The Relief of Lucknow in November 1857 was one of the great set-pieces of Victorian imperial history. It had every dramatic feature: a heroic struggle against desperate odds, innocent women and children threatened by a merciless enemy, and an exotic cast including Highlanders regardless of the heat in kilt and bonnet, and bluejackets manhandling heavy guns into action under fire. After Delhi, Lucknow was the storm centre of the Indian Mutiny, when the Honourable East India Company's Bengal Army massacred its European officers, and proclaimed the end of British rule in India. A narrow focus on events at Lucknow, however, gives a misleading impression of the part played by the Royal Navy in the restoration of peace to Bengal. The sepoy rising in the summer of 1857 provided a showcase for the Royal Navy's ability to react to imperial emergencies, foreshadowing naval participation in later land campaigns in New Zealand and Africa.

Two ships landed naval brigades to help suppress the Mutiny. HMS *Shannon* supplemented the Army's firepower, supplying half the siege train for the Relief of Lucknow in November 1857 and the subsequent clearing of the city in March 1858. HMS *Pearl's* Royal Marine sharpshooters and bluejacket field gunners formed the core of a scratch force of Gurkhas and Sikhs, and were for a time the only British troops operating north of the Gogra River. Their guerrilla campaign against fugitives from the main operations around Lucknow opened a new chapter in naval operations ashore, looking forward to twentieth century counter-insurgencies. In their different ways both the naval brigades that fought in Bengal exemplify the resource and responsiveness that made naval units such effective participants in Victorian small wars.

The Indian Mutiny was one of several imperial emergencies to confront the British during the 1850s. British politicians of all persuasions much preferred arguments about tax reform, drains, or theology to the problems of imperial defence, and cut the armed services to the bone. Despite the notorious unreliability of the native Bengal regiments, British troops were withdrawn from India for service elsewhere, giving the rebels their chance. The Indian Mutiny struck at the strategic heart of the British Empire. Possession of the Indian sub-continent not only guaranteed immense wealth, it conferred Great Power status. The sepoy revolt simultaneously threatened Britain's wealth and her position in the world.

The British responded to the threat by diverting forces intended for the Second China War to India. Among them were two new ships, 'calculated to obtain great speed under sail or steam and to carry very heavy metal': the steam frigate HMS *Shannon* (51 guns) and the steam corvette HMS *Pearl* (21 guns).[1] Such vessels were an attractive proposition for an enterprising captain compared with a battleship, doomed to spend most of her time swinging at anchor. *Shannon* could make 12 knots. Her thirty-one day passage from the Cape to Singapore in 1857 averaged 213 miles a day, one of the best then known. The 'Pax Britannica' is usually associated with the phrase 'send a gunboat', but faster, more powerful vessels like *Shannon* and *Pearl* provided the strategic reach that allowed the Victorian navy to respond to later crises in New Zealand during the 1860s (HMS *Niger* and *Pelorus*), Zululand in 1879 (HMS *Active*, *Shah*, and *Boadicea*), and Burma in 1885 (HMS *Woodlark* and *Turquoise*). HMS *Pearl* had been with the Pacific squadron at Callao, before sailing for China, but neither she nor *Shannon* saw much action at Canton. On 16 July 1857, the day after the massacre of 400 European women and children at Cawnpore, both ships received orders that sent them racing for Calcutta. In such an emergency warships with space for large complements could act as troopers. *Shannon* took 300 Royal Marines from Hong Kong, and *Pearl* three companies of the 90th Light Infantry from Singapore.

Shannon won the race, arriving at Calcutta on 8 August, cheered by an anxious European population. Sir Colin Campbell, Commander-in-Chief in Bengal from mid-August, thought *Shannon* and *Pearl* 'as good as the right wing of an army', over-awing the city with their heavy guns, while the marines from Hong Kong secured the citadel.[2] All hands had sharpened cutlasses during the voyage, inspiring rumours that their services would not be confined to Calcutta. Captain William Peel VC of the *Shannon* had distinguished himself with the Naval Brigade in the Crimea, and now offered naval assistance to the hard-pressed Indian Government. Captain Edward Sotheby of Pearl recalled a conversation at dinner, with the Governor-General:

> 'I hear, Captain Peel, that your band aboard the *Shannon* plays the Sevastopol March'. Peel answered, 'No, my lord, it now plays the Delhi March'. Upon which the Viceroy said to Peel, 'Will you come into my private room after dinner', And in that room they planned to form a Naval Brigade to march to Delhi. Three or four days afterwards they formed the Shannon's Naval Brigade consisting of 500 men and four 68 pounders, and were on the route to assist in quelling the mutiny – A few days after the Viceroy asked me if I could do the same, and I formed a smaller brigade of 250 men and some light guns.[3]

On 18 August 1857 the first echelon of *Shannon*'s naval brigade filed aboard a river steamer and her tow, a flat-bottomed iron barge with a thatched roof. They wore their usual clothing, except for white cotton covers over their sennet hats to protect the back of the neck against the sun. Water-bottles and haversacks were acquired later. A more serious deficiency was a lack of modern small arms. The marines had Minié rifles, but *Pearl*'s seamen carried smoothbore percussion muskets, and one of *Shannon*'s three companies of small-arms men only took cutlasses. It would be almost three months before either brigade saw action, something of an anti-climax after their dash to Calcutta. Campaigns in nineteenth-century India were leisurely affairs, although Peel's men took as little baggage as possible:

> ... each of us has a seaman's bag only, and a blanket, and we have no native servants, without which everybody says we shall never get on.

The Battle of the Alma, 1854. Captain William Peel was ashore during the Russian War of 1854-6, where he won the Victoria Cross. He landed with a hand-picked party of sailors - his gig's crew - to help bridge a river at Alma for the French. (National Maritime Museum, London: Neg No PX9230)

> But it is on that, in a great measure that we rest our hopes of success, as we shall thus be dependent entirely on our own resources.[4]

Meanwhile the naval brigades drilled aboard their flats, before the sun became too hot, shot at pariah dogs along the riverbank, and hardened feet unaccustomed to boots with painful route marches. Drill and marches featured throughout the campaign. After the Relief of Lucknow Peel's brigade still paraded for an hour's drill every day, before a critical audience of soldiers.[5] *Pearl*'s brigade:

> ... formed our force in fighting order, and drilled like the devil, morning, noon, and night; marched out to practise the men, and get them into the ways of battalion drill: in fact turned the British tar into a soldier.[6]

Sailors were naturally trained as gunners, but few were acquainted with horses, the usual means of moving field guns ashore. The available animals were unbroken, and sailors had to improvise harness with rope brought from the ships. Sotheby formed a field battery with four brass 12-pounder howitzers borrowed from the army, and forty-six of his most horsey bluejackets. One of them wrote:

> ...busily engaged fitting harness for our horses and getting them to work together in the guns and we succeeded tolerably well for before we left Myrwa we could go through every evolution connected with horse artillery.[7]

Authentic military vehicles were scarce. Both brigades used native carts or hackeries held together with string, and pulled by recalcitrant bullocks capable of two miles per hour, when beaten vigorously. Later in the campaign *Pearl*'s carpenter adapted captured limbers to naval use, '... an example of that readiness with which a sailor can turn his hand to anything and get out of a difficulty while many a man would be thinking about it ...'[8] *Shannon*'s brigade could not find carriages strong enough for their 68-pounder shell guns, so re-equipped with standard army siege guns: six 24-pounder guns, two 8in howitzers, and some 'infernal machines' made from rocket tubes lashed onto a hackery.

Sir Colin Campbell's first duty as Commander-in-Chief was to rescue the beleaguered British garrison at Lucknow, the capital city of Oudh. He had 4500 men, a strong force by Mutiny standards, but outnumbered eight to one by an enemy well equipped with artillery, and holding strong defensive positions. If Sir Colin were to succeed without crippling losses, he would have to make full use of the naval brigade's guns to clear the way for his infantry.

Infantry-artillery co-operation demanded high standards of gunnery and inter-service co-ordination. The infantry formed up behind the gun line, while the latter played at long bowls with the enemy, then charged through the gaps between the guns, after a final salvo. Something went wrong during one attack on the outskirts of Lucknow. As the 93rd Highlanders rushed forward:

> ... one of the guns went off killing one bluejacket and wounding two others and also wounding one of the 93rd. It appears that the gun hung fire and in the confusion and smoke the men went up to the muzzle and the gun went off killing No.3 on the spot and wounding No.4 and also the man that was serving the vent.[9]

Peel leading the naval brigade into action at Lucknow. 1857. (National Maritime Museum, London: Neg No PZ500)

Nevertheless, the Highlanders took their objective, and developed a close working relationship with the naval brigade. In subsequent assaults on the Secunderbagh and Shah Najif Mosque the soldiers laid onto the 24-pounders' drag ropes, and hurried them forward under a perfect hail of lead and iron. A Royal Marine veteran remembered Peel saying, 'It's no use unless we are close up, we must bring the whole place about our ears and then get to close quarters'.[10] Sir Colin Campbell thought the action almost unexampled in war, Captain Peel behaving very much as if he had been laying the *Shannon* alongside a hostile frigate. Nevertheless the Shah Najif only fell after the 'infernal machines' showered the crowded ramparts with rockets. Peel suggested that if they frightened the enemy half as much as the men firing them, there would be no rebels left in Lucknow by evening.

Campbell linked up with the garrison on 17 November 1857, but had insufficient force to evacuate the numerous civilians, and defeat the remaining rebels. He fell back on Cawnpore, where the naval brigade had another chance to display its novel approach to streetfighting. Tantia Topi, the only rebel leader with any strategic skill, had swept down on the small force left to cover Campbell's communications, bottling them up in their entrenchments. Rebel guns were firing into the camp with uncomfortable accuracy, so Peel's return on the afternoon of 29 November was a welcome reinforcement for the garrison. The naval brigade immediately set about counter-battery work, taking three 24-pounders into Cawnpore to mix it with the rebels, as lesser gunners might have done with field pieces. After a rocket barrage, forty men ran a loaded 24-pounder, muzzle first, down the street to within 300 yards of the enemy gun position, which they silenced with four rounds. Such aggressive tactics were not without risk, however. A shell took the legs off two sailors and wounded another, while the marine sharpshooters in their red tunics got a good peppering.

The naval artillery played a similarly forward part in Campbell's decisive victory over Tantia, outside Cawnpore on 6 December 1857. Opening fire at 800 yards they advanced their guns with the skirmishers, several hundred yards ahead of the main body. They used a combination of drag ropes and bullock teams, 'always kept handy, much to the disgust of the native bullock drivers'. The rebels responded feebly, '... as if they were quite surprised at heavy guns coming along taking the lead like ours did ...'[11] Several sailors were hit, and their shipmates became impatient, calling out: ' 'Damn these cow-horses' – meaning the gun bullocks – 'they're too slow! Come, you 93rd, give us a hand with the drag ropes as you did at Lucknow!'[12]

Meanwhile the Royal Marines and other infantry kept up a tremendous fire of musketry among the broken ground on either side of the battery, until the enemy could no longer stand the naval guns' persistent advance, and fairly ran. The battle secured Campbell's lines of communication, allowing him to move decisively against the rebels at Lucknow. The naval brigade again provided close fire-support, now augmented by their 68-pounder shell guns, which the carpenter's crew had mounted on East India Company gun carriages. The 423-strong brigade now reached its peak firepower: eight 24-pounder and six 68-pounder guns, two 8in siege howitzers, and eight rocket tubes. Hackeries carried 100 rounds per gun, with another 400 in reserve. Peel admitted to a great deal of anxiety as to whether the 3-ton 68-pounders would answer, fearing they would be too heavy to handle, but they sat better on the carriages than the 24-pounders, and were as easily handled and transported. No one had ever worked 8in guns in such a way on land before, but the twenty-man detachments rattled them about famously, '... with the usual quickness common to a sailor'. Peel was confident they would 'show to the world that British seaman could fight on land as well as on the deep'.[13]

The return visit to Lucknow (3-16 March 1858) followed the established pattern, the naval brigade methodically softening up the rebel defences for the assaulting infantry. At the Martiniére the 68-pounders did their work so well that when the attack went in, there was not a sepoy left in the building. Moorsom shells, a new type of percussion shell, went off splendidly, the mud walls being just hard enough to burst them. As at Cawnpore, detachments hauled their guns down streets enfiladed by small-arms fire to breach rebel barricades. Sometimes Indian sappers cleared the way, sometimes the seamen acted as their own pioneers, hacking holes through garden walls with crowbar and pickaxe, to engage the enemy beyond. The last formed bodies of rebels left Lucknow on 17 March, and the

Peel's sailors in action with their guns at Kali Naddi in 1858. The 68-pounder shown here did not actually come into use until later - the gun should be an Army 24-pounder on a field carriage. (National Maritime Museum, London: Neg No A2423)

merchants ransomed the city. *Shannon*'s naval brigade handed their guns over to the Royal Artillery, and set off down country. Captain Peel accompanied them in a dhooli, or canvas litter, for a rebel sniper had shot him in the thigh. The wound was not serious, but a previous occupant of the dhooli had infected it with smallpox, and Peel died at Cawnpore. He had been the mainspring of the *Shannon*'s naval brigade, who always felt they were specifically Peel's naval brigade. He had combined old-fashioned gallantry with a modern egalitarianism. One of his marine detachment in the Crimea recalled his saying, 'Every man must pull his pound in emergency no matter what his rank – Sergeant you clap on that rope', an attitude that endeared him to the common man.[14]

The experience of HMS *Pearl*'s naval brigade was quite different from the *Shannon*'s. It was months before Captain Sotheby's force made contact with the enemy, and many despaired of ever seeing a mutineer. Isolated beyond the Gogra River, they felt they had been brought upcountry for nothing, left in the background with no chance of a crack at the rebels. Like the Shannons, however, the Pearls would depend for success upon their skilful combination of artillery with infantry. *Pearl*'s brigade formed the nucleus of a miniature army, the Saran Field Force, under overall command of a Colonel Rowcroft. Sotheby's men fought as an all-arms force of Royal Marines and naval small-arms companies, and a naval field gun battery. Four hundred and fifty Gurkhas made up the numbers, with fifty Sikh police that a flying column of bluejackets had rescued from a mob. Their first action was at Soanpur (26 December 1857). Faced by overwhelming numbers of rebels, Rowcroft's tactics were resolutely offensive, relying on the rifles of the Royal Marines and the accurate shellfire of Sotheby's seamen to break up rebel formations before they got close enough to use their short-ranged smoothbore muskets. The Field Force formed a shallow line, the sailors in the centre with four 12-pounder howitzers and a Gurkha battalion on each flank. Marines and Sikhs skirmished ahead with their rifles, while a couple of companies of Gurkhas stayed behind in reserve. This formation, and the action that followed, set a pattern for the rest of the campaign:

> At ten came into action by the enemy opening fire on our skirmishers, keeping up a sharp fire shelled the enemy out of their position after trying to surround and outflank us – followed them through the woods and town of Soanpoor [*sic*], pursued them to Mujowlee and over the Chota Gunduck to Sulempore where we captured a gun ... if we had been a little quicker we might have destroyed the whole party.[15]

Midshipman Montagu, who took part as Sotheby's aide de camp, thought Soanpur was not a very worthy engagement:

> The fact is, the natives had no leaders and no organisation in these particular districts. They relied on their numbers to smother our forces, to harass our communications, and to make themselves obnoxious.[16]

The shift to guerrilla resistance became pronounced after the Pearls' most significant action at Amorha on 5 March 1858. So many rebels had turned out that Rowcroft formed his line one rank deep, to present a wide enough front:

> We opened fire first to try the range and then advanced the line a few yards. They then opened fire from their guns which were quickly answered with shell and again advanced as they had the range too well our men at the same time cheering along the line and keeping up a smart fire as they advanced while the shell from our guns did great execution among them and they began to fall back carrying their dead and wounded with them. The naval brigade and Ghoorkhas [sic] now charged them in line and they retreated in confusion while our artillery shelled them as quick as they could serve the guns.[17]

This time the British had cavalry on both flanks, who chased the beaten sepoys seven miles off the battlefield. There was only one naval fatality, Mr Fowler the Second Master, but the rebels lost about 500 dead, and so many guns that they never took the field in such strength again. After Amorha the rebel forces north of the Gogra resorted to guerrilla tactics. They faded away into the jungles like so many ghosts, relying on the climate to wear out their opponents. The weather was very hot, the thermometer showed 117 degrees, and the naval brigade's hospital was full:

> ... we took every precaution to keep the men out of the sun, but the heat and exposure to damp swamps – the frequent forced marches against parties of rebels who were constantly endeavouring to harass us but seldom waited to be attacked was telling on our men.[18]

The rainy season in July brought cooler weather, but washed out the roads. When flying columns went out to prevent rebels establishing themselves in the villages, the sailors lashed guns and limbers onto elephants to get through the waist-deep mud, and wished they had brought their boats. It was a brutalising war, in which neither side gave nor received quarter: 'Our constant companion being a gallows which was rigged up at every place we halted and we served all according to their deserts'. As in later counter-insurgency campaigns

March into India

Naval brigades sometimes came in small sizes; here, four of *Pearl*'s men rout a much larger force of mutineers. (Author's collection)

the result depended on who could win over the people of the surrounding countryside. The farmers grew tired of sepoys stealing their corn, while the sepoys showed no mercy to any of their own people who sold food to the British, or betrayed rebel movements:

> ... whenever we halted at a village we were more a source of apprehension than safety to them for although they know that we would pay them for everything we got and that they were safe enough while we remained yet the moment we left they would be exposed to the mercyless [sic] fury of the rebels ... [19]

Nevertheless, the villages nearest the naval brigade's monsoon quarters were quick to recover:

> ... swarming with people belonging to the place and others who have come to the place for the sake of safety... as well as a great many who have come from different places to drive a lucrative trade with our troops ...[20]

Seapower Ashore

Dryer weather in the autumn restored mobility. The renamed Gorakhpur Field Force, 'obliged to do the work of double their number' formed flying columns to chase bands of rebels driven out of Oudh and made bolder by desperation. The sepoys' rapid movements made their interception almost impossible, 'as they were so active and not encumbered with baggage'.[21] Reinforced by Brasyer's Sikhs, who had fought alongside *Shannon's* Brigade at Lucknow, Sotheby's men showed their operational flexibility in November by reverting to an exclusively artillery role, even the marines acting as gunners. Two days before Christmas 1858, *Pearls'* field gunners took part in the last serious action of the Mutiny, at Tulsipur, handling their teams and guns with such dash that the soldiers swore, with expletives deleted by Pearl's chaplain, they would believe sailors capable of anything in future. On New Year's Day 1859, Sotheby received orders to return to his ship, after a sixteen-month campaign and twenty-six actions.

HMS *Shannon's* heavy guns recapitulated a theme familiar in joint operations since the eighteenth century, but the naval brigades that fought during the Indian Mutiny did more than simply provide additional firepower, or a handful of extra bayonets. The Royal Navy's broad experience and training allowed seamen to act interchangeably as gunners, riflemen, or as pioneers, depending on their mission. Edmund Verney observed how *Shannon's* naval brigade could go anywhere, with a few cavalry for reconnaissance, while an infantry regiment needed detachments of gunners and sappers. When a Major of the 90th Light Infantry could find no-one to mend a broken tent pole, he paid *Shannon's* carpenter a sovereign to do the job. The garrison artillery at Cawnpore lacked gun sights, so their naval detachments lashed bits of wood, found beside the Kalpi Road, onto the gun carriages. Perhaps the most remarkable display of naval flexibility was the bridging of the River Gogra by *Pearl's* brigade, to allow a Gurkha army to join Campbell at Lucknow. There were plenty of river craft at Gopalpur to make a bridge of boats, but parties of rebels prowled the riverbanks, which bristled with antique fortresses of uncertain military value. Sotheby's men received the job of tracking the boats fifty miles upstream to link up with the

March into India

Gurkhas, watchful Royal Marines covering the overgrown banks from a barricaded river steamer. It was generally supposed the sailors would be in their element, and '... in the event of their getting into difficulty, would no doubt be well able to get out of it ...'[22] The brigade arrived without incident, briskly disposed of the local rebels, then turned-to as engineers to construct the bridge.

Some critics objected to such diversion of the Royal Navy's resources. In 1903 Laird Clowes claimed that military shortcomings had forced the Navy to take on duties that impaired its ability to carry out its proper tasks. The Admiralty had objected to the use of sailors ashore during the siege of Sevastopol, but accepted the emergency use of naval assets in Bengal. The Board congratulated *Shannon's* Brigade on sharing in '... the arduous services which the existing state of affairs in India has called for from all Her Majesty's subjects ...'[23] Captain Sotheby had no doubts about the naval contribution to the Mutiny's suppression:

> When we left our ship Delhi and Lucknow and most of the principal towns were in the hands of rebels, before we left we had the satisfaction of leaving the country in peace – though all the duties our men had to perform were quite of a military character, it was done cheerfully and the behaviour of the men was excellent ... the manner that our men worked and managed the guns was quite the admiration of the military. They always fired with the same precision and were as much at home as on board the ship.[24]

Pearl's chaplain thought the campaign a practical example of how the Navy could be turned to account in a great emergency:

> ... seamen from their pliability of character and habitual obedience to command, can easily adapt themselves to any circumstance; and instead of spending their time at cutlass drill or shifting topsails in a peaceable port by way of exercise are ready at any moment, when there is no enemy to meet on their own element, to man a battery or take the field ... five hundred miles from their ships and thereby render incalculable service to the state ...[25]

When Laird Clowes penned his criticism in the altered circumstances of the early twentieth century, powerful rivals had

A typical gun crew in their emplacement, serving a 24-pounder during the Indian Mutiny. (National Maritime Museum, London: PAD 5908)

appeared in home waters, compelling the Royal Navy to narrow its strategic horizons. No such compulsion applied during the 1850s. General-purpose units like *Shannon* and *Pearl* were free to respond to crises like the Indian Mutiny in a variety of ways. These ranged from regular naval activities, like rushing troops to the critical point, or silently overawing opposition with the menace of seaborne firepower, to more substantial commitments ashore. Traditionally the Royal Navy's heavy guns had augmented the Army's siege train. Naval brigades in India showed that the large ship's companies of the time could adapt to other shore roles. Inspired by Peel's reckless leadership *Shannon*'s gun detachments fought as assault troops, engaging the enemy at close quarters over open sights. HMS *Pearl*'s brigade not only fought as orthodox gunners and light infantry; they built bridges, and suffered the frustrations of guerrilla war that would become commonplace for later generations of British soldiers and sailors. Seamen from both ships learned to work with a variety of exotic draught animals, and developed close relations with British and Indian soldiers. If Pearl's chaplain can be suspected of pardonable hyperbole in writing of her 'incalculable service to the state', his reference to the 'pliability' of her seamen is no more than the unvarnished truth.

Notes

1. Lieutenant Edmund Verney, *The Shannon's Brigade in India* (London 1862), p1.
2. Rear-Admiral V A Montagu, *A Middy's Recollections 1853-1860* (London 1900) p148.
3. RNM 1990/143(1) Captain Edward Sotheby: Anecdotes. Total numbers landed were: - *Shannon*: 24 Officers, 500 Seamen, 50 Marines, 10 x 65 cwt 8in shell guns, 8 rocket tubes (4 x 24pdr and 4 x 12pdr), 1 x 6pdr field gun, 1 x 24pdr field howitzer. *Pearl*: 19 Officers, 200 Seamen, 39 Marines, 2 x 12pdr field howitzers, 1 x 24pdr field howitzer.
4. Commander W D Rowbotham, *The Naval Brigades in the Indian Mutiny 1857-58* (Navy Records Society 1947), p264: Lt Nowell Salmon 16 Aug 1857.
5. Midshipman E S Watson, *A Naval Cadet with HMS Shannon's Brigade in India* (London 1988), p52.
6. Montagu, p155.
7. RNM 1985/291 James Chappell, *Diary of Commission of HMS Pearl 1856-59* (undated entry).
8. Reverend E A Williams, *The Cruise of the Pearl round the World, with an Account of the Operations of the Naval Brigade in India* (London 1859), p98.
9. NMM JOD/154/1-2 Ordinary Seaman J P Hoskins, *Journal of HMS Shannon's Brigade in the Indian Mutiny* 14 Nov 1857.
10. Private Henry Derry RMLI in *Globe & Laurel* ix (1902), p17.
11. Watson, p57.
12. Sergeant W Forbes Mitchell, *The Relief of Lucknow* (London 1962), p89 – first published 1893 as *Reminiscences of the Great Mutiny*.
13. See Rowbotham, p149: Peel-Sir Michael Seymour 1 Mar 1858, and Hoskins 17 and 23 Feb 1858.
14. Sergeant William Turner RMLI, *Globe & Laurel* xv (1908), p27.
15. RNM 1990/143(1) Sotheby, *HMS Pearl in the Indian Mutiny* 26 Dec 1857.
16. Montagu, p165.
17. Chappell (undated entry re Amorha).
18. RNM 1990/143(6) Sotheby: Journal 1826-1864 10 May 1858.
19. Chappell, 23 May 1858.
20. Chappell, 1 Jul 1858
21. RNM 1990/143(6) Sotheby 2 Sep 1858.
22. Williams, p111.
23. Rowbotham, p145: Admiralty minute 25 Dec 1857.
24. RNM 1990/143(6) Sotheby Jan 1859.
25. Williams, p298.

CHAPTER 7

The Long Arm of Seapower:
The Anglo-Japanese War of 1863-64
by Colin White

On the afternoon of 11 August 1863, a small British squadron of seven ships arrived off the mouth of Kagoshima-wan, the great fjord at the southwestern tip of Japan. Ahead went the tiny gunvessel HMS *Coquette,* sounding the deep waters in search of a safe anchorage. Following her was mixed bag of corvettes and sloops, together with one large vessel, the steam frigate *Euryalus*, flagship of Rear-Admiral Augustus Kuper CB.[1]

Kuper was then just 54, a comparatively early age in those days for a man to receive one of the key foreign commands in the Royal Navy's worldwide network of squadrons. Of German stock, he had entered the Royal Navy under the patronage of King William IV and had seen active service in the First China War of 1840-2 and the Crimean War. Particularly experienced in amphibious operations and river campaigns, he was now Commander-in-Chief, East Indies and China, a vast command stretching from the Red Sea in the west to the Sea of Okhostsk in the northeast and encompassing India, Burma, Malaya, Borneo and China.[2] To patrol this enormous area he had some fifty ships, most of them under 1000 tons. Normally, they were scattered all over the station but now Kuper had ordered a concentration of as many vessels as possible in Japanese waters and had steamed there to take personal command.

Ever since western merchants had arrived in Japan in the mid-1850s, in the wake of Commodore Perry's mission of 1853, there had been tension between them and the more traditional Japanese leaders, who opposed opening up Japan to western influences. The foreigners were corralled in a special settlement at Yokohama but, even there, they were subject to repeated attacks. Then, on 14 September 1862, a party of Britons on a sightseeing tour were caught up in a street-brawl with the samurai of one of the great feudal princes of Japan, the Daimyo of Satsuma. A young merchant, Charles Richardson, was killed and the fashionably piled-up hair of one of the ladies was severed from her head by a sweeping sword. The British demanded an indemnity of £25,000 and the surrender of the men who had killed Richardson. But Satsuma was one of the leaders of the Jo-I, an influential group passionately opposed to the growing western influence and he determined to make a stand against the hated foreigners. So Kuper had now come to Satsuma's stronghold at Kagoshima, with a British envoy, Lieutenant-Colonel Edward Neale, on board to attempt to force him to see reason.

Three days of inconclusive negotiations ensued. Satsuma refused even to meet the British, remaining in his summer home in the mountains and sending envoys to negotiate for him. In the meantime, Kuper moved his squadron closer to the town of Kagoshima, anchoring about 1200 yards from the shore, and sent the *Euryalus*'s Master, William Parker, to take soundings so as to establish how close to the town and its defences the ships could go. The Japanese were openly using the time gained by their delaying tactics to reinforce their batteries. Slowly the tension mounted until eventually Neale realised he was getting nowhere. So, on the evening of 14 August he gave Kuper permission to take direct action. Early the following morning, Kuper sent part of his force to seize three steamers belonging to Satsuma and brought them back to his anchorage to use as bargaining tools. The barometer had been falling throughout the previous two days and now a strong wind was blowing from the east. At about noon, the squadron was hit by a sudden squall and, at that very moment, the Japanese batteries at the eastern end of the town opened fire on the *Euryalus*, the only ship within range.

Kuper was now in a dilemma. Three of his ships had prizes lashed alongside, which left him only four ships with which to deal with the Japanese defences. And those defences were strong enough to require all the force at his disposal (see map on page 148). Along the foreshore

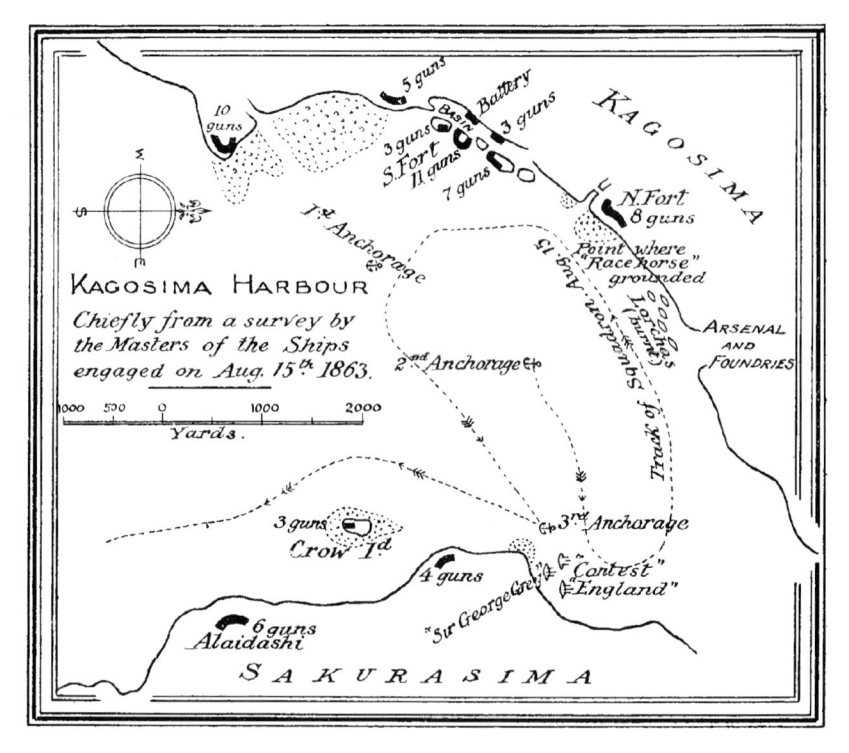

Map of the attack on Kagoshima, 15 August 1863. (From William Laird Clowes, *The History of the Royal Navy*, Vol VII)

of the town of Kagoshima were two forts connected and supported by a line of five smaller batteries. The southwestern approach to the anchorage was defended by a fort on a convenient promontory mounting eleven guns, while the eastern channel was even more strongly defended by two small forts on the main Sakura Island and another battery on the outlying Crow Island. All these forts and batteries were fairly basic by contemporary western standards, with little protection for the gunners and magazines, but the seventy-six guns which they mounted – some of them 32-pounders and 10in mortars – were perfectly capable of inflicting heavy damage on the unarmoured British ships. The admiral's dilemma was further heightened by the fact that the wind was fast rising to gale force and it was obvious that a typhoon was approaching.[3]

Kuper nevertheless decided to attack at once. As the Japanese shot and shell began to fly among the *Euryalus*'s rigging, he signalled to the *Coquette*, *Argus* and *Racehorse* to cast off their prizes and burn them. He wrote later in his dispatch:

> ... I considered it advisable not to postpone until another day the return of the fire of the Japanese, to punish the Prince of Satsuma for the outrage and to vindicate the honour of the flag ...[4]

At 12.55pm came the signal to weigh anchor, form line of battle and to clear for action, orders which the squadron took nearly *two hours* to accomplish! Admittedly, by then clearing for action was more complicated than in Nelsonian times but, even so, such a long wait at such a crucial moment seems inexcusable. To cover this confusion on the part of his ships, Kuper, at 12.20pm, had ordered the *Perseus* to engage the batteries to draw their fire. For nearly 1½ hours, Commander Augustus Kingston circled his 17-gun sloop in front of the North Fort, one of the largest in the Kagoshima line, until finally, at 2.15pm, Kuper ordered him to withdraw and to take his place in the line of battle, which was now bearing down, in strict order of seniority, from the northeast. In a high wind and in heavy seas that kept the decks continually awash, the squadron steamed slowly down the Kagoshima foreshore in line ahead engaging the batteries in succession at a range of only 500 yards.

In the *Euryalus* at the head of the line, Master William Parker, using the rough charts he had made earlier, took the flagship in nearer and nearer; but even this was not good enough for Kuper, who leaned over the bridge-rail and shouted 'Go in closer Parker! Go in closer!'. Despite heavy rolling, poor light and frequent rain squalls, the British shooting was accurate and, as the rearmost ships came into action, they found that the fire of the northern batteries was already slackening as a result of the punishment they had received from the ships at the head of the line. Then, within the space of ten minutes, a series of disasters struck the flagship. By then, she had outstripped her slower consorts and was steaming alone at the head of the line with a broad sheet of water between her and the *Pearl*, her next astern. The most powerful Japanese batteries were concentrated at the southern end of the town and, as the *Euryalus* came within range of them at 3.00pm, she was hit repeatedly by a number of shot and some particularly well-aimed 10in mortar shells. A roundshot killed Captain John Josling and Commander Edward Wilmot as they stood beside Kuper on the bridge; a shell exploded in the gunport of No. 3 Gun on the main deck, killing seven men outright and wounding a further twelve. The starboard boom boats – which, contrary to the invariable custom of earlier wars, were not being towed astern – were destroyed by another shell, sending up a shower of lethal wooden splinters which killed two men and wounded four more. Finally, and possibly worst of all because of its effect on morale, the 7in breech-loading Armstrong pivot gun on the forecastle blew out its breech piece, knocking down its entire crew and concussing them severely. One authority has suggested that the sudden hail of direct hits was due to the fact that the *Euryalus* was passing a range marker buoy put down by the Japanese.[5] However, none of the contemporary accounts mention such a buoy and none of the other ships suffered in a similar way. Probably, the *Euryalus* suffered so badly because she presented such a splendid target, steaming alone within about 400 yards of the shore.

In the meantime, further down the British line, the *Racehorse*'s engines failed and at 3.10pm, driven by the fierce wind, she drifted helplessly onto the shore right under the guns of the North Fort. Luckily, the fort had suffered the most from the concentrated fire of the heavier ships and so was almost silenced but even so, the *Argus* – which together with the *Coquette* came to the rescue of their consort – lost her mainmast before finally, at 6.00pm, the *Racehorse* was refloated. The rest of the squadron, following in the wake of the *Euryalus*, turned at the southern end of the batteries and steamed north to Sakura Island, where they anchored out of range of the guns.

Although no other ship had suffered nearly as many casualties as the flagship, only the *Havoc* had escaped completely without loss. The final list was eleven killed and fifty-two wounded, of whom two later died of their wounds – a very high number for so minor an operation involving so few ships. The Japanese losses are not known but it is likely that they were high also. Quite apart from the fact that their batteries were completely unprotected, the heavy rolling of the ships had caused many of the British shell to fall into the town, where they killed civilians and also started fires. The flimsy wood and paper houses were soon alight and, by 6.30pm, Kagoshima was a mass of flames that were fanned by high winds throughout the night as the typhoon reached its peak.

The following morning, Sunday 16 August, the ships buried their dead and, then, at 2.30pm, prepared for action once more as some Japanese soldiers had been seen erecting new batteries on Sakura Island, commanding the squadron's anchorage. However, Kuper was not contemplating any further action for when, at 3.30pm, the order came to weigh anchor, the *Euryalus* led the squadron out of the bay, engaging the flanking batteries on Sakura Island on the way and also shelling Satsuma's palace. Once again, the British gunnery was good and, at 4.00pm, as the squadron headed southwards, one of the parting shots blew up a magazine. After spending another night at the Seven Islands anchorage, and effecting as many repairs as possible, the British finally left Kagoshima Bay at 2.00pm on 17 August and set course for Yokohama.

Diplomatically, the Kagoshima expedition was a failure. Certainly, Satsuma had lost three valuable steamers together with a number of junks and his capital and palace had been burned. But the Japanese were used to earthquakes and fires and, accordingly, built their houses of flimsy material so that they could be reconstructed easily. The important fact was that Satsuma had not been forced to give in to the British demands. Moreover, his men had had the great satisfaction of seeing the severely damaged British ships withdraw from the scene of the action. In later years, it was claimed that this action had first inspired the Japanese to build a navy of their own, because it had taught them the full destructive power of the western ships, which before they had tended to despise. But this was only hindsight. On 16 August 1863, Satsuma's retainers at Kagoshima celebrated a great victory over the hated foreigners and Kuper and Neale had to admit that they were no closer to obtaining their indemnity or the surrender of Richardson's killers.

Tactically, the battle was also open to much criticism. The British squadron had been caught unprepared, which was inexcusable in view of the mounting tension of the previous three days. It is obvious that Kuper had not formulated any proper form of attack, since his ships simply scrambled into action in order of seniority. This left the smaller and weaker vessels at the end of the line, where they would be very exposed if any accident occurred – as happened in the case of the *Racehorse*. The ships had also gone in too close to the batteries; 500 yards was an excellent range for the old-fashioned Japanese smoothbores and mortars, whereas the up-to-date British rifled guns would have been just as efficient at three times that distance and even their smoothbores would have been accurate at 1000 yards. Most telling of all, the Kagoshima batteries had not been permanently disabled, merely temporarily silenced by the deaths of their gun crews. The activity of the Japanese in mounting new batteries on Sakura Island on the morning of the 16th had shown that they were by no means defeated or demoralised.

Kuper realised just how close to failure he had come. He had been greatly shocked by the heavy loss of life and especially by the deaths of Josling and Wilmot, the former a particular protégé of his.[6] And he had realised that ships, on their own, could not hope permanently to silence shore batteries manned by an enemy as determined and courageous as the Japanese had shown themselves to be. His first despatch, of 22 August, contains a significant passage:

> ... Having thus accomplished every act of retribution and punishment *within the scope of the operations of a small naval force* [my italics][7]

and, in his next despatch dated 26 August, when he had had time further to reflect, he gave a lucid and balanced appraisal of the sort of force which was needed for such operations. He wrote:

> A mere naval force, composed chiefly of small vessels, the crews of which will not admit of a landing party being detached to follow any success afloat, would be of little service in Japan: and to attack batteries without having means of securing their ultimate demolition by the assistance of a land force would be a useless sacrifice of valuable life.[8]

Kuper had, in fact, learnt a most important lesson, which was to have a decisive effect upon the ensuing operations in Japan. In accepting that bombardments had to be supported by a landing in force, he had grasped an essential tactical maxim, which eluded many other Victorian naval officers. Naval bombardments of shore defences occurred very frequently throughout the nineteenth century and they were rarely completely successful, because they were rarely followed-up properly.

Returning to his base at Yokohama, Kuper found that the tension between the Japanese and the westerners was as strong as ever. Another Daimyo, Choshiu of Nagato, had closed the Straits of Shimonoseki, the main route between Yokohama and China, to western vessels and an attempt by a small French squadron to force him to back down had been repulsed. The westerners were learning the hard way that their opponents were both strong and determined. In the meantime the naval build-up was continuing. British and French reinforcements arrived and in the spring of 1864, the growing allied fleet was further swelled by a Dutch squadron of four ships. Among the British reinforcements was the sail and steam battleship HMS *Conqueror* with a battalion of Royal Marine Light Infantry on board and the French transferred troops from China. A combined operation was taking shape.

Eventually, by August 1864, Kuper and his allies felt strong enough to undertake a major operation in the Straits of Shimonoseki and, on 28 August, Kuper led a squadron of ten ships out of Yokohama. On the morning of 1 September they rendezvoused with the four Dutch and three French ships off the island of Himeshima. In the afternoon the collier *Pembrokeshire* arrived from Shanghai and the allied fleet restocked its fuel supplies.[9] The batteries defending the Straits of Shimonoseki constituted one of the strongest systems of fortifications in Japan (see map on p155). In particular, the eight batteries overlooking the narrowest part of the Straits were so placed as to be capable of sweeping the entrance with concentrated fire. Battery 8 – mounting at least twenty guns, most of them 32-pounders – was the most powerful single Japanese work the Europeans had yet encountered.

There were however, some important weaknesses in the system. First, although the sides of the Straits were steep and high, none of the batteries had been built on top of them – from where they would

Planning the bombardment of Shimonoseki. Rear-Admiral Augustus Kuper, standing centre, the French Admiral Jaures, seated second from the left, and the British envoy Alcock pointing at the map. (National Maritime Museum, London: Neg No C8583/C

have been able to fire plunging shots onto any ships below. Instead, they had been built on low ground close to the shoreline, where they were on much the same level as any attacking ships. Worse, many of them had been placed at the *foot* of the sheer cliffs so that any enemy shot or shell which went over simply hit the solid rock face and rebounded into the middle of the gunners, or exploded, sending

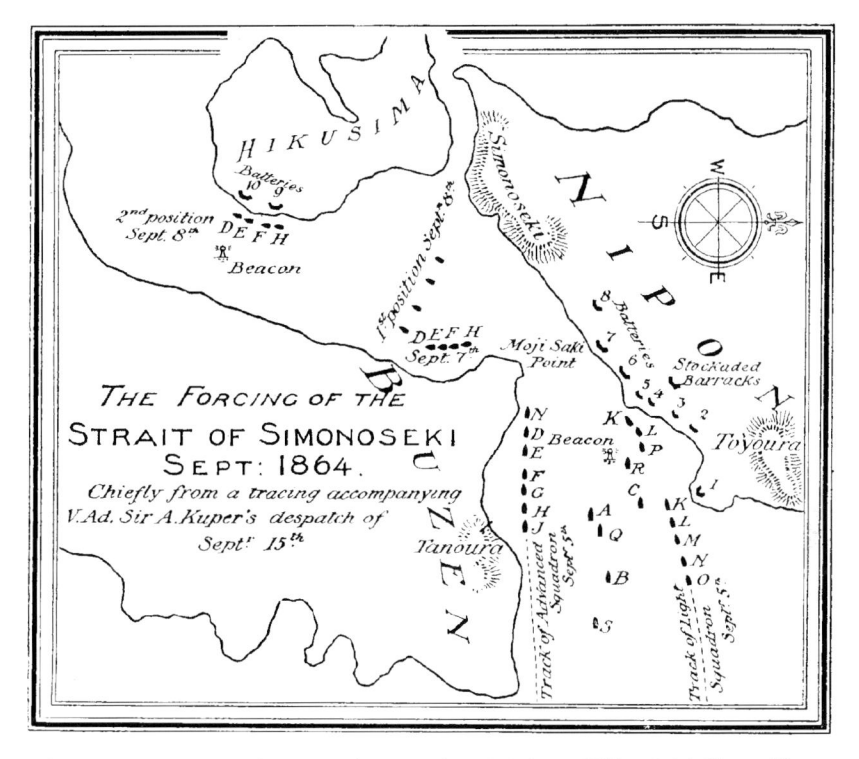

The forcing of the Straits of Shimonoseki, September 1864. (From William Laird Clowes, *The History of the Royal Navy*, Vol VII)

down showers of lethal splinters. Second, although the batteries were capable of delivering concentrated fire to their front, none of them had been designed to support their fellows with flanking fire and so it was possible to capture them one by one. Finally, and most important of all, the Daimyo of Buzen, whose lands were on the southern side of the Straits refused to help Nagato in his fight, which meant that the allied ships were able to hug the southern shore and did not have to contend with crossfire.[10]

Kuper divided his powerful fleet into three distinct but supporting squadrons. An advanced, or 'corvette' squadron, under Captain John Hayes in the *Tartar*, and consisting of the French *Barossa*, *Leopard* and *Dupleix*, and the Dutch *Metalen Kruis* and *D'Jambi* was to attack the batteries at medium range – 1000 yards – by advancing up the southern side of the channel. At the same time, a 'light' squadron, under Commander Augustus Kingston in the *Perseus*, with *Coquette*,

Bouncer, the Dutch *Medusa* and the French *Tancrède* in company was to take the batteries in the flank from close inshore on the northern side. The heavier ships, *Euryalus*, *Conqueror* and *Sémiramis* (flagship of the French Admiral Jaurès) were to remain in the centre of the channel, giving covering fire to the light squadron; while the Dutch *Amsterdam* and *Argus* were held in reserve to tow out any disabled ships. The Royal Marines were to be landed to capture the batteries as soon as they had been silenced and a party of Sappers and Miners was to supervise the destruction of the Japanese guns and the demolition of the fortifications. Every important feature of the operation – the range of 1000 yards, the special outflanking squadron and the strong landing force – demonstrated how well Kuper had learned the lessons of Kagoshima.

The plan worked smoothly. The allied fleet attacked at 2.00pm on 5 September, when the tide was at its highest, and by 2.30pm all the ships were in their appointed positions. The *Conqueror* grounded twice on uncharted shoals and had to remain at extreme range, but her presence added effect to the attack and she was also a convenient transport for the Royal Marines. She was also able to fire a few broadsides at long range – and so became the last of the old 'wooden walls' ever to fire her guns in anger.

Although the Japanese batteries on the southern side of the Straits did not take part, the fire from the northern batteries was as furious and as accurate as at Kagoshima and all the allied ships were hit several times, although nearly always at very long range. In the *Barossa*, for example, there were six hits on the quarterdeck alone but no one was killed or wounded. Indeed, there were hardly any casualties on this first day – most of the losses occurred during the land fighting which followed. On the other hand, thanks to Kuper's careful positioning of his ships, the Japanese were subjected to a withering crossfire and earned the admiration of their foes by the way in which they stood to their guns. Commander John Moresby of the *Argus* wrote:

> It was a marvel to me that they held out so long for, excepting the traverses between the guns, there was not the slightest protection from our shellfire which struck them full in the face.[11]

Moresby had been rather disappointed to be told to stay out of the fight, especially since he had served under Kuper before and had expected his old chief to give him a place of honour. Eventually, presuming on their friendship, he signalled to the flagship 'Permission to engage' and received the welcome reply 'Affirmative. Join the Inshore Squadron.' Kuper had obviously decided that the Japanese fire, although still very hot, was not likely to damage any of his ships too severely for, a little while later, he allowed the *Amsterdam* to join the light squadron as well. This enabled him, at 4.45pm, to transfer the *Coquette* to the head of the corvette squadron where she took soundings as the larger ships began to move slowly up the straits to attack the westernmost batteries. By then the fire from all the batteries, except No. 8, was slackening and the smaller batteries, 4, 5 and 7, had ceased firing altogether. Kuper decided that the day was too far advanced to land his special parties and so, at 5.35pm, he made the signal to disengage. However the *Perseus* and the Dutch *Medusa* had by that time crept close inshore, abreast of the central batteries, and they could see that No. 5 Battery had been abandoned altogether. So, disregarding Kuper's order, Commander Kingston and Captain de Casembroot decided to send a party ashore to spike the guns. This gallant sortie was accomplished without loss.

The following morning, the large No. 8 Battery – virtually untouched by the bombardment of the previous afternoon – opened fire again at about 5.20am. Its shot fell around the *Coquette*, which was still heading the line of corvettes, and struck the *Tartar*, wounding eight men.[12] At once, the naval bombardment began again but, this time, the Japanese fire slackened within half an hour and Kuper realised that the right moment had come for him to launch the second stage of his attack. At a given signal, the boats from the British ships began to gather around the *Euryalus* and the Royal Marine battalion, reinforced by the smaller detachments of marines from the individual ships, under the overall command of Lieutenant-Colonel William Suther RM, embarked. They were followed by a naval brigade made up of small-arms men from the *Euryalus* and *Conqueror* under the command of Captain John Alexander – in all, a force of about 1000 seamen and marines. At the same time, the French were embarking 350 and the Dutch 200 seamen and marines. The boats were then towed ashore by the lighter ships of the squadron, to a point just below the silenced No. 5 Battery. There, the parties landed without incident and proceeded to spike all the abandoned guns and to wreck the gun carriages. The only mishap occurred to the *Perseus*. At 10.40am she was driven onshore by a sharp current while landing some of the boats. She remained firmly stuck until finally, in the evening of 7 September, Moresby, in the *Argus*, managed to tow her off.

The work of spiking proceeded well and, by 4.00pm, Kuper decided that the time had come to re-embark his forces before night fell. The French and Dutch sailors and marines had already departed when the British naval brigade – which had just returned from dismantling the guns of No. 3 Battery with the help of the Sappers and Miners – was attacked in the rear by a strong force of Japanese troops. The attack was beaten off and, at that moment, Colonel Suther arrived from the western batteries with the Royal Marine battalion. He and Captain Alexander agreed that it would be foolhardy to leave so strong enemy force at large in the vicinity of their embarkation point and they therefore decided to pursue their assailants. The Japanese retired up a long narrow defile and took refuge in a well-fortified stockade at its head, which the two commanders at once decided to attack. A charge was made, with Midshipman Duncan Boyes carrying the colours, supported by the Captain of the Afterguard, Thomas Pride. Ordinary Seaman William Seely went ahead of the charge to reconnoitre and, though severely wounded, insisted on taking part in the fighting. Eventually, after some hard hand-to-hand fighting, in which the Japanese apparently used bows and arrows as well as rifles, the stockade was carried and its defenders driven off into the neighbouring hills. Captain Alexander was badly wounded in the right foot during the battle and, altogether, eight men were killed and thirty-three wounded. Boyes, Pride and Seely were recommended for, and later received, the Victoria Cross.

The embarkation now continued. Night had fallen and it was decided that, instead of risking the men in open boats, the *Argus*

Sailors and Royal Marines pose for a group photograph in Battery 5 at Shimonoseki, a few days after its capture. (National Maritime Museum, London: Neg No C8583/D)

should take them on board and deliver them to their various ships. Moresby later bore eloquent witness to the difficulty of this operation:

> I think it was about the most anxious job I have ever carried through. The darkness was impenetrable, the tide running through the Strait at six knots an hour, and we had to cross it and sheer alongside the various ships. Our decks were crowded and on the bridge were one or two of the senior captains of the fleet. They kindly made various suggestions, seeing the serious difficulties to be overcome; but my

nerves were highly strung just then, and I had to request perfect silence. By great good luck, we did the trick without an accident.[13]

The entire range of the lower batteries was now in allied hands and all their guns had been disabled. There now remained the task of reducing the remaining two batteries on Hikusima and, on 7 September, Kuper ordered the *Tartar, Dupleix, D'Jambi* and *Metalen Kruis* to proceed up the straits to attack them. They arrived in position at 5.30pm and, the following morning, Jaurès and Kuper shifted their flags to the *Coquette* and joined them there. They opened fire at 9.30am but the batteries did not reply and, at 11.30am, a boat was seen approaching from the town of Shimonoseki, bearing a flag of truce. On board, was an a envoy from the Daimyo, with a letter written by order of Nagato undertaking to reopen the straits and protesting that he had been acting on orders from the Mikado and the Shogun. Kuper and Jaurès – who conducted the negotiations jointly, since there was no senior diplomat present – insisted that they needed a guarantee from the Daimyo written in his own hand and they agreed to a two-day truce, so that such a letter could be written and delivered. Accordingly, at 1.40pm, flags of truce were hoisted in the allied ships and all hostilities were suspended.

However, Kuper was determined to destroy the batteries completely. On 7 September, he had sent working parties ashore to blow up the magazines and to throw down the walls and he had also given orders that as many of the guns as possible should be embarked in the ships of the fleet. Despite the truce, he ordered the work to continue and, by nightfall on 10 September, sixty-two guns had been carried away. Eight were discarded because they were too badly damaged; but the remaining fifty-four were later divided up among the allies as trophies. On the 10th, Nagato's Chief Counsellor, Mori Idzuno, came aboard the *Euryalus* and delivered to Kuper the required letter from his master undertaking not to close the Straits again. With the work of demolition now complete, Kuper and Jaurès agreed to withdraw their ships, since the object of their mission had been accomplished. However, as a final precaution, the fleet remained at anchor in the eastern approach to the Straits for a further 10 days.

The *Perseus* was sent back to Yokohama to be properly checked for any damage she might have received when she grounded. Finally, on 20 September, the whole fleet weighed anchor and sailed eastwards, leaving the *Barossa*, *Tancrède* and *D'Jambi* on patrol.

Kuper now decided to make a show of force to as many Japanese as possible and, instead of returning to Yokohama by the direct sea route, he took his ships through the Inland Sea, emerging at the eastern end near Osaka. Jaurès had decided to return by the direct route; but there still remained eight British ships and three Dutch corvettes, which steamed in line ahead with the *Bouncer* and *Osprey* out in front making soundings. Kuper even insisted on having the *Conqueror* with him in this stately procession, taking advantage yet again of her imposing appearance; but on 22 September, she ran firmly aground. All efforts to tow her off failed and she had to unload all her upper deck guns into the *Leopard* and *Bouncer* before, finally, she could be refloated again.

The voyage lasted seven days and had a magical quality that the sailors remembered in after years. Moresby recalled how they had steamed:

> through broad sheets of water, connected by passages among the islands so narrow and intricate that as the leaders swung round the headlands it seemed to those astern as if their course lay over the land.[14]

The fleet anchored off many towns, but Kuper gave strict instructions that no-one was to land. However, each ship was soon surrounded by boats full of inquisitive spectators and enterprising merchants. Eventually, on 27 September, the long line of ships emerged into the open sea and on 1 October, led by the *Euryalus*, they steamed into the Bay of Yeddo and anchored off Yokohama. As the British ships passed the flagship, the crews manned the rigging and cheered.

The War in Japan of 1863-4, provides a fascinating glimpse of Victorian Seapower in action. It was one of the last occasions when a full squadron of the old-style 'cruisers' – frigates, corvettes and sloops – went into battle and it is intriguing to see how those half-mechanical, half-sailing ships performed. The teething troubles of the

Armstrong guns caused much investigation at the time and led, eventually, to the abandonment of the new breech-loaders and the reinstatement of muzzle-loaders for another twenty years. But there is no evidence that any comparable analysis was made of the performance of the ships themselves. In fact, they had not proved very efficient. On the way to Kagoshima, the squadron had found it easier to keep in company under sail than when steaming. At the battle itself, the *Euryalus* had forged ahead of her slower consorts, thus exposing herself to concentrated fire with disastrous results. At Kagoshima again, the *Racehorse*'s engines had failed at a critical moment; while at Shimonoseki, the *Perseus* had been unable to combat a fast crosscurrent and had been driven ashore. Tactically, the main interest of the war is the classic use of ships in conjunction with landing forces at Shimonoseki. But, sadly, the lessons of this well-handled battle were not properly analysed or appreciated. It is, for example, fascinating to speculate what might have happened at the Dardanelles in 1916 if similar tactics had been employed there. Strategically, the conduct of the war can hardly be faulted. It was then, and remains still, a classic example of the use of seapower to further a country's political ends.

BIBLIOGRAPHY AND SOURCES

The Anglo-Japanese War has not been much studied. The most complete published account is in Volume 7 of *The Royal Navy* by W Laird Clowes (pp190-209), which includes extensive extracts from Kuper's despatches. There is a shorter, more modern, account in *Send a Gunboat* by A Preston and S Major.

Contemporary reports, and comment can be found in *The Times* and the *Illustrated London News* and the latter has some superb engravings, based on sketches done on the spot. For a vivid, more personal, view of Shimonoseki by Commander John Moresby of HMS *Argus*, see *Two Admirals* by J. Moresby.

However, most of the material from this monograph is drawn from the original despatches and logs housed in the PRO. Full references for these will be found in the footnotes.

Notes

1. The main sources for the movements of the British ships are the ships' logs in the Admiralty 53 series. Admiral Kuper's despatches are ADM 1/5824 and 5825 and his journal is ADM 50/287.
2. For a fuller biography of Kuper see *Illustrated London News*, 20 Feb 1864.
3. The details of the Japanese fortifications is taken form the very full list attached to Kuper's official despatch (ADM 1/5825).
4. ADM 1/5825 Kuper to Admiralty 22 Aug 1863.
5. A Preston and S Major, *Send a Gunboat* (London 1967), p75.
6. He mentioned their deaths three times in his official despatch and each time in terms of personal sorrow.
7. ADM 1/5825 Kuper to Admiralty 22 Aug 1863.
8. ADM 1/5825 Kuper to Admiralty 26 Aug 1863.
9. Kuper's despatches for the Shimonoseki operation are in ADM 1/5876. His journal is ADM 50/288.
10. This analysis of the Shimonoseki fortifications is based on a survey made on the spot by Major Wray of the Royal Engineers, a copy of which is in ADM 1/5876.
11. J Moresby, *Two Admirals* (London 1890), p117.
12. ADM 53/8240 Log of HMS *Tartar*.
13. Moresby, op. cit, p238.
14. Ibid, p239.

CHAPTER 8

Admiral Beatty and Brown Water: The Sudan and China 1896–1900

by Richard Brooks

Admiral of the Fleet David, Earl Beatty is a major figure in the conventional history of the Royal Navy. During the First World War he led the battlecruisers into action at Dogger Bank and Jutland, and in 1917 succeeded Sir John Jellicoe as Commander-in-Chief of the Grand Fleet, the most powerful naval force ever assembled at that time. After the war Beatty became First Sea Lord, struggling to preserve the Royal Navy from a succession of economy-minded governments. Few naval officers can be so thoroughly identified with the First World War at sea, or the assertion of British maritime power by conventional means. Beatty's early career, however, included two episodes far removed from the clash of dreadnoughts.

The Royal Navy of the late nineteenth century played an essential role in the small wars of the period. Its warships were everywhere, providing strategic depth for beleaguered coastal enclaves, or reaching inland along the great rivers, to support military operations in the heart of Africa and Asia. Beatty took part in two such campaigns. He commanded a Nile river gunboat from 1896 to 1898, and led HMS *Barfleur*'s naval brigade at Tientsin, during the Boxer Rebellion of 1900. These very different passages from his life show the variety of operational means at the disposal of the Victorian navy, the wide range of enemies it faced, and the versatility of its officers and men.

The Sudan had been an Egyptian dependency until the Mahdist Revolt of the mid-1880s wiped out the Egyptian garrisons, and killed the British general, Charles Gordon, at Khartoum. In 1896 Egypt's economic and military recovery allowed the Anglo-Egyptian army under Sir Herbert Kitchener to begin the reconquest of the lost province. Kitchener's advance was deliberate and certain, slowed by the need to develop his communications as he went. To secure his natural line of advance along the Nile Kitchener built up a powerful flotilla of river gunboats commanded by British officers, among them the young Lieutenant Beatty. During the action at Hafir in September 1896 Stanley Colville, commanding officer of the Nile flotilla, was disabled. Beatty pressed home the attack with all the dash he would later show with his battlecruisers. The river was too low for naval operations in the winter 1896/7, so Beatty took some leave, returning in July 1897 to help work the flotilla through the cataracts, or rapids, that block the Nile between Dongola and Abu Hamed. For the next twelve months the gunboats asserted Anglo-Egyptian naval supremacy between the River Atbara and Khartoum, before leading Kitchener's final advance in August 1898. Beatty was the only naval officer to serve throughout the campaign, more than two years elapsing between his original secondment to the Sudan in July 1896, and the climactic battle of Omdurman in September 1898, just outside Khartoum.

The Boxer Rebellion, on the other hand, was an emergency, short-lived but acute. Naval involvement lasted only a few months, but was far more trying for the participants than service on the Nile. Chinese insurgents known as the Society of Righteous Harmonious Fists, hence Boxers, overran the area surrounding Peking and the foreign trading settlement at Tientsin, threatening the lives of Europeans and Chinese Christians. Warships from most of the world's navies gathered off the mouth of the shallow Peiho River. Beatty was among the forces sent up to defend the international trading concession at Tientsin, with HMS *Barfleur's* naval brigade. They arrived on 11 June 1900, just before the Boxers cut the railway and telegraph. Sniping and incendiarism began at once, followed by heavy fighting when 15,000 regular Chinese soldiers joined the Boxers. International reinforcements fought their way into Tientsin on 23 June, allowing the garrison to relieve a naval force that had optimistically set off for Peking to evacuate the diplomatic legations there, but soon found itself in need of rescue. One casualty of the abortive dash to Peking was Captain John

Abu Klea class gunboats in action at Hafir: one of these was commanded by Lieutenant David Beatty. (Author's collection)

Jellicoe, wounded in a bayonet charge. Beatty accompanied the rescue column, despite two bullet wounds in his left arm. After another three hair-raising weeks, the allies stormed the Walled City of Tientsin to raise the siege on 13/14 July. Most of the British naval brigade, including Beatty, had returned to their ships by 20 July. The severity of his wounds prevented him joining the relief of the Peking Legations in August.

The naval forces committed in the Sudan functioned as technical advisors. Beatty was one of a handful of naval personnel assigned to an ostensibly Egyptian flotilla. Only a small proportion of the crew of each vessel were British: a naval or military officer, two engineers, and one or two Royal Marine non-commissioned officers as gunnery instructors. The rest were recruited locally: Egyptian gunners, Arab sailors, and black Sudanese stokers. There were three classes of gunboat, besides some unarmed steamers. The oldest were four stern-wheelers, dating back to the Gordon Relief expedition of 1884-5, and named after the desert battles of that period. Two new types of gunboat appeared during the campaign, three stern-wheelers and another three twin-screw craft. The latter drew less water, but were more complex, requiring more frequent repairs to their engines. The later classes were heavily armed with quick-firing guns and Maxims, their height providing good command over the flat banks of the Nile. A British shipyard constructed the new gunboats in numbered sections, to be carried as far as possible by railway, to bypass the first and second cataracts before assembly. In August 1896, the whole army in camp at Kosheh collected on the river bank to watch Colville supervising the construction of *Zafir* by a combined team of sappers and marines, seconded by Lieutenant Beatty and a civilian engineer sent out by the contractors. Another group of marines helped assemble the twin-screw flotilla near Berber in May 1897, mounting guns, shipbuilding, painting, and rigging the new gunboats like regular dockyard mateys.[1]

The naval brigade at Tientsin followed a quite different pattern. It was a self-contained formation of ground troops, comprising Royal Marines, bluejacket small-arms men, and field gun and Maxim crews. In addition there was a small headquarters with technical and medical staff, and a dozen stokers trained in first aid to act as stretcher bearers. Including detachments previously landed from the cruisers *Aurora* and *Orlando*, there were some 430 officers and men to defend the British part of the settlement.[2] Compared with the Nile gunboats' quick-firers, the guns used by the Royal Navy in China were a disgrace to the service: two 9-pounder muzzle-loading field guns designed in 1871, three Maxims, and *Orlando*'s Nordenfeldt, a hand-cranked machine gun with five barrels. The ships on the China station had yet to receive the 'new' 12-pounder field gun that would become familiar to generations of visitors to the Royal Tournament.

The command arrangements for the two interventions were as disparate as the forces themselves. In the Sudan, Kitchener directed a well-oiled machine with his customary energy, assisted by some of the most able officers in both services. Colin Keppel replaced Colville after the latter's wound. Lieutenant Walter Cowan described him as:

> ... the most loveable and inspiring leader that any sailor could ever hope for and life up and down that river and with the Egyptian Army officered by the pick of the British Army was full of incident and spectacle, and never a day not filled up to the brim with achievement of some sort; Lord Kitchener supplying the driving force and requiring the utmost from everyone...[3]

Colville and Keppel had both served as sub-lieutenants during the Gordon Relief Expedition of 1885, providing a firm basis of expertise in riverine warfare, reinforced by Charles Hope Robertson, the other Commander RN on the Nile in 1896, who had commanded a gunboat on the Shiró River in East Africa. The situation at Tientsin was quite different. Beatty took over the defences of the British settlement on 12 June 1900 with only his observations of the Sudan campaign to guide him. International command arrangements were chaotic, Beatty commenting on ' ... the difficulty of controlling and inducing any concerted action out of so heterogeneous a force ...'[4] He noted that international distrust hampered efforts to raise the siege; '... first one was not ready, then another, so sickening each other that relations were severely strained. We ourselves were as bad, if not worse, than any, and were most unreasonable ...'[5] And one Russian officer '... a most delightful man with charming manners, diplomatically a thorough Russian who could lie scientifically and candidly, a trait which made it very necessary to believe what one saw only ...'[6]

Beatty's own presence at Omdurman and Tientsin arose from a chance example of Victorian naval patronage. Beatty had been Colville's watchkeeping midshipman during HMS *Alexandra's* Mediterranean commission of 1886-9, and on promotion to Lieutenant followed him to HMS *Trafalgar* in 1895. When appointed to the Nile flotilla, Colville requested Beatty's services. In the peaceful 1890s, such a chance of active service was unbelievably good luck, especially for Beatty who had fallen behind his contemporaries at Greenwich, preferring the pursuit of West End actresses to the

Fateh class gunboats which were built in kit form on the Thames and assembled in Egypt. (Author's collection)

mysteries of maritime navigation. Colville and Beatty were both promoted for their work on the Nile. When Colville became Captain of HMS *Barfleur* on the China station, Beatty joined him as Commander, responsible for managing the ship's company, and if necessary leading it into action ashore.

The Boxer Rebellion appears superficially similar to the Mahdist Revolt. Both movements expressed popular resentment of foreign penetration of the local culture and economy, and opposed Western rifles with spears and swords. The Chinese, however, were a far more dangerous enemy. The Boxers may have been an ill-armed rabble, but Western military assistance had made the Chinese soldiers of 1900 a very different proposition to those of the 1860s, whose weapons included wooden swords and rocket-propelled spears. At Tientsin the Chinese army shelled the settlement incessantly with modern 4in guns that outranged the opposition. Five shells hit Beatty's billet, 'one crashing through my room, smashing everything inside and setting fire to my bed'. The Chinese supported their infantry attacks in the latest style, 'the whole place being alive with shells and fragments of shells flying about, and a hail of bullets, so that anyone rising to fire at the advancing Chinese was immediately struck down'.[7] Beatty himself was hit twice leading a sortie to silence two particularly troublesome Chinese field guns. One bullet narrowly missed the artery in his left shoulder, and another lodged in his left wrist.

The Mahdist state, by contrast with the Celestial Empire, was isolated and ill-armed. Its leader, the Khalifa, was out of touch with modern weapon developments. A modern Sudanese army officer writes:

> ... He had never been able to assess the effect of Maxim machine guns or anything like the Nile flotilla with the best gunners of the British Navy, who were themselves the best in Europe ...[8]

Most of the Khalifa's weapons had been captured in the 1880s. They were obsolete and poorly maintained. Artillery pieces were brass muzzle-loaders, ineffective beyond 700-1000 yards, although the Emir Mahmud was said to have promised a wife to any gunner who could put a shell into a gunboat. Shells manufactured in the Khalifa's arsenals were erratic, their wooden plug fuses often failing to detonate. At Hafir one penetrated *Abu Klea*'s magazine without exploding, and Beatty himself went below to throw the projectile overboard, an exploit that in the Crimea might have gained him the VC. Passive countermeasures against the gunboats were similarly unsuccessful. An Egyptian officer held prisoner by the Khalifa since the 1880s offered to construct a submarine mine from an old boiler stuffed with gunpowder, but accidentally blew himself up, along with one of the Khalifa's few serviceable steamers. The Dervishes had nothing to put against gunboats on the river, disappointing contemporary hopes for a centennial re-enactment of the Battle of the Nile.

The main enemy on the Nile was nature: the climate and the capricious river itself. The thermometer in August 1896 reached 120 degrees Fahrenheit, a southerly wind like the draught from a furnace delaying the native sailing craft that carried most of Kitchener's supplies. The Nile rose and fell every summer and winter, its course interrupted by the Cataracts just passable at high water. Kitchener's offensives conformed to the river, his major strategic initiatives beginning in August. The Nile, however, was late in 1896 and 1897, adding to the difficulties of tracking gunboats up cataracts. The river dropped fifty feet in 500 yards at the worst part of the Second Cataract, the water cascading across a series of basalt steps. Fourteen hundred men worked for an hour and a half to haul *Metemmeh*, her fires drawn and bulwarks strengthened, through the narrow channel:

> ... Lieutenant Beatty stood in the bows ... anxiously guarding against the bow hawsers being fouled, and every officer on board had charge of a rope to see that it was hauled upon and slackened in obedience to a signal. It was an anxious moment, and the slight craft creaking and swaying from side to side in the grip of the torrent as if she would be swept below, but little by little the combined strength of the men began to tell, and upon a zigzag course she moved slowly ahead ...[9]

Beatty was less fortunate at the start of his second tour in 1897. He found *El Teb* ill prepared to ascend the Fourth Cataract: '... no material for stopping holes, no carpenters, no engineers' stores, and heavily loaded ...' The ill-coordinated efforts of locally recruited tribesmen swung the boat out into rough water in midstream, the hawser parted, and she immediately capsized, before whirling away to finish up on a rock five miles downstream:

> ... of course, every mortal thing was lost with her, a terrible piece of luck, and left me stranded with only what I stood up in to commence a long and tedious campaign, and no opportunity of being able to replace it ... but I must be thankful I still remained above water myself.[10]

Beatty had been lucky; three of his Egyptian sailors had drowned in the wreck.

The Navy's work on the Nile covered the whole spectrum of operational activities. Combats like that at Hafir in September 1896 were infrequent, and the flotilla's direct contribution to the victory exaggerated. The Dervishes had ambushed the gunboats, hitting *Abu Klea* in eighty-six places, and driving *Tamai* back when Colville attempted to run past the forts. Thick mud walls defied the Maxims, which failed to stop Dervish gunners putting a shell through the shield of *Metemmeh*'s 9-pounder, and another through her cabin, carrying away the crown of the Captain's hat. Colville himself was shot in the arm by a sniper up a date palm. The gunboats were more useful as riverine super-cavalry, exploiting their mobility to throw the enemy off balance. Running past Hafir under covering fire from Egyptian field artillery, they forced the Dervish commander to retreat, their relentless pursuit to Dongola and Merowe reducing the outmanoeuvred Mahdist army to an exhausted rabble.

The gunboats gave Kitchener a choice between military and naval offensive strategies. In Dongola the flotilla went first, and the army followed to consolidate. The following year, land forces struck across the desert to seize Abu Hamed before the Nile rose, the flotilla bringing up reinforcements as soon as they could pass the Fourth Cataract. When a handful of irregular camelry bluffed their way into Berber in September 1897, the gunboats rushed a battalion of Sudanese infantry upriver to occupy the bridgehead. Once established, the flotilla dominated the Nile above the Fifth Cataract with a continuous routine of raids and patrols: '... a handful of black Sudanese soldiers with a British Bimbashi would be tossed into your steamer, and away you would go, directed by the briefest of always verbal orders from Lord Kitchener to attack or reconnoitre some Dervish fort or concentration ...'[11] The enemy never knew when their supply craft were safe. The Khalifa sent an army to recover Berber, but the flotilla made the river line too warm for them, driving them across the desert onto the Atbara River. Then the gunboats prevented their return by destroying the Dervishes' supply depots left along the Nile bank. The Atbara was too shallow for gunboats, but Beatty himself accompanied the night advance, which resulted in the Battle of Atbara (8 April 1898). He took a bombardier

HMS *Orlando*'s Nordenfeldt machine gun at Tientsin in 1900. (Author's collection)

of the Royal Marines Artillery and fourteen Egyptian gunners with a rocket tube and several camel loads of Hale's 24-pounder war rockets, probably the smallest naval brigade on record.[12] In August 1898 Kitchener once more exploited the gunboats' mobility to move the army and all its supplies forward 125 miles to Wad Hamid across the trackless desert. Dressed in their underwear to save space, the Sudanese and Egyptian infantry packed aboard the steamers and barges like sardines. River transport allowed Kitchener to abandon his lines of communications, and economise on detachments from the field army. The steamers gave him strategic freedom of manoeuvre, as they plied to and fro with the army's impedimenta, including a 5in howitzer battery and a floating field hospital. This strategic contribution to the campaign has been overshadowed by the stirring events of the Battle of Omdurman, but it was crucial. The gunboats' sometimes spectacular interventions on the battlefield were just one element in the firepower that destroyed the Khalifa's army. Without the Navy's logistical support Kitchener's magazine rifles and Maxims would never have reached Omdurman at all. The flotilla resumed their strategic function immediately after the battle. An intrepid column of French Senegalese troops had appeared at Fashoda, 500 miles beyond Khartoum on the White Nile. Kitchener took five gunboats, including Beatty's *Fateh*, to move them on, politely but firmly, from what had once been Egyptian territory, before the Mahdist Revolt. Only sea power made such a show of force possible. Keppel's gunboats were the long fingers of the Royal Navy, reaching into the heart of Africa, backed up by the muscle of the Mediterranean Fleet, which deterred escalation of the crisis.

The naval brigade at Tientsin, on the other hand, played a purely tactical role, fighting as infantry or field gunners. The straggling perimeter of the international concession struck Beatty as ill-adapted for defence, but he had a firing step built inside garden and warehouse walls, and distributed Maxims and 9-pounders in commanding positions:

> ... of Fatigues we had enough to keep us going morning, noon, and night, unloading trains from Taku, loading trains to be sent on to C-in-C, building Barricades to all the Streets, digging trenches, throwing epaulments, and making gun positions.[13]

The initial Boxer attacks:

> ... came on quite heedless of the Volleys we opened on them, never replying because the poor beggars had no arms to reply with, and coming up to within 300 and 400 yards armed with swords, spears, and torches. So there we squatted, knocking them over as they came along apparently quite unconcernedly.[14]

Matters became more serious when the Chinese regular army joined in. Five thousand of them attacked the railway station which was defended by a mixed force, including two companies of bluejackets:

HMS *Alacrity*'s long 12-pounder on a Scott mounting in formal pose, with Chinese ponies to pull it. Sailors used whatever draught animals were available – elephants, camels, bullocks – as well as their own brawn to haul guns. (National Maritime Museum, London: Neg No E0809)

> ... with the exception of myself it was the first time that any had ever seen a shot fired, it was a high trial, and they stood it well, steady as a rock and cool as cucumbers, as if they had been at it all their lives.[15]

The reputation they earned was not without drawbacks. Beatty found his men humbugged by constant calls for assistance:

> ... apparently it was considered advisable by all the different nations that when they thought it necessary to ask for reinforcements (which was very frequent) to get the best they could by applying to us.[16]

It had been impossible to evacuate the civilian population, who were prone to panic: '... out of their houses they poured in a dreadful state of excitement, anxiety and terror, some with nothing on but nightshirts and pyjamas.'[17] Subsequently women and children were tucked away in cellars, safe from Chinese artillery fire. Fortunately there was plenty to eat as the godowns contained large quantities of rice and flour. When the fighting was over the owners demanded compensation from the Admiralty for their damaged goods, including some crates of stout that had unaccountably vanished, as if they expected the Navy to pay for saving the concession!

The attack on the Walled City on 13 July provided a foretaste of the tactical stalemate of 1914-18. The Royal Navy provided artillery support with 12-pounder guns landed from HMS *Terrible* and 4in guns from HMS *Algerine*, all mounted on carriages improvised by Captain Percy Scott. Unlike *Shannon*'s guns in 1857 these fired indirectly, from positions out of sight of their targets, while Captain Edward Bayly, Senior Naval Officer at Tientsin, controlled their fire by telephone from the roof of the Gordon Hall. The British military commander attributed the eventual success of the attack largely to the naval guns, but Chinese rifle fire from the Walled City was unsubdued, pinning down the attackers a mile outside.[18] *Barfleur*'s marines and bluejackets were still acting as infantry, '... lying out in the open without any cover in a stupid place, as the bullets kept falling all around.'[19] Despite Beatty's characteristic anxiety to close with the enemy, his main contribution was to recover the wounded of the 9th US Infantry under fire. Beatty himself helped to carry a stretcher, one arm still in a sling. Captain Bayly rather spoiled the image of allied goodwill by suggesting that if recently arrived Americans had spent more time looking around and less time drinking, their wounded would not have had to ask the way to the hospital.

The Royal Navy's own casualties in China reflect the critical situation: a sixth of the men committed during the rising were killed or wounded, 359 out of 2207. Beatty reckoned the international garrison of Tientsin, some 2400 strong, lost 100 men a day in the first five days of the siege. The Chinese habit of killing their prisoners did little to relieve the defenders' anxiety, cut off from everywhere, and their ammunition fading away: '... in fact we knew nothing and had to act in the dark and simply hold on.'[20] Every tree and wall in the battered concession was studded with bullets, its buildings burnt

A Maxim gun on an improvised mount aboard a British river gunboat during the Boxer Rebellion. (National Maritime Museum, London: PU9528)

down or riddled with shell holes, the streets barricaded with bales of rice, peanuts, and textiles. Life in the Nile flotilla was quite peaceful by comparison: one British sergeant was killed at Hafir; another was invalided home after some Jihadia riflemen ambushed the *Fateh*; one suffered serious sunburn. Only one gunboat was permanently lost, when the overloaded *Zafir* sprung her plates, and sank leaving only her funnel above water. The Egyptian ration beef cooked like leather, and the marines had to endure ginger ale at five pence a bottle, but the flotilla was part of an irresistible military machine; communications down the Nile were secure, allowing the *Army and Navy Gazette* to publish regular reports on Kitchener's progress.

Beatty's spells of active service made him the youngest Captain in the Royal Navy. He had served only six years as Lieutenant, half the average, and two years as Commander, rapid promotion that opened the way to high command. In the Sudan he had experienced matters far outside the usual orbit of a junior Lieutenant in a battleship in peacetime. He had commanded his own ship in action, seen the application of naval power to land operations, and developed cordial inter-service relations. In a chance riverside encounter on the eve of Omdurman Beatty had lobbed a bottle of champagne to a thirsty cavalry subaltern. Twelve years later Winston Churchill, late 4th Hussars and now First Lord of the Admiralty, rescued Beatty from self-imposed unemployment by appointing him his Naval Secretary, an opening that led directly to high command in 1914.

At a strategic level, the relatively trivial naval deployment in the Sudan gained a disproportionate strategic advantage, a few key personnel seizing control of the Nile, the only line of communication in a country otherwise devoid of transportation or water. At Fashoda the gunboats defused an international crisis that could have led to war with France. In China Beatty met an emergency entirely different from Kitchener's remorseless advance. The enemy was subtle and well armed; the international command chaotic. The emergency demanded troops, not sailors, but the Boer War had overstretched the British Army, much as the Indian Mutiny had done forty-three years earlier. Had the Navy not been prepared to act against the Boxers the consequence could have been a catastrophic loss of face. Bayly described Beatty as the life and soul of the defence of Tientsin, young midshipmen and ordinary seamen behaving like veterans under his inspiration.[21]

Beatty was not unique in profiting from his chance of active service, however. His fellow officers included other future Admirals: Herbert Hood and Walter Cowan on the Nile, Roger Keyes and Christopher Cradock in China. Cradock would go down with HMS *Good Hope* at Coronel in 1914; Hood would be killed at Jutland leading the 3rd Battle Cruiser Squadron; Keyes' Zeebrugge Raid raised naval morale in 1918, and Cowan's 1st Light Cruiser Squadron shepherded the High Seas Fleet into Scapa Flow, to surrender in

November 1918. Colville ended his career safely as Commander-in-Chief Portsmouth, flying his flag in HMS *Victory*. The varied experience of such officers underline the personal connections between conventional naval history and episodes like those besides the muddy waters of the Nile and Peiho. Beatty, however, went further than any of them, except Jellicoe, another victim of Chinese marksmanship.

TYPES OF NILE GUNBOAT 1896-98

Year/Name	Type	Guns	Draught	Comments
1884:				
Abu Klea	Stern-	1 x 9pr Krupp	2ft 6in	Beatty 1896
El Teb	wheel	2 x .45in		Renamed *Hafir*
Tamai		Nordenfeldt		Flagship 1896
Metemmeh				
1896				
Fateh	Stern-	1 x 12pr	2ft 9in	Beatty 1897-8
Nasir	wheel	2 x 6pr		
Zafir	128 tons	3 x .45in Maxim		Lost 28 Aug 1898
1898				
Sheik	Twin-	2 x 12pr	2ft 0in	
Sultan	screw	1 x 4in How		Flagship 1898
Malik	140 tons	4 x .45in Maxim		

NOTE ON SOURCES

Rear-Admiral W S Chalmers *The Life and Letters of David Beatty Admiral of the Fleet* (London 1951) quotes extensively if not always accurately from Beatty's own accounts of the Sudan Campaign and Boxer Rebellion. The National Maritime Museum holds Beatty's original Journal of Service in the Boxer Rebellion and a memoir of the Nile Campaign by Admiral Sir Walter Cowan. The Royal Naval

Museum holds the papers of Captain Edward Bayly, SNO at Tientsin during the siege.

A useful essay on *The Operations of the Gunboats during the Nile Campaign* appeared in Brassey's Naval Annual 1900, and *Globe and Laurel* published several letters from RMA participants. 'Ismat Hasan Zulfo provides a valuable Sudanese perspective in *Karari* (F Warne 1980).

NOTES

1 *The Globe and Laurel*, Anonymous letter, Vol V 1898, pp89-90.
2 Total RN presence at Tientsin during the first siege 18-23 June 1900 (excluding officers):

Ship	RN	RM
Barfleur	128	21
Aurora	128	–
Orlando	100	28
Total	356	49

3 NMM BTY 1/1 Admiral Sir Walter Cowan, *Recollections*, p3.
4 NMM BTY/1/3 Earl Beatty, *Journal of Service in the Boxer Rebellion*, 11 June.
5 Ibid, 11 July.
6 Ibid, 17 June.
7 Ibid, 18 & 22 June.
8 'Ismat Hasan Zulfo, p153.
9 *Army and Navy Gazette* (12 Sep 1896), p763.
10 Rough Record of Proceeding – Nile Expedition 2nd Phase quoted in W S Chalmers, p26.
11 Cowan, op cit, p3.
12 *The Globe and Laurel*, Anonymous letter 1898, Vol V, p68.
13 Beatty Journal, 12 June.
14 Ibid, 15 June.
15 Ibid, 18 June.
16 Ibid, 20 June.
17 Ibid, 15 June.
18 *London Gazette*, 5 Oct 1900, p6109: Brig A R F Dorward, Capt J H T Burke 15 Jul 1900.
19 Beatty Journal, 15 June.
20 Beatty Journal 22 June.
21 Sir Roger Keyes, *Adventures Ashore and Afloat* (London 1973), pp254-5

CHAPTER 9

'Ex Africa Semper Aliquid Novi': The Second Boer War 1899-1901
by Arthur Bleby

By 1899 diplomatic relations between the Republic of the Transvaal and Great Britain had been deteriorating for some years. The Transvaal had re-equipped its army with the latest artillery from Krupps and Creusot and had in store 37,000 new Mauser 7mm magazine rifles and ample ammunition. The Orange Free State, which had a military pact with the Transvaal, had also purchased 20,000 Mausers. In May, at a conference in Bloemfontein between President Steyn of the Orange Free State, President Kruger of the Transvaal and the British High Commissioner in South Africa, Sir Alfred Milner, no agreement could be reached. War was now inevitable.

The British garrison, scattered in cantonments across the Cape Colony and in Natal numbered 12,000, and Milner sought reinforcements. The War Office proposed to mobilise the 1st Army Corps and a Cavalry Division (about 35,000 men in all) but the government agreed to send only 10,000 men, drawn from British regiments in India and the Mediterranean. Having waited for the spring flush of grass to appear on the veldt to provide forage for the Boers' ponies, on 27 September 1899, President Kruger informed President Steyn that the Transvaal commandos had been called out. They invaded Cape Colony, investing the small British garrisons at Mafeking and Kimberley, and advancing into Natal towards the main British base at Ladysmith, where General White was attempting to organise both the peacetime garrison and the reinforcements from India. The British 1st Army Corps was ordered to mobilise on 7 October.

Public shows of firepower were always part of the Navy's demonstration of capability and intent, and a way of winning public support. Here a large crowd takes a break from the beach tearooms to watch a senior officer's wife pull the lanyard to fire a long 12-pounder. (National Maritime Museum, London: Neg No C7195/24)

The Navy at the Siege of Ladysmith

In Simonstown the Royal Navy was asked prepare a naval brigade. Formed of seamen and marines from HM ships *Doris* and *Monarch* of the Cape Squadron, and *Powerful*, which was on her way home from China, the naval brigade left for Stormburg on 20 October taking with them two 12-pounder field guns. HMS *Terrible*, on passage to China, had arrived on 14 October. *Terrible*'s commanding officer, Captain Percy Scott, aware that the Boer artillery of Creusot and Krupp guns outranged the British field artillery, had, in anticipation of action, already devised field mountings for the long-barrelled 12-pounder guns which formed a part of the secondary armament of both *Terrible* and *Powerful*. Even bigger guns were needed and on 24 October the governor of Natal sent an urgent request:

> ... in view of heavy guns being brought by General Joubert from North I would suggest the Navy be consulted with a view to their sending detachment consisting of Blue-jackets with guns firing heavy projectiles at long range.

Scott quickly devised a mounting for 4.7in guns as well, and within 36 hours two of these were on their way to Durban in *Powerful*. By 7.00pm on 29 October, the 4.7in guns on 'transportable' mountings, three long 12-pounders on improvised field mountings and a naval 12-pounder field gun had been entrained for the front. Two trains were required for 17 officers, and 267 ratings (guns' crews, a rifle company of seamen and a medical party including stokers as stretcher-bearers), who arrived at Ladysmith at noon on 30 October.

They found the railway station being shelled by a 6in gun, the roads partially blocked by casualties, and the army retreating on Ladysmith. Hauled by eight-span ox teams and led by a local boy on his bicycle, three long 12-pounders were hurried forward. They were no sooner unlimbered on the gun line and readied for action when the artillery was ordered to retire. A Boer 6in gun began to shell the sailors and their guns, the intensity of fire increasing as they began to move. Then a shell dropped very close to the leading 12-pounder, overturning the gun and knocking off a wheel, wounding the crew and dispersing the ox team. The remaining two guns unlimbered again and, covered by the rifle company, silenced the Boers. The brigade remained in this uncomfortable position between the Boers and the retreating army until the gun had been righted, repaired and another ox team found to tow the gun into camp.

Meanwhile, the other guns, including the naval 12-pounder field gun and four Maxims, were moved directly to their defensive positions. However, as the two 4.7in guns and a procession of ox carts moved off, the leading cart dropped a wheel into a roadside gully: it was not until next day that they arrived in camp. Soon the railway line and telegraph line were cut and 22,000 Boers with five Creusot 6in and seventeen 75mm guns invested Ladysmith on 2 November. Twelve thousand British troops manned a fourteen-mile defensive perimeter with only the Navy's two 4.7in and three long 12-pounder guns able to offer any reply to the Boer bombardment. Captain Hedworth-Lambton RN, commanding the brigade, knowing that ammunition for the guns was limited, enforced strict orders that fire could only be opened in retaliation. With just five long-range guns it was impossible to give continuous cover to the whole perimeter, so the 12-pounders were moved daily to alternative positions to engage the Boer guns. The 4.7in guns were dug in at the naval camp facing north, but alternative sites were dug for them and from time to time one of these would also be moved.

Six weeks later, on 15 December, the distant sound of battle was heard from the direction of the Tugela where, at Colenso, General Buller was making his first attempt to relieve Ladysmith, and, on the night of 5/6 January, a 4.7in gun was resited to command the southern approaches to the town. Mr W Sims, Gunner RN, Mr C C Sheen, Engineer RN, and thirteen ratings, plus twenty-five sappers, escorted by seventy Gordon Highlanders, moved the gun to the hill and began to dig a gunpit. At 2.40am digging was stopped when the party was alarmed at work by the sound of bullets passing overhead. The sappers and the Gordons found their rifles and manned the gunpit, and the Imperial Light Horse extended along the crest of the hill to meet the attack. Mr Sims, cutting loose the oxen and driving them away, then mustered his seamen and led them back to the gunpit. Here he fell them in, numbered them off, detached them in half sections right and left, and conducted volley fire by half sections – all strictly by the Whale Island drill book. By daylight the Boer attack had spread along the southern face of the hill and they were established in a flanking position. Boer artillery shelled the British positions, especially the artillery, the British artillery shelled the Boer infantry, and then the Navy joined battle by firing their big guns at the Boer artillery. By 11.00am the Boers were gradually being pushed back, the volume of fire diminishing, and it was thought that the attack was over. At noon General Hamilton, who had taken immediate command of the defence, feeling it safe to thin out his line, ordered Sims and his men to retire down the hill, leaving the sappers in the gunpit. However, a party of Boers crept up, charged into the pit and a hand-to-hand scrimmage began. Alarmed by the sudden increase in the volume of fire and alerted by a number of men running past him shouting that the Boers were in the pit, Sims gave the order to fix bayonets, extended his men in line and countercharged, clearing the gunpit at bayonet-point and firing on the retreating Boers. The battle was over by 2.30pm.

Ladysmith had survived the heaviest attack: the British casualties in this one battle were 14 officers and 1350 other ranks killed and 31 officers and 240 other ranks wounded. The Navy lost one stoker killed and one able seaman severely wounded. The Boer losses were uncertain, but reports placed the number at least 700. Afterwards, life in Ladysmith fell into the lethargy and idleness of a town under siege: the brigade was reduced to siege rations of horse meat and biscuit, the horse meat being served in various forms, chervil (horse meat soup), horse sausage, potted horse tongue as well as minced, stewed and roast horse. When the Boers captured the town's water works, Mr Sheen, the engineer, designed an extempore distillery which worked until the coal ran out. Then water had to be drawn from the muddy and contaminated waters of the tributary to the Tugela: poor rations and bad water took their toll, with sickness increasing and morale declining.

The sound of battles from Spion Kop and Vaal Krantz were heard on 24 January and 5 February, and from 14 to 28 February there was the sound of intermittent gunfire as General Buller mounted the advance which was to relieve Ladysmith. At dawn on 28 February the Boers were in full retreat and that afternoon they were seen to be rigging sheerlegs over a 'long Tom', as the enemy's 6in guns were known. The Navy's guns swung into action for the last time on this tempting target, a direct hit bringing the sheerlegs down. Shortly after 6.00pm two squadrons of cavalry rode into town and the siege was over. The naval brigade was ordered back to their ship and on

7 March were accorded the honour of being played to the railway station by the pipes and drums of the Gordons. In the course of the siege they had lost one officer and five ratings killed or died of wounds but a further two officers and twenty-five ratings died of disease.

Sir George White wrote in his dispatch:

> Captain the Hon. Hedworth Lambton, RN, commanding the Naval Brigade reached Ladysmith in the nick of time, when it became evident that I was not strong enough to meet the enemy in the open field. He brought with him two 4.7-inch and four 12 pounder guns which proved to be the only ordinance in my possession capable of equalling the range of the enemy's heavy guns. Although the ammunition was strictly limited Capt. Lambton so economised it that it lasted out to the end of the siege and under his direction the Naval guns succeeded in keeping at a distance the enemy's siege guns, a service which was of the utmost importance.

The Naval Brigade with Buller

A naval brigade had also participated in General Buller's campaign to relieve Ladysmith. Buller had reached Cape Town on 31 October 1899 ahead of 1st Army Corps. The Boers had invaded from the north, Mafeking and Kimberley were under siege, and the Boers in Natal were investing Ladysmith. Both Cape Colony and Natal were wide open to further Boer advances. Buller decided that he had no choice but to split his Army Corps into three separate forces. One under General Methuen to advance to the relief of Kimberley, the second under General Gatacre to clear the Stormberg area of Cape Colony, while the third under his personal command would relieve Ladysmith.

On 7 November HMS *Terrible* relieved HMS *Powerful* at Durban and Captain Scott, RN, became the commandant of the town which was placed under martial law. His energetic steps to place Durban in a state of defence included landing 450 officers and men, with two 4.7in guns on improvised field mountings and sixteen long 12-pounders, who were deployed outside the town where they remained until General Buller called them forward to join his army

'Ex Africa Semper Aliquid Novi': The Second Boer War

Long 12-pounders on parade at Frere Camp, Colenso, Buller's headquarters for the relief of Ladysmith. Note the improvised gun carriages and the farm carts for limbers. (National Maritime Museum, London: Neg No C7195/20)

at Frere. On 12 December this naval brigade marched the short distance from Frere to Chievely, the column of guns, ammunition wagons and baggage wagons stretching for two miles, and they established camp on a kopjie which became known throughout the army as Gun Hill. On 13 December the guns were moved to another kopjie about two miles nearer the Boer positions, dug in and a few ranging shots were fired at the Boer positions. This position became known as Shooters' Hill.

To reach Ladysmith Buller would have to cross the Tugela River and then fight through a maze of kopjies. At Colenso, to his front there were three possible fords (drifts), an intact footbridge and the blown railway bridge. Fifteen miles to his left was another possible crossing, Potgeiters Drift, where the barrier of kopjies appeared less formidable. A further five miles on was Trichards Drift. The Boers, under General Botha, were in cleverly-concealed trenches covering all three drifts and the intact footbridge at Colenso and had anchored their left flank on Mount Hlangwain. When Buller heard the news of British defeats at Magersfontain and Stromberg, he decided that he should attack without delay at Colenso.

Buller planned a two-pronged attack with the Irish Brigade under General Hart on the left crossing the river at Bridle Drift while General Hildyard moved to cross the river by the intact footbridge and Wagon Drift beside it. Two 4.7in guns and four long 12-pounders were ordered to a position on a slight eminence, which became known as Naval Gun Hill, 4500 yards from the Boer centre. Six other long 12-pounders were placed under Colonel Long, the Commander Royal Artillery, with two 12-pounders remaining in position on Shooters' Hill to protect the camp. At about 5.30am the guns on Naval Gun Hill began firing, but there was no return fire and no Boers could be seen. Hart led his troops towards Bridle Drift and Long, his two batteries and the Navy's 12-pounders also moved forwards.

When Hart was about half-way to Bridle Drift he altered his line of advance and led his troops towards a deep oxbow bend in the river, effectively a salient. When they were well inside, the Boers opened fire from the front and both flanks. Thrown into confusion, the British suffered very severely for an hour, and Hart's only reaction was to order more men into the salient. Buller, from Naval Gun Hill, watched this action and rode over to Hart to order him to withdraw his men. Three of the Boer's 6in Creusot guns brought heavy fire down on the horse batteries supporting Hart and they were forced to retire, but when the 4.7in guns on Naval Gun Hill shifted target to the Creusots they soon ceased firing.

On the other flank Long, supporting General Hildyard's attack, had advanced the guns under his command too close to the Boer positions. He was forming his gun line with the two Royal Horse Artillery batteries at a range of 500 yards, when the Boers opened a devastating fire. In the advance the naval brigade's guns, being ox-drawn, were outpaced by horse-drawn batteries moving at the trot, and they struggled to cross a donga. Two guns with their limbers were across, two guns and their limbers were jammed with wheels locked and their ox teams mixed in a melee, but the rear guns were halted on the enemy side. When the Boers opened fire, native drivers bolted for cover leaving the ox teams unmanageable, but the two guns already across the donga and the two yet to enter were brought into action. Borrowing artillery gun teams, the third and fourth guns were extricated from the donga and these also joined in the action. The jammed wagons had, temporarily, to be abandoned as any effort to clear them brought down intense artillery and rifle fire.

The gun crews of the Royal Horse Artillery took heavy casualties but fought on for about an hour before, ammunition exhausted, the survivors took cover with their wounded in a shallow donga close in the rear of the guns, waiting for the reinforcement and re-supply of ammunition for which they had asked. General Buller, riding back from his meeting with General Hart, found the naval guns in action but the Royal Horse Artillery guns in the open, apparently abandoned on their firing line. He rode off to organise infantry support and then back to supervise the recovery of the guns. Three of his staff officers with gun teams and limbers cantered to the guns and in the face of intense rifle fire hitched up and brought off two of them, at the cost of two officers wounded, one mortally. Two further gun teams were dispatched, suffered over fifty percent casualties in both men and horses, and failed to reach the guns. An independent attempt from a battery on the right flank also failed. Throughout this the naval 12-pounders tried to subdue the Boer rifle fire, but without much success.

At this juncture a Boer shell burst very close to Buller. He was hit and very severely bruised in the ribs by a shell fragment and was probably concussed. This may have affected his judgement for suddenly he ordered the army back to camp at Chievely, abandoning the guns and wounded on the battlefield, personally ordering the naval 12-pounders to retire. This was easier said than done. There were still two guns over the donga, two wagons jammed in the donga, and four guns and some wagons beyond the donga with no means of traction. Artillery gun teams were again borrowed and the guns were moved out of range, while the guns' crews readied the wagons for removal. The two in the donga were separated and manhandled out, but on the enemy's side. They, and the other wagons on that side, were turned ready to be hitched up and hauled away, even though the wagons had a large turning circle which at first brought them closer to the Boer positions. Finally all were recovered and Lieutenant F C A Ogilvie, RN, brought his detachment with their guns and wagons safely back to camp at Chievely. Surprisingly after all this action the naval brigade had only three men wounded.

The withdrawal of the army was covered by fire from the 4.7in guns and 12-pounders on Naval Gun Hill. They remained in position until the infantry had passed through and then moved off to take up their old position on Shooters' Hill. The four naval surgeons in the brigade were detached to help care for the wounded in the field hospital at Chievely. Buller moved the army back to Frere and ordered Lieutenant Ogilvie with his six 12-pounders to accompany him, the 4.7in and remaining 12 pounders staying in position on Gun Hill. For the next twenty-five days the 4.7in guns harassed the Boers, usually shooting at dawn and dusk when visibility was at its best. From time to time the guns, laid at dusk, fired blind during the night.

On 10 January 1900, having been reinforced with another division, Buller began his second attempt to relieve Ladysmith with a flank march towards Potgieters Drift and Trickhardts Drift, starting the series of moves that led to the battle of Spion Kop. The naval brigade was split into batteries to be attached to individual divisions and give long-range artillery support. It was during these operations that the naval brigade demonstrated its ability to overcome obstacles and move its guns over almost any ground and up the steepest of slopes.

General Warren proved himself to be incompetent. His advance was sluggish, and his manoeuvres indecisive and meaningless. After his failure at Spion Kop, Buller re-united the two wings of his army and on 5 February attacked the lightly-held Boer position at Vaal Krantz. The attack was to be under cover of artillery massed on the south bank of the Tugela. For the naval brigade this movement over rough country and up steep hillsides meant much manhandling of their guns. Then for three days the guns kept up what a Boer general later described as 'the heaviest bombardment I saw during the war'. The infantry crossed the Tugela and secured a position on Vaal

Krantz, but to advance further required artillery support and not even the naval brigade could position their guns for this purpose. After a council of war Buller withdrew his troops across the river and marched back to Frere. The naval brigade re-occupied Gun Hill.

While Buller was engaged to the west the Boers had strengthened their position to the east of Colenso and occupied Hussar Hill, Green Hill and Monte Cristo which gave additional security to Mount Hlangwane. Buller rested his army and reconnoitred the ground before beginning, on 14 February, his third and finally successful attempt to relieve Ladysmith. Lord Dundonald's Mounted Infantry, supported by Lieutenant Ogilvie and his 12-pounders seized Hussar Hill. When it was secured Ogilvie dug in his guns, and by the close of the 16th, after two days of dogged fighting supported by the naval guns of Gun Hill and on Hussar Hill, the infantry had cleared Green Hill of Boers. That evening the naval brigade was reinforced by the arrival from Durban of a 6in gun on an improvised travelling mounting. This gun was also dug in on Gun Hill and came into action at a range of 16,000 yards to silence the Boer Creusot 6in gun. For the next ten days it was to dominate the Boer heavy artillery. By the evening of 18 February the Boers had been driven from Monte Cristo and Hlangwane.

With this bank of the Tugela clear Buller re-grouped. The naval brigade's guns, except the 6in, were called forward to give close support to the infantry. The first British troops crossed the Tugela on 19 February and the next day Buller began to batter at the Boer positions on the hills ahead of him. Four days of bitter battle brought little reward and on the 25th Buller and Botha agreed a truce to allow the treatment of the wounded and removal of the dead. Buller now pulled back over the Tugela and threw a pontoon bridge over the river in a position which would allow his troops to cross and attack on a wider frontage. The naval brigade concentrated on Hlangwane, being strengthened by two 4.7in guns on transportable mountings, which were dug in overnight and under fire.

A barrage was begun at 7.00am on 27 February, the sappers completed work on the bridge, and the infantry began to cross at 10.00am. Once over the Tugela the troops defiled to the right and, as

Six of HMS *Terrible's* eight midshipmen armed with Longley Enfield rifles have swapped their dirks for bayonets and donned sennet hats. Soon they will also exchange their blue reefer jackets for more practical khakis. (National Maritime Museum, London: Neg No C7195/15)

they reached their allotted positions, turned to the left and began to climb the hill facing them. By nightfall, and after hard fighting, all the positions had been taken, the Boers were in full retreat, and the road to Ladysmith was open. Next morning Dundonald with his mounted infantry were sent forward to reconnoitre towards Ladysmith and, having brushed aside the Boer rearguard, rode into town.

There was now a pause in operations while the Ladysmith garrison, back on full rations, recovered their strength, re-equipped and re-organised. The naval brigades, however, began to break up. The 'Powerfuls' who had been in Ladysmith throughout the siege embarked on 7 March to return to Portsmouth. The 'Terribles' left on 11 March to resume their passage to China. Some guns were handed over to the army, and the naval brigade was reduced to ten officers and ninety men, sufficient to man two 4.7in guns and four 12-pounders. On 21 March this reduced naval brigade moved up the railway to Elandslaagte in pursuit of the retreating Boers. An artillery dual began in which one Boer gun was destroyed and the others silenced at a cost of two seamen killed and two wounded. Eleven days later Boer artillery and infantry was beaten off and the naval brigade destroyed another gun.

On 11 May Buller advanced, the naval brigade marching with Buller as he manoeuvred the Boers out of successive positions back to and beyond Laings Nek, clearing Natal of the invaders. On 22 June the brigade was further reduced when men from HMS *Forte* were recalled to their ship and their 4.7in guns were also handed over to the army. The 12-pounder guns were given defensive roles on the lines of communication where they remained until October when, having handed over these too, the sailors entrained for Durban flying a paying-off pennant on their train.

Belmont, Graspan, Modder River and Magersfontein

When Buller left Cape Town he had given General Methuen the task of guarding the railway line from Cape Town to Kimberley, upon which he would be completely dependent for his supplies, and of lifting the siege of Kimberley. Besides infantry Methuen had a regiment of cavalry, a company of mounted infantry and two batteries of artillery, including a naval brigade with four long 12-pounders from the seamen at Stormburg. Methuen set up his headquarters at Orange River Station on the railway and began his march towards Kimberley on 21 November. As Methuen marched out, the naval brigade's train arrived, and the sailors were faced with a night march to catch up with the main body, an experience they did not enjoy; 'A night march with obstinate mules is a very trying experience'.

When they did catch up with the main body it was already in action against the Boers in position high on a line of kopjies covering the railway line. Captain Prothero, in command, brought his guns into action. Not satisfied with his initial position Porthero ordered the guns to limber up and moved to the left between two kopjies. The guns now had the Boers in sight at 1700 yards and after a short engagement they joined in a general retreat. Ordered forward to engage the retreating Boers but faced with very bad going, Captain Prothero, whose men had been without food or sleep for thirty-six hours and were exhausted by their exertions, abandoned the pursuit.

After a night's rest the advance continued up the line of the railway, halting at dusk to bivouac about three-quarters of a mile short of two dams from which the force watered. When the commissariat wagons came up supper, a meagre ration of tinned meat and ship's biscuit, was issued, and soon after supper an ADC brought orders for the next day. These began '... the enemy, about four hundred strong, hold a hill on our line of advance two miles to the north. The brigade will lead the attack supported by the K.O.Y.L.I. and a field battery ...'. Methuen was unaware that a contingent of Transvaal Boers had arrived and joined the Free State Commandos. The naval brigade stood-to at 3.00am on 25 November and led off the whole force, leaving the guns and fifty seamen on the train. They marched about a mile to the right of the railway track while an armoured train and the train carrying the Navy's guns kept abreast of them. The Boers were position on three kopjies: the two nearest the railway line were low but from the second of these a spur ran up to the third, the highest and most forbidding of the trio. The Boers position on the upper slopes, well concealed by bush and protective rock formations, dominated the open ground which offered no cover to the advancing naval brigade. A battery of field artillery and two 12-pounders (all that the fifty seamen could unload from the train) were in action on the left and a second battery was on the right shelling the highest kopjie. The brigade moved right and, followed by the King's Own Yorkshire Light Infantry and a half battalion of the North Lancs, marched diagonally across and towards the Boer position. At 7.45am they were about 700 yards from the foot of the

'Ex Africa Semper Aliquid Novi': The Second Boer War

This 6in gun was made up in the railway yards at Durban. (National Maritime Museum, London: Neg No C7195/30)

highest kopjie in the order from the left of 'C' company (Royal Marines Light Infantry), 'B' company (Royal Marines Light Infantry), 'A' company (Royal Marines Artillery), and 'D' company (bluejackets), when the field battery ceased firing. As the Boers opened fire, the brigade, led by Prothero, halted, turned half left to face the enemy, wheeled right to come to within about 600 yards of the foot of the kopjie, assumed the prone position, and opened fire. Then Prothero ordered his men to carry out a series of rushes which got them through the zone of concentrated fire at the foot of the kopjie. Fixing bayonets they began the steep climb up the kopjie in places hauling themselves up on hands and knees, all the time under fire from the front and left flank. When they were about 25 yards from the summit the Boer fire ceased and the summit was taken at the rush. With no liking for close-quarter fighting, the Boers ran from the bayonet, but took cover a few hundred yards back to open fire again. British infantry following the naval brigade cleared the spur to the left, leading to a general retreat by the Boers.

After a day's rest Methuen resumed the advance, only to find the Boers dug in in concealed positions covering the crossing places of the Modder river, from where a Boer gun opened fire on his wagon train. The naval 12-pounders on a low ridge about 5000 yards from the southern bank of the river engaged and silenced this gun, but so began a day-long artillery duel. The Boer gunpits were difficult to spot, as they were using smokeless propellant, and they frequently shifted their positions. To solve this problem the naval brigade moved their guns ever closer to the Boer positions, but then came under heavy rifle and pom-pom fire: they retired in good order, keeping up a brisk fire from three guns while the fourth moved. The infantry advanced to within about 1000 yards of the Boer trenches before the volume of fire halted them. The British right and centre, trapped in the open, were pinned down all day. Only on the left did the infantry have any success, after about three hours forcing a passage of the river and securing a bridgehead. By nightfall there was a stalemate but at dawn it was found that the Boers had stolen away.

Methuen paused on the Modder River, bringing up supplies and reinforcements and sending out reconnaissance patrols along his future line of advance. He also sent a message to the naval Commander-in-Chief at the Cape asking for guns heavier and with a longer range than the 12-pounders. Another 4.7in gun on a field mounting was sent up and on arrival it was positioned on the north bank of the river to carry out daily bombardments of the Boers. On 9 December this gun accompanied a reconnaissance in force and opened random fire, hoping for return fire to reveal Boer positions. The Boers were not provoked into a reply and a twelve-mile long defence line dug in at the foot of, and not in accordance with Boer custom on the crest of, Magersfontein ridge remained undetected. Methuen planned a night march and dawn attack on the Boers and issued orders for this to take place in the early hours of 11 December, moving forward the 4.7in gun and five batteries of field artillery to within three miles of Magersfontein to bombard the crest and forward slopes. At midnight on 11 December on a moonless night, in an African thunderstorm and facing into a gale-force wind, the Highland Brigade formed up in close order, 3600 men packed into a column 45 yards wide and 160 yards long, kept in a cohesive whole by ropes held by the right- and left-hand men of the flanking files. They made slow progress but, about an hour later, as the sky began to lighten, had reached the point at which they were to extend. However, General Wauchope, commanding the Highland Brigade, decided to continue to advance in close order, giving the order to extend only when the leading files were within 500 yards of the hidden Boer trenches. As the leading files began to open out the Boers opened fire and the Highland Brigade was thrown into disorder. Fortunately, probably because of the bad shooting light, the Boers were firing high but the volume of rapid fire drove the Highland Brigade to ground, and for nine hours there was a stalemate. The Highland Brigade lay prone out in the open, unable to move without drawing fire. The Royal Artillery advanced their guns to within 1000 yards of the Boers to give support and from further back the naval 4.7in joined in. However, at about 1.00pm a party of Boers was detected working round the right flank of the Highland Brigade and two companies of the Seaforths were ordered to move back to face this threat. This defensive move was seen and interpreted as a retirement by other tired, thirsty and painfully sunburnt men who also began to retire. The rest of the afternoon was spent in efforts to reform the Highland Brigade.

Methuen held his position until dawn next day, hoping that, as at the Modder, the Boers would retreat during the night, but a balloon, flown at dawn to reconnoitre the position, reported the Boers still there. Methuen's greatest problem was in watering his force and he decided to return to the banks of the Modder. After a truce in which to bury the dead and collect the wounded the army moved back to camp where Methuen received orders to remain on the defensive. Life in camp, which was to last two months until 11 February 1900, was not comfortable. The ground quickly turned to a fine dust which was stirred up by any movement of man or beast and sandstorms or dust devils were frequent. Drinking water was always in short supply and the river water had to be boiled before use.

The naval brigade was stationed north of the river and on 15 December began a routine of harassing fire on the Boer trenches and exchanging shots with their guns. Another 4.7in gun came up from Simonstown and this was sited to cover the right rear of the army. Two of the 12-pounders were sited on the extreme right flank on the north bank, all in gun pits and protected by small detachments of Royal Marines. On 3rd February Commander W L Grant of HMS *Doris* brought up two more 4.7in guns. At Enslin they collected wagons, water carts, two hundred and eighty four oxen with forty-two native drivers and four colonial conductors. There they began to prepare for the forthcoming campaign which was to be conducted by Field Marshal Lord Roberts with Kitchener as his Chief of Staff.

Roberts' Campaign

The campaign began on 11 February when Roberts, leaving Methuen supported by two 4.7in guns and two 12-pounders to mask Magersfontein, moved east across the veldt to attack the Boer supply depot at Jacobsdal. General French and the cavalry were ordered to ride round Magersfontein and relieve Kimberley. By 15 February this was done, the Boers marching eastward in an attempt to get ahead of the British army and between Roberts and Bloemfontein. On 16 February there was a skirmish between British infantry and Cronje's forces who broke contact and slipped away at nightfall, leaving seventy-eight loaded supply wagons in British hands. Next morning the cavalry made contact with the Boer column and drove it into the loop of the Modder river at Paardeburg. Here Cronje laagered his whole force together with his baggage train and the wives and families who had joined their husbands in the camps before Kimberley and at Magersfontein. Trapped by the British, Cronje entrenched his position.

Roberts was at Jacobsdal recovering from a chill, Kitchener was with the troops at Paardeburg and assumed command of operations there. With the support of two 12-pounders and 6th Division's artillery, Kitchener launched a series of uncoordinated frontal infantry attacks on the Boer trenches, all of which were beaten off. By the end of the day nothing had been achieved and the heaviest casualty list of any day in the Boer War had been incurred. Kitchener's plan for the next day was more of the same, but fortunately Roberts recovered and took charge. While Kitchener was launching bloody attacks on the Boers, the naval brigade was marching from Magersfontein to join up with Grant's guns at Jacobsdal. They were settling into their bivouac on 18 February in the expectation of rest when they received marching orders and at 9.30pm moved off on an all-night march, halting at 6.00am. The oxen were turned out to graze and all hands were at breakfast when Lord Roberts and his staff cantered up on their way to Paardeburg. Roberts asked the Navy, as soon as possible, to move on for another ten miles to strengthen the artillery surrounding Cronje. But the oxen had to be allowed to feed and to chew the cud, so it was not until the afternoon that they could move again. Not until 8.00pm did they bivouack, having been under way for fifteen of the last twenty-two hours. At Paardeburg, the naval brigade with one 4.7in gun and three 12-pounders were placed in a very exposed position 1300 yards from the Boer trenches. For seven days, every time a gun was fired Boer rifles replied. However, Grant with three 4.7in guns and one 12-pounder was sent over the Modder to a position within 3000 yards of three Boer guns and a pom-pom. When they opened fire, their first shell burst amongst the Boer wagons.

When Roberts learnt that there were women and children in the laager, he offered them safe conduct out of danger, an offer which was refused. So, on 22 February Roberts began a deliberate bombardment directed at the Boer transport, food dump and ammunition reserves. The fall of shot was observed from a balloon which signalled corrections by flag. The Boers in their trenches and the women and children sheltering under the river bank were comparatively safe, suffering mostly from the noise, the smell of putrefaction from dead animals, and from the squalor created by their own lack of hygiene, but after five days General Cronje surrendered to Roberts.

Roberts' army had been on short rations and struggling with severe water problems. The only source of water was the river, thick with mud and increasingly contaminated by effluent and decaying animal carcasses. Boiled and clarified with alum it was safe to drink but disgusting taste could not be disguised with the meagre quantity of tea or coffee issued with the rations. On 26 February the first column of supply wagons arrived in camp and two and a half days rations were issued – to last five days. However, Grant's guns' crews did not suffer quite the same deprivations. About two miles from their camp there was a large flock of sheep grazing on the veldt. An officer with Grant was to write:

> The guileless Bluejacket (the Stokers – good luck to them! were the most successful criminals) seldom returned without one. Their invariable explanation was that 'it had followed them into camp' but this was a very elastic term and included, perfectly correctly, those occasions on which the unwilling animal was towed in on a piece of rope; less accurately when it was pushed from behind by one and towed by the ears by another; and still less accurately, perhaps, when, as often happened it was too dead beat from following them so far, and was brought in on their shoulders.

There was a leg of mutton in the Wardroom every night. Later, Grant was ordered to re-join the rest of the naval brigade and his line of march was through the remains of the Boer laager. There were quick eyes and light fingers amongst the guns' crews. 'Oh! I picked it up in the laager' became a catchphrase within the brigade to explain otherwise inexplicable acquisitions.

The Boers were concentrating their forces at Poplar Grove, the last natural defensible position before Bloemfontein. Roberts began his move on 5 March, sending the Cavalry Division in a wide flanking movement, the Highland Brigade with the Navy's 12-pounders down the north bank of the Modder and the 4.7in guns to a position on a kopjie 7000 yards from the Boer centre with orders to remain concealed until daybreak on 7 March. At 4.00am the gun's crews ran their pieces onto the summit and waited until Lord Roberts gave them the order to fire the starting gun which was the signal for the cavalry to begin their sweep round the Boer flank. President Kruger of the Transvaal had, that morning, arrived in the Boer camp. The Boers, appreciating the threat from the cavalry, began to abandon their trenches, mount up and ride off. Kruger being hustled into a light Cape cart in which, at the gallop, he led a general retreat. The 4.7in guns had little to do until, towards the end of the action Lord Roberts personally directed them onto a target marked by some prominent anthills on the veldt below. As the second round burst on target about 200 Boers broke cover and raced to the rear. There was just time before they vanished over a convenient ridge for two more shots to speed them on their way. The 12-pounders attached to the Highland Brigade were in the open and came under fire from two guns, one on each flank. In action to right and left they had a busy time but incurred no casualties and eventually the Boers abandoned their guns.

Roberts' way to Bloemfontein was now clear and, though their boots were in deplorable condition – some men with bare feet wrapped in puttees – and they were on short rations, they covered the seventy miles in just four days. Roberts, who needed some time to refit his army and solve his considerable administrative and logistic problems, readied his army for the next phase of the war. The naval brigade too settled into camp life, and their khaki drill uniforms were replaced by khaki serge and their disintegrating sennet hats by felt bush hats. On the raised left brim of these the sailors embroidered a foul anchor and the Royal Marines a bugle – these badges became almost the only distinguishing marks of the members of the brigade. The seamen from *Powerful* left to rejoin their ship, although her Royal Marines remained with the brigade. The reinforcements included Midshipman Cunningham, the future Admiral of the Fleet Viscount Cunningham of Hyndhope. However, an epidemic of enteric fever which developed at Bloemfontein did not spare the brigade, eighteen officers and men being admitted to hospital, and it was no longer possible to man all the guns with seamen. To their delight one of the 4.7in guns was handed over to

A 4.7in gun dug in on its 'transportable mounting': the size of the baulks of timber indicate the achievement in getting the gun to the front. On the right is a 'cruiser scope' on a tripod mounting: the sailors allegedly made pocket money by charging soldiers for a glimpse of the enemy. (National Maritime Museum, London: Neg No C7195/11)

the Royal Marines Artillery, leaving infantry duty to the Royal Marine Light Infantry.

On 22 April Grant's guns were ordered to join the Highland Brigade which was sent to prevent General De Wet and his men from joining up with the Boer forces in the Transvaal. Grant's guns never rejoined the naval brigade, but instead enjoyed four months hard campaigning against a very mobile force of Boers. In nine days from 22 to 30 May they marched 129 miles, fighting on five days and ending the march on one-third rations. After two months of sparring with De Wett around Heilbron they began another series of marches, covering 250 miles in fifteen days, during which the gun wheels began to collapse. One gun was sent to Pretoria for repair, while the other was dismantled and carried on wagons, Grant giving his assurance that, if required, the gun would be remounted and fired within an hour. The last trek now began, lasting twenty days with action on ten of them and 187 rounds fired. On 30 September Grant handed over the guns and equipment to the army, and on 2 October he and his men entrained for Simonstown.

At Bloemfontein on 2 May the remainder of the naval brigade received orders to leave two 12-pounders for garrison duty and for the remainder to prepare to march. By now they had developed their own march routine: since the main body the army moved about a mile an hour faster than the ox drawn guns, the brigade would set off about two hours before the main body, halt at noon for four hours for the oxen to graze before resuming the march to arrive in camp about two hours behind. Army standing orders laid down that ammunition wagons were never to be separated from the guns but baggage wagons were to be a part of the baggage train. The seamen and marines were determined that they would not be separated from their baggage, which in any case they required for the rigging of their camp and preparation of supper after their late ending to the day's march. So, in every ammunition wagon there was also camp equipment, bedding, clothes and provisions. In this, as in their constant foraging for food and disregard for any authority in matters concerning their comfort, the brigade irritated the staff. On one occasion a heated argument about baggage brought the advance of the column to a halt and finally involved both Lord Kitchener and Lord Roberts. The divisional commander himself rode forward to find out the cause of the hold up, and he agreed that the naval brigade's baggage wagons always go with the guns. This did not satisfy the staff officer who referred the matter to Lord Kitchener who, in turn, reported the facts to Lord Roberts. As one of the fifteen ammunition wagons passed by, a tarpaulin cover flapped, exposing a case clearly marked 'Van Houten's Cocoa'. Lord Roberts, remarking 'Yes – they mark it very funnily', rode off.

For the naval brigade 29 May was probably the worst day in the whole campaign. They were to cross the Klip river using an old and rotten wooden bridge which the sappers had passed as strong enough to carry guns. The 12-pounders with their mule teams crossed safely as did the leading 4.7in gun with its seamen crew, the bridge groaning under the weight. The Royal Marines gun was halfway across when its left wheel broke through the planking and the gun heeled over at 45 degrees and stuck. Two divisions were trapped behind and firing had broken out ahead. It took four hours to move the gun, first by cutting away the rest of the bridge and dropping the gun into the riverbed. Then it needed a double team (sixty-four) oxen and several hundred soldiers from the trapped divisions to haul it up the riverbank. Meanwhile the seamen's gun was hauled to the sound of firing but never caught up with the retreating Boers. As night fell it was being brought back to camp following the tracks of a field artillery battery, when the surface of a soft patch of ground, which could take the weight of a field artillery piece, was not equal to the seven-ton weight of a 4.7in gun. Bogged down and unable to extricate the gun, its crew spent a cold and hungry night. The 12-pounders pushing on hard had penetrated the outskirts of Johannesburg, but they found themselves behind the Boer lines and had to make their way back through the Boer positions.

The next day the gun was extricated from the bog into which it had sunk, an evolution which required the combined efforts of every officer, man, ox, and mule before it was free and they could return to camp. The next day they marched past Lord Roberts in the defeated Johannesburg and into camp on the far side of the town. The march was an infuriating experience, taking four and a half-hours, with frequent unexplained halts, to reach Johannesburg. It was not until 3.00pm that the naval brigade passed the saluting base and headed, hopefully, for camp. They were supposed to follow the field artillery but never caught up with them and marched on until dusk when they halted and spent another cold and hungry night. They had overshot the camp by three miles.

The advance on Pretoria was continued on 3 June and on 4 June met with resistance on the Quaggaport Hills where De La Rey had established a defensive line. Under cover of this resistance General

Botha evacuated his men from the town and retreated up the railway line towards Portuguese East Africa taking most of his stores and ammunition with him. Lord Roberts confidently expected that, with the capitals of both Boer states in his hands, the Boers would sue for peace, but after a week, when they had not done so, Roberts moved to attack General Botha on Diamond Hill on the British left flank. The guns of the naval brigade were badly positioned and out of range, so they were moved forward some 7000 yards and next morning duelled with a 6in gun mounted on a railway truck. This chugged up the track into range and then back to reload, until at extreme range a shot from the a naval 4.7in gun hit the railway line. That evening the Boers evacuated their positions and rode off into the veldt.

The brigade was now ordered into camp near Pretoria. Near their lines there was a flock of guinea fowl which the officers promptly shot for the pot, but these were allegedly tame birds and the owner complained to the authorities. As a result the brigade was ordered to shift camp to a distant and less comfortable site from which they could 'protect the railway'. Here they built themselves a hutted camp, using timber and corrugated iron sheet, and their main pastime was cricket. The advance eastward towards the Portuguese East Africa border began on 22 July and on 25 August, near Belfast, Roberts met Buller advancing from Natal. Roberts ordered the combined armies to attack General Botha, occupying a defensive position straddling the railway and protecting President Kruger's temporary capital. The Boer position was anchored on near-impassable land cut up by deep ravines on the north and a stretch of boggy land to the south, and the British were committed to a frontal assault. The brigade was stationed on Monument Hill (the Monument marking the highest point of the Transvaal and offering a convenient aiming point and range marker for the Boers). There were, as far as the brigade was concerned, two days of confused action during which they engaged targets of opportunity when not engaging Boer 'Long Toms'. When, on the second day, the infantry penetrated the Boer position the commandos rode off, the larger section under Botha to the north while the rest broke south, leaving a screen to protect the Presidents of the Orange Free State and Transvaal as they moved up the railway to Portuguese East Africa.

After Belfast the naval brigade was again split up. The bluejacket gun was attached to the cavalry and marched to Barbeton, the most difficult march of the campaign, particularly the pass known as the Devil's Knuckle, so steep that the ascent required triple ox teams to get the gun and wagons to the top of the pass. The descent was a goat track and even with the greatest care Cape carts and wagons capsized. One wheel of the gun collapsed and was replaced by a wagon wheel which lasted, fortunately, until the armourer managed to repair and refit the gun wheel at Barbeton. The other 4.7in gun remained on Monument Hill. The two 12-pounders were attached to the 11th Division and marched in pursuit of the two presidents, reaching the border on 24 September. It was littered with the partially destroyed stores, ammunition and weapons discarded on 23 September when the Boer army had crossed into Portuguese territory.

On 30 September, handing over transport to the Army Service Corps, the guns and their crews entrained for Pretoria. There were elements of farce in this journey – the engine driver was an alcoholic, the engine could barely move the train, and the stokers, improvising brushes, turned to and boiler-cleaned the engine after which it was still necessary to push the train up any steep gradient and finally, due to the inebriation of the driver the train was in collision. It took the naval brigade two and a half-hours to clear the line, 'the never failing drag ropes proving most useful'

Once at Pretoria the naval brigade was re-united and paraded to receive the thanks of Lord Roberts and of General Pole-Carew (with whom they had been connected since Belmont and Graspan). The guns were handed over to the Royal Artillery and the naval brigade entrained for Simonstown. The Royal Navy's part in this war was over.

BIBLIOGRAPHY

Admiral Richard Bacon, *A Naval Scrapbook* (London 1925)
Michael Barthrop, *The Anglo-Boer War* (Poole 1987)
W Baring Pemberton, *Battles of the Boer War* (London 1975)

Lieutenant E A Burne, RN, *With the Naval Brigade in Natal* (London 1902)
Sir Arthur Conan Doyle, *The Great Boer War* (London 1908)
Admiral of the Fleet Lord Cunningham of Hyndhope, *A Sailor's Odyssey* (London 1951)
T T Jeans, *Naval Brigades in the South African War* (London 1901)
Rayne Kruger, *Goodbye Dolly Grey* (London 1959)
Colonel Marling VC, *Rifleman and Hussar* (London 1931)
Major-General Moultan, *The Royal Marines* (London 1972)
Peter Padfield, *Aim Straight* (London 1966)
Thomas Pakenham, *The Boer War* (London 1979)
P C Smith and B Oakley, *The Royal Marines* (Tunbridge Wells 1988)
J Symonds, *Buller's Campaign* (London 1974)
H H Wilson, *With the Flag to Pretoria* (London 1900-2)

CHAPTER 10

The Royal Naval Division
1914-19
by Chris Page

The Royal Naval Division (RND) was an unique formation: the majority of the Division throughout the War were sailors, with naval ranks – Leading Seaman rather than Corporal, Chief Petty Officer rather than Sergeant, Lieutenant Commander rather than Major. And yet, almost none of them had ever served at sea. The Ratings grew beards, they referred to 'going ashore' when they took leave, worked naval watch systems, went to sick bay when ill, called the field kitchen 'the Galley', and wore naval cap badges with their khaki etc. When deployed to Antwerp by rail, there was even discussion as to whether units should disembark from the port and starboard side of the train! The Battalions carried the names of naval heroes, rather than numbers, as in the Army.[1] Initially the Division consisted of brigades of men from the Royal Naval Reserve, the RNVR, and the Royal Marines. Subsequently, due to a shortage of sailors, a third brigade was formed of soldiers from various regiments. Notwithstanding its usual traditions, and a discipline more like that found in some of the Dominion divisions which upset some of the more senior Army officers, it proved to be a very effective elite fighting unit. Winston Churchill, its founder, said that the Division came to be regarded, 'In the glorious company of the seven or eight most famous in the British Army'.[2]

From the start, the RND attracted some interesting people, including Bernard Freyberg VC, who went on to become Governor General of New Zealand, Rupert Brooke, A P Herbert, and Arthur Asquith, son of the Prime Minister, and one of our most gifted and courageous citizen soldiers of the First World War.

The Division did not exist before 1914. Before the outbreak of war, the First Lord of the Admiralty, Winston Churchill, realised that there would be between 20 and 30,000 naval reservists for whom there would be no immediate jobs at sea, and the Committee for Imperial Defence agreed that they should be formed into a division for emergency deployment for possible tasks including minor amphibious landings, coastal raids and defence of ports. On 30 August 1914, Churchill signed the mobilisation order for the Royal Navy, but already by then a mixed bag of naval reservists had been assembled, the equivalent of two brigades, and were under canvas near Deal, in Kent. It should be remembered that this was at a time when the British Expeditionary Force stood at only six divisions, and Kitchener's call for volunteers had not begun to bear fruit.

The Division was formed around cadres of officers and NCOs from the RN and RM, supported by a sprinkling of retired officers of high quality, mostly from the Brigade of Guards. A very large proportion of the Reservists were miners from the North of England, or from Scotland, and Northern Ireland, and this trend continued with every reinforcement of the Division throughout the war.

As the RND was not part of the War Office establishment, the Admiralty set up a Committee under Winston Churchill to administer it. Not surprisingly, therefore, the organisation and training did not proceed at what may be termed an ideal rate: there was not even a nominated Divisional Commander. At last common sense prevailed, and on 1 October 1914 it was decided that the Royal Marines should administer the Division.

Antwerp, October 1914

It was a surprise to most of these partly-trained men to be woken at 5.15am on 4 October to march to Dover. Some of the officers were feverish from a typhoid jab the previous day, and the men had only had their rifles for a week. The two naval brigades arrived in Dunkirk and unloaded all their kit. By 11.00pm they were in a train to Antwerp. It had been decided to try to delay the German advance on the Channel

Seapower Ashore

Eastbourne (Sussex) Division RNVR 'D' Company Howe Battalion, in the streets of Vieux Dieu, an eastern suburb of Antwerp, 6 October 1914. Note the old-style bandoliers and naval caps. The Royal Navy had copied the style of its greatcoats from the Russians in the war of 1854-6. An officer is peering at the camera, directly beneath the White ensign. (Imperial War Museum: Q14772)

ports by shoring up the Belgians in their fortress. The plan was for them to hold the line of the River Nethe around Antwerp while the French Army and the British 7th Division counter-attacked the German flank eventually to relieve them. The battalions had no cavalry, artillery, engineers, medical equipment or transport.

They detrained at Antwerp at 9.00am on 6 October, and marched through cheering crowds to the suburbs, where they spent a night, before being moved nearer the enemy to take over part of the line of trenches about 7 miles south-east of the city which joined the ring of forts to the east and south. Major General Paris, of the Royal Marine Artillery, had been appointed the Divisional Commander, and he was to prove extremely popular. The troops were in no great danger, even though there were under bombardment. It became apparent that there was no way of stopping the Germans, and, later that evening, the order came to withdraw. The RND began to march under fire to St Gilles-Waes station about 30 miles away to the West. After 13 hours on the road the exhausted battalions caught the train to Ostend, arriving in Dover on 11 October. At least, most of them did: three battalions of the 1st Brigade, totalling about 1500 men, had marched to internment by crossing the Dutch border to avoid capture, including the whole of the Brigade staff, and over 900 more had been compelled to surrender to the encircling Germans. Seven officers and 53 men had been killed and 3 officers and 135 men wounded. A heavy price to pay for a mission for which, with hindsight, the troops were dangerously inadequate in training and numbers. In retrospect, the RND got off lightly. There would be occasions in the future when it would not be so lucky.

A catastrophe had been narrowly averted, and on its return home, there developed a powerful lobby against the Division and its champion and creator, Churchill. He faced down his critics, and it was decided that the Division would remain in existence. Training recommenced, and recruiting began to replace those battalions lost at Antwerp. A depot for the new recruits was set up at Crystal Palace, and it was decided to concentrate the Brigade and Divisional training at the new Blandford Camp, on Salisbury Plain, early in 1915. The Division was allocated medical teams and engineers, but remained dispersed, pending the move to Blandford. After the RND's return from Antwerp, the Army either showed its impatience with this unprofessional outfit, or decided that the needs of the New Army divisions took priority, and removed the majority of the regular and ex-regular officers who had been with the RND from the start. This was a serious blow, but the outcome was that the RND was thrown largely on to its own resources to find its officers. Now, and subsequently throughout the war, they selected candidates solely on the grounds of merit. A great number of the most distinguished officers in the RND were promoted from the ranks. They were also fortunate at this time that, not only had there already joined many men of obvious officer-like qualities, but in the re-establishment of Hawke Battalion, a large number of the Public Schools' Battalion were included among the recruits.

Blandford Camp formed a dedicated base for the Division, unlike some other New Army formations, where recruits could be trained and the wounded recover before being returned to (usually) their old unit, where each element of the front-line battalions was represented in microcosm, and where a genuine *esprit de corps* and friendship between officers and men was engendered, which was to last through the War.

Gallipoli 1915

Before the Division could be fully concentrated at Blandford, it was on the move to Gallipoli, as part of the British attempt to seize the Dardanelles. Unfortunately, two days before the landings, Rupert Brooke died of septicaemia. He was buried by his friends, including Asquith and Freyberg, on Skyros Island.

It had been decided that the RND would not be part of the initial landings around the southern tip of the peninsula, but would be used to create a diversion to the north, near Bulair, to occupy Turkish reserves. General Paris sent 300 men from Hood and Howe battalions to act as beach parties for the landings further South. Already, Anson and the Plymouth RMs had been transferred to assist the 29th Division, who were tasked with landing on the southern beaches. On 24 April the RND transports set sail for Bulair where they arrived at daylight on the fateful 25th.

The demonstration originally proposed was that a platoon or more of the Hood Battalion would land during the night, light flares, and generally make a lot of noise. Freyberg, however, pointed out that this would be suicide, as the force had already been steaming up and down in full view of the shore, and a warm welcome would be guaranteed. He volunteered to swim ashore and light enough flares

Surgeon A H Crook outside a dugout, Antwerp, October 1914. (Imperial War Museum: Q14780)

to make the Turks believe that something was about to happen, and then return to the ships. He had to swim about two miles, and lit one lot of flares after stumbling about naked on the exposed shore in near-zero temperatures; avoiding the Turkish fire, and that of the British diversionary barrage, he swam another quarter of a mile to light the second set of flares, and with no ship in sight, working on a compass bearing only, began the long swim back, hoping to bump into a British boat. By some chance he was picked up after a further two hours in the water, nearly dead from cold. The ruse worked, and the Turks kept two of their four divisions in the north of the Peninsula. Freyberg was awarded the DSO for this heroic act.

When the landings took place in the south, the RND beach parties found themselves in the very thick of the action right from the start; at V beach, Sub-Lieutenant Tisdall, of Anson Battalion, won the VC for rescuing many men under heavy fire. The Plymouth Battalion of the Royal Marines was landed on Y beach, on the western shore of the peninsula, with an Army battalion, the 1st King's Own Scottish Borderers, and a company from the 2nd South Wales Borderers, as a flanking party. The force behaved with great gallantry, but with a little more dash at the beginning, when their landing had been virtually unopposed, they could possibly have unhinged the Turkish defence: having lost about one third of the force in repulsing several Turkish night attacks, the exhausted troops were withdrawn. A few days after the landings, the RND went ashore and took their place in the line.

For the next few weeks, the Allies tried to fight their way up the Peninsula from the south, and to break out from the Anzac landing, which had gained a foothold on the west coast. For all this period the RND, while heavily involved, was used by the C-in-C piecemeal by battalions and brigades attached to other formations, French, British and Australian. At least four major actions took place during May. Lance Corporal Parker of the Portsmouth Battalion of the Royal Marines won the VC, at Anzac, for extreme courage in assisting wounded and bringing up supplies, while serving as part of the four battalions of the RND sent to assist the Anzacs. In the middle of May the remnants of the Division (less Hawke, Benbow, and Collingwood Battalions, which were still on the high seas), were concentrated under General Paris on the Achi Baba Front, which now took on characteristics of trench warfare, soon to be equally familiar on the Western Front. The Division held the line on the left of the French, who were on the right of the line. Then came the 42nd Division and the remains of the 29th Division, on the left. During a series of night advances towards the end of May, the line was pushed forward nearly half a mile, so at least the rest areas were more safe from shellfire. At the end of May the three other Battalions joined the Division, which for the first time was now constituted in accordance with its establishment, with two naval brigades and one Royal Marine brigade. Nevertheless, because of losses, the Division was still weaker than on 25 April, when the land campaign began. Before the arrival of the three extra battalions, the Division was down to under 5000 men. The addition of these fresh, but inexperienced, troops bolstered the numbers them for the next major attack, the third battle of Krithia.

Officers of Hood Battalion at Blandford Camp, early 1915. Rupert Brooke is second from the left in the second row, Arthur Asquith is at the extreme left of the back row, and Bernard Freyberg is seated, third from the left. (Imperial War Museum: Q71074)

As before, this took the form of a straightforward trench-to-trench assault along the whole front. The basic problem was the same as earlier: any hold-up in any part of the attacking line opened the unit next in line to catastrophic enfilade fire from uncaptured Turkish positions. For the RND, this meant that they were utterly dependent on the success of the French on their right flank capturing the high ground of the Kereves Dere Ridge. The start of the attack was to be noon: the day was very hot, and the assault troops were obliged to wait for hours in stinking trenches beset by millions of flies and watching the maggots crawling over the bodies of the dead of earlier battles. The bombardment was described as 'desultory', and its lack of effect was discovered at 11.20am, when a feint attack was made along the line: immediately the parapet was swept by a hail of small-arms fire from unsuppressed Turkish positions. The bombardment resumed, and at 12.00pm Howe, Hood, and Anson Battalions advanced on the RND front into a hail of fire.

Sub-Lieutenant (later Commander) Hedderwick in a front-line trench, Gallipoli 29 May 1915. Hedderwick was Mentioned in Despatches for his service at Gallipoli: wounded on 4 June 1915, he rejoined the seagoing Royal Navy. (Imperial War Museum: Q61116)

With desperate losses, they reached and captured the Turkish front line. Only about 20 officers and 300 men had survived, and they were under severe fire. The reinforcing battalion, Collingwood, new in action and up to full strength, advanced across no man's land to support: they were cut down, mainly from fire from the uncaptured ridge on the right, which the French, despite gallant attempts, had not taken. After further actions in the second and third Turkish lines, it was obvious that the captured positions could not be held, and the troops withdrew. Five officers and 950 men, from 70 officers and 1900 men who started the attack, returned to their own front line. This had a knock-on effect for the unfortunate 42nd Division, exposing their right in turn. In view of these losses, General Paris disbanded the Collingwood and Benbow Battalions to make up the numbers in Hood, Howe, and Anson, and reduced the naval brigades to three Battalions each. The disbanded Battalions were never reconstituted.

So trench warfare resumed, until the next attack on 12 July, for which the RND was in reserve for the newly arrived 52nd Lowland Division. 'Support' in this case was a euphemism for following up a moderately successful and gallant attack to eliminate troublesome Turkish positions. Two battalions of the Division went into action, the Portsmouth Royal Marines and Nelson Battalion, and twelve officers were killed, and only one of Nelson's was unwounded.

At last, on 25 July the Division was relieved and sent back to rest. It now numbered 129 officers and 5038 men, about half strength. So ended the RND's first extended spell of action on the Peninsula: they took no part in the later struggles at Anzac and Suvla. This is hardly surprising: conditions were desperate and dysentery was rife. Much more influential on the future of the RND at this time, however, were two other decisions, one made by the Admiralty, and the other by the War Office: the first was an order for all stokers of the Fleet reserve to be recalled for duty with the Fleet; this affected only about 300 men, but had the effect of withdrawing the hard core of trained and disciplined men remaining from the earliest days of the Division. The second decision was the refusal of the War Office to provide reinforcements for the Division; the Army had always looked askance

'White House', a position at Gallipoli captured by the Hood Battalion on 6 May 1915. (Imperial War Museum: Q61127)

at the RND, and it was not surprising that they did not bend over backwards to get the Admiralty out of a hole. This meant that, for the rest of the campaign, the RND was fit only for garrison service. For a while it looked as though it was to be broken up. This impression was reinforced when the RND was reduced to two Brigades only, the 1st with Drake, Nelson, Hawke and Hood, and the 2nd Brigade composed of 1st and 2nd Royal Marines, Anson and Howe. Both Brigades served in the front line for the rest of the campaign, taking casualties from Turks and illness, and were among the last to be evacuated in January 1916. During the Dardanelles Expedition, of the 16,000 men who had passed through the Division, over 13,000 had become casualties, or sent to hospital because of illness. When they left, they had suffered 7198 killed and wounded, of whom 133 officers and 2358 ratings died.

The Western Front 1916-1918

The Division arrived at Mudros Harbour, Lemnos Island, in the Aegean, on 10 January 1916 with an uncertain future in prospect. There was continuing pressure from both the Army, and from some parts of the Navy, for the Division to be broken up. The reasons that this did not happen are not easy to divine, but it seems as though the performance of the Division at Gallipoli had been good enough to persuade the Army that there was merit in retaining the formation, perhaps in reduced numbers, and for its originally-designed functions. From the Navy point of view, the immediate pressure on manpower had receded, but the key to the Division's retention was the unflagging support of Winston Churchill, backed to a large degree by continuous lobbying by people of influence. Among sources were Violet Asquith, close friend and confidante of Churchill, and, of course, her brother, Arthur, about to be promoted Commander to take over 2nd Hood Battalion. Arthur kept up a personal correspondence with his father, the Prime Minister, and he and Violet had direct and indirect private access to him; Violet married Asquith's Private Secretary, Maurice Bonham Carter in November 1915. Both also had the ear of Hankey through the formidable Margot, wife of the PM.

Finally, it was decided to send the Division to France, and they arrived in the pleasant villages north-west of Arras in June, and began a major reorganisation: for the first time it was complemented with field artillery, trench mortar companies (heavy and medium), machine gun units, and allocated an ammunition column. On 19 June the Division received a number, and came under full control of the Army. It would henceforth be known as the 63rd (Royal Naval Division). Its composition was now in three brigades, the 188th, with two marine and two naval battalions; the 189th, all naval personnel, and the 190th, a new addition of soldiers, with the 1st Honorable Artillery Company, 4th Bedfords, 7th Royal Fusiliers, and 10th Royal

Dublin Fusiliers. General Paris remained in command. In the rear areas, and the trenches between Vimy and Lens, the Divion trained for the inevitable time when they would be required for the Somme campaign.

In early October the RND arrived in the Fifth Army area in the line from Serre almost as far as Beaumont Hamel, where, despite terrible losses, no gains had been made in the first attack on 1 July. By October 1916, Haig had decided that no further progress could be made in the Southern sector of the Somme until the salient remaining around Beaumont Hamel, St Pierre Divion and Serre had been reduced. He was keen for one further major success to strengthen his hand at the forthcoming Chantilly conference, at which the war plans for 1917 would be agreed with the French.

On 14 October, General Paris was severely wounded by a shell, and was replaced by a 'real' Army General, Cameron Shute, recently promoted after having commanded a brigade at Guillemont, an earlier Somme battle. Shute was a difficult man: he could not come to terms with the RND's different ways, and resolved to shake them up, and in so doing alienated them. He even tried to get them to shave off their beards! On 7 November Shute wrote a scathing memorandum about his new command to Corps Headquarters including such comments as 'There are no smart Battalions, no real sailors among them, receiving nearly double Army pay, standard of physique and training below that of the Army';[3] while admitting there was 'no crime' he commented that discipline was 'lamentable'. Naval titles were 'ridiculous', and he opined that 'The Division can never come up to Army standards unless Army officers are drafted in'.[4] He finished with the comment that the Division was not in a satisfactory state, and that all RN and RM personnel should be transferred to the Army. It is interesting that, after so damning an assessment of its competence, Shute issued final orders for the Division to attack a hitherto impregnable enemy position, manned by enemy divisions assessed as 'good' and 'excellent, only three days later. As if this were not enough, the weather was appalling, raining and icy; the trenches were inadequate, with almost no dug outs, and deep in freezing mud. In addition, all three brigades were either in the line, or engaged in exhausting working parties during the run-up to the battle.

The basic plan for the attack depended on that great discovery of the Somme, the creeping barrage, which when followed by determined infantry, gave a good chance of success of breaking into static enemy trench systems. Holding on in the face of the inevitable German counterattacks was a different matter. It was to be a major effort involving five divisions from Serre to St Pierre; all RND Brigades would be involved, the two naval/RM Brigades in line on a front of about 1200 yards, with the soldiers of the 190th supporting them. The Division's final objective was the far side of the village of Beaucourt, over a mile away. By the 13 November, the RND Battalions were down to about 500 men each as a result of casualties and sickness. Nevertheless, there were some positive aspects: the Germans did not expect an attack on what they believed to be an impregnable position, there was a huge amount of artillery support, and a great deal of thought had gone into the planning and briefing, so that everyone knew what had to be done. To improve the chance of surprise, the artillery carried out a heavy bombardment of the German lines just before dawn every morning for several days before the attack.

There was not enough room in the front line for all the attacking troops, so, the night before the attack, many of them lay out in no man's land for up to 12 hours in the freezing cold with no protection from the elements or German fire. Mercifully, the enemy did not get wind of anything untoward, and the casualties among the assault troops were only due to the occasional chance shell. As dawn approached a heavy mist began to develop, and at 5.45am the intense barrage opened, as it had for several previous days, and the troops stood up and walked into the gloom, as close to the creeping barrage as they dared. On the right there was good progress and Hood, led by Freyberg, was in the German third line in a few minutes.

On the left and in the centre, the attack was held up mainly by a large strongpoint which had not only survived the bombardment, but continued to fire even through the creeping barrage, and it took a long time, and cost many lives, before the RMs and Howe managed to get into the German third line. Unaware of the hold up Freyberg led his Hoods and some Drakes (about 450 in all) on to the next objective which they took on schedule by 6.25am, capturing well over 400 prisoners, more than Freyberg's effective strength. The rest of the story of the battle is of Freyberg pressing on his front, capturing all his objectives with relative ease, while the rest of the Divisions slogged up the centre and left. Only the next morning, when a tank managed to approach to within point-blank range of the strongpoint did the garrison of over 400 surrender. Freyberg meanwhile dug in and awaited the order to go forward to capture Beaucourt, the final objective, which was stormed by 8.30am on the 14th. Throughout the rest of that day, they were subjected to heavy shelling, while on the left, the loss of the redoubt enabled the rest of the German positions to be taken. By early morning on 15th, the Division was relieved. There were 3000 casualties in the two naval brigades alone, and over 800 in the army brigade. In the month of November, total casualties in the Division were 100 officers and 1600 men killed, and 160 officers and 2400 men wounded. During this battle, known as the Battle of the Ancre, the RND alone took 1600 prisoners. Haig's hope had been to take Beaumont Hamel and 3000 prisoners. Instead, he got 6300 prisoners and three fortified villages, Beaumont, St Pierre, and Beaucourt. The other Divisions in the attack also did very well, particularly the Highlanders of the 51st, who took Beaumont Hamel. Freyberg, four times wounded, received the VC for what General de Lisle, himself a VC, called 'probably the most distinguished personal act of the War'.

The factors which led to success here included German complacency of the strengths of their positions, the achievement of tactical surprise, crucially, the amount, and accuracy, of the artillery support and the heavy mist, which prevented the German artillery from receiving any SOS messages, and, in conjunction with the fact that the Ancre by now was a flooded morass, increasing the range at which the German machine guns on the slopes east of the river had to fire, resulted in fewer casualties than might have been expected from there. Improved British tactics in following close to the barrage, ensuring dug outs cleared, carrying plenty of Lewis guns, etc, played an important part but most importantly, the calibre of battalion and company leadership, not just by Freyberg, and the determination and esprit of the troops was key to their success.

They arrived back in billets much depleted in numbers, but wiser, and confident that they had 'shown Shute what they were made of'. Ludendorff described the defeat as 'a particularly heavy blow, for we considered such an event no longer possible, particularly in sectors where our troops still had good positions'.[5]

Despite the excellent performance of the Division in this action, Shute was moved to write again to II Corps on 1 December that, 'the gallantry of the RND on the Ancre only emphasises the need to reorganise'.[6] On 21 December, the new Corps Commander, Jacob, endorsed Shute's proposals to Gough, saying 'I do not wish to recommend any modification in proposals made. The proposals made by the GOC 63rd Division should be carried out without delay'.[7] Shute's proposals were then forwarded to the Admiralty and the War Office, which resulted in a meeting in a Committee Room of the House of Commons between their representatives in early February 1917, at which the Admiralty defended the retention of the Division, and criticised Shute for his handling of it. The hand of Churchill and the Asquiths can be detected in this. The outcome was that it was Shute who went, and the RND which remained. Shute was relieved by Lawrie on 19 February. Lawrie proved to be a popular choice and commanded the Division with high distinction until nearly the end of the War. Shute went on to command a Corps in 1918.

While these machinations were in progress, Shute was busy filling RND Battalion commander's jobs with Army officers, and trying to find volunteers to transfer to the real Army. All this stopped in January, when it is recorded that 'The zeal of the reformers suddenly abated',[8] and the Division began to revert to its previous ways. Shute had been told to relax a little. Reinforced by new drafts, they again took the line in the middle of January, virtually in the same places they had captured in November. As we all know, the winter of 1916/17 was one of the very coldest on record, and the ground had been frozen continuously since mid-December. In these conditions it was decided to renew the attacks on the enemy at the earliest opportunity, and Hood and Hawke were given the job of undertaking what was planned as a surprise trench raid to capture the German positions, 'River' and 'Puisieux' trenches, on the slopes north of Grandcourt. The latter trench was only 300 yards away, while 'River' trench was a further 100 yards; the attack was scheduled to start at 11.00pm on 3 February and last for 8 minutes. It was completely successful: despite resolute enemy defence once more from unidentified dug-outs and strong points the Brigade took all its objectives. However, the 8 minute battle lasted in fact over 50 hours, and involved all four Battalions. Casualties totalled over 650.

The other two Brigades of the Division pressed on and found the village of Grandcourt abandoned, the first signs of the retreat to the Hindenburg line. The Division carried out one more attack, on 17 February, in support of a push on Miraumont. The RND's part in this operation is described as 'brilliantly successful'[9] but still the Royal Marines suffered heavy casualties. After this, the RND was rested.

After another period of recovery and reinforcement, the Division moved up to Arras, and took over the line in front of Gavrelle, a small heavily fortified village on the Arras-Douai road, on 14 April. Today Gavrelle is not a very inspiring place: a new main road, built as a by-pass, allows thundering juggernauts to be heard day and night, and some of the reconstructions after the war were not undertaken as sympathetically as in certain other towns. But it was much worse in 1917, occupying a gentle rise in the ground on whose crest stood the famous windmill, and overlooking the British lines across a flat plain which stretches west for over two miles. As before, the omens were not good: some of the attacking troops had been in the line for eight days in foul weather, and had had insufficient sleep and much digging for the two nights immediately prior to the attack, with little food and water, and under constant shelling. The objectives were demanding: to capture the village as a part of a more general attack and press on to a line 300 to 600 yards the other side, setting up a defensive flank to the north. At least a large amount of artillery was available: five heavy artillery groups in addition to the Division's own artillery. The 189th Brigade would be on the right, and the soldiers of the 190th on the left.

Observing that the wire was not properly cut, Commander Sterndale Bennett, of Drake Battalion, and the youngest battalion commander on the western front, reported the fact to Brigade HQ and ended with the bland enquiry 'Is the attack cancelled?'.[10] The question was assumed by Brigade HQ not to require an answer. Nevertheless Bennett readjusted his attack plan at the eleventh hour, to attack on a narrower frontage, protecting his flank with a Stokes mortar barrage. By means of these tactics, and by following an effective creeping barrage, the first objectives were taken in ten minutes. Only on the extreme left was the advance held up by the wire and flanking fire. After 10 minutes, Asquith, who had relieved Freyberg in command of Hood Battalion decided not to wait any longer and led his Battalion forward, arriving in the second German line about the same time as the first wave attackers. This was almost urban fighting, with buildings falling around the troops, and close-quarters sniping and machine gunning, all of which made it very difficult to reorganise the men for the next push. Somehow Bennett and Asquith did so and pressed on into the village, sending back hundreds of prisoners. By now the RND troops were out of range of their own field artillery and were under fire from the Windmill on the left. The position was precarious, so Asquith carried out a reconnaissance of the enemy trenches along the front and decided that there was no way through; returning to his own positions, he walked up the main road to the Mayor's house, entered it and found the garrison of ten men asleep, and took them all prisoner. It is an interesting comment on the psyche of soldiers in action that they can sleep within 200 yards of a major fight, if they think they are not in danger. The term reconnaissance gives little idea of the scale of Asquith's achievement: it meant walking in broad daylight along the whole of the battalion front, under constant sniper and shell fire, making notes, and getting close enough to enemy positions to estimate their numbers. Asquith's companion on this reconnaissance was killed next to him by a sniper. Lewis guns were installed here which gave the troops much better covering fire. Even so, the situation was precarious, and had the Germans attacked from the Windmill, the would probably have overrun the British positions.

A defensive flank was set up to try to hold the positions gained: by now it was mid-morning and the enemy began a series of determined counterattacks with first-class troops, including the elite 2nd Guards Reserve Division, which lasted throughout the day, all of which were repulsed with very heavy casualties in scenes reminiscent of the first day of the Somme, with the Germans on the receiving end this time. The occupying troops were also under continuous bombardment, and so when the order came for a further advance the commanders on the spot decided to ignore it. The night was relatively quiet, but the following morning saw the Germans again massing to retake the village. At about 3.00pm, after a prolonged and heavy bombardment, they advanced, and were once more repulsed with severe losses. So ended a battle in which the RND had taken nearly all of their objectives: enemy losses had been high, but the cost to the Naval Division was over 2000.

The RND had not yet finished with Gavrelle, however: as a part of a more general attack on 28 April, both left and right of the town, it was decided that there would be a push north-east, with the specific aim of capturing the Windmill position which dominates the area. The 188th and the 190th Brigades did the job, in co-operation with the 2nd Division. With tremendous gallantry, the Windmill was carried by the 2nd Marines, who continued to hold it despite ferocious counterattacks, and severe casualties. Anson, pressing forward on their right were quickly cut off and had to fight their way back to their own lines, which they did, driving back over 250 German prisoners in the process. Further to the left the attack failed because of enemy wire, a strong point on the railway, and determined counter attacks. Before dawn on the next day further efforts were made by a composite battalion of the 10th Dublins and the 4th Bedfords. One more section of trench was gained, but at severe cost. Particularly notable during this phase was the outstanding courage of Second Lieutenant Pollard of the HAC who won the VC for repelling a massed German attack with only four other men. He had previously won the DCM and the MC. Second Lieutenant Haine of the same battalion also received the VC for outstanding gallantry in leading a successful bombing (hand grenade) attack which resulted in

The Royal Naval Division: 1914-19

The only photograph of Asquith in the trenches at Gallipoli. (Asquith Papers)

the capture of previously impregnable enemy trenches. That night, the Division was relieved. The Marines' casualties in this action were over 1100.

Throughout the period from 15 to 29 April, the Division was almost continuously in action, and suffered over 3800 casualties, of whom 40 officers and over 1000 men were killed. After resting, the RND returned to garrison the line at Gavrelle. The time between Gavrelle and Passchendaele was spent reorganising, followed by continual spells in the front line in the Gavrelle area: the HAC left to join the Guards Division, and the Dublin Fusiliers had been removed to reinforce the 16th (Irish) Division. These two battalions were eventually relieved by the Artists Rifles and the 1/4th King's Shropshire Light Infantry, respectively. The chance was taken to give some leave; some of the old salts of the Division had had none since mobilisation.

Meanwhile, the battles around Ypres had reached a crucial point, and it was decided that the final push to take the village of Passchendaele would be undertaken by the Canadian Corps. To support them on the left, XVIII Corps were to push up through the marshy ground, now a morass of mud and shell holes. The RND arrived towards the end of October and took over from the 9th Division. They moved up into the line for the attack scheduled for 26 October. Their sector ran from Wallenmolen Cemetery, now non-existent, to a destroyed stream called the Lekkerbotterbeek. Jerrold, the RND historian, wrote that the 'Division was never confronted with a task which, on the lines laid down for them, was more impossible of fulfilment'.[11] In this relatively low-lying area the conditions were appalling. There were few trenches, the front line positions of both sides consisting of isolated posts in a sea of mud. Those of the Germans, however, were based on heavily-fortified farms and pill-boxes. Speed of progress during an attack was a matter of pot luck on the condition of the terrain, which meant that following any sort of creeping barrage was almost impossible. In addition, the very nature of the ground reduced the effectiveness of the artillery. The 188th Brigade would make the first assault. Its objectives were all the German posts on the west side of the flooded Paddebeek stream, about 500 yards away. Once these were taken, the enemy posts across the stream would be attacked. At midnight immediately prior to the attack it started raining again, and the thoroughly soaked troops went forward at 5.45am, on a frontage of over 1500 yards, with the Ansons on the right, and the 1st RMs on the left. By 7.20am, some gains had been made, the RMs taking Banff House (a concrete-reinforced farmhouse) but other positions were retaken by enemy counterattack. Asquith was watching the attack as the CO of Hood, the support Battalion, and after the second wave of the 2nd RMs and Howe seemed to have got bogged down, he undertook a reconnaissance, accompanied by one other officer and one man, the purpose of which was to confirm which posts were held by our troops and which were not. As a result isolated garrisons were relieved, contact established with the Canadians on the right, and the artillery was able to defend those positions in British hands while bombarding those still occupied by the Germans. Asquith made one more reconnaissance that day, to confirm that a position previously held near Varlet Farm was not in enemy hands, and to lead up a relieving party for the seven men, all that remained of the attackers who had stormed the place in the first minutes of the action. The gains had been minute for the cost, and even these would not have been held without the information generated by the reconnaissance.

Despite the failure of the 26th, another attempt was made by the 190th Brigade at dawn on the 30th, with very few gains, and severe losses, despite the gallantry of the attacking troops, of whom the 1/4th Shropshires were fighting their first action. Over 30 officers and nearly 1000 men had been killed and more than 80 officers and 2000 men wounded. Still, the pressure had to be kept up, for without success on the left, the Canadians would not be able to push on to Passchendaele, so the 189th Brigade went into the line. The operations of the next four days and nights achieved practically all the originally intended objectives at very little cost.

To discover the reason for the change in fortunes it is necessary to look at the tactical changes made after the first costly attacks: these came about mainly as a result of a report by Asquith, after his experiences of the 26th. His report concluded that attacking at dawn behind a creeping barrage in the swampy conditions could not succeed: the isolated enemy posts were able to support each other and call down artillery when needed. Asquith realised that, in the unique circumstances of this particular battlefield, success would only be achieved by the application of highly-mobile parties, using surprise, attacking German positions individually at night. This required two other vital ingredients, high-calibre leadership and prior reconnaissance. XVIII Corps approved the experiment. One by one the enemy strongpoints were picked off by small parties at night after expert and lengthy prior reconnaissance. In these conditions, the relatively dispersed enemy posts had difficulty communicating with each other, and the element of mutual support was lost. By these methods, isolated concrete fortresses, largely impervious to shellfire, which had previously been able to mow down whole battalions with little loss to themselves, had become death-traps for their garrisons. Previously, almost all the other major, formal, attacks during Third Ypres came at dawn and involved a creeping barrage. Operations finally ceased when the Canadians captured Passchendaele.

Meanwhile the Battle of Cambrai began: after stunning British gains, the Germans counterattacked and recaptured much of the territory they had lost. The salient around Flesquieres was still in British hands, jutting into the Hindenburg Line along an improvised position on Welsh Ridge, and it was here that the RND took over the line in the middle of December. On the 30th, the Germans made a surprise attack, dressing the leading waves in white to provide camouflage in the snow, and made serious lodgements in the line. In the major counterattack which was required to retake the key parts of the line, Commander Buckle, on Anson Battalion, won his first DSO. The cost was a further 63 officers and 1355 men killed, wounded and missing. Estimates of the German attacking strength vary, but probably amounted to fifteen battalions and some storm troops. German casualties were 'very heavy',[12] according the official history.

After their efforts, the RND was allocated a smaller sector for defence, and the 190th Brigade, which had suffered badly in the action at Welsh Ridge, was withdrawn. During this period of rest, four more officers were killed, including a Battalion Commander. At the end of January, the requirement for reinforcements was reduced by the controversial decision to form Infantry Brigades in the British Army from three battalions, rather than four, as previously. Howe and Nelson were disbanded, and their sailors absorbed in the other Naval RNVR Battalions, and the 1/4th King's Shropshire Light Infantry were transferred to the 19th Division.

By the middle of February, the Division, back up to its new strength, found itself again in the Flesquieres salient in V Corps, adjacent to the left hand Corps of Gough's Fifth Army. In early

March the enemy started bombardments in preparation for his major offensive on the 21st. The salient was drenched with nearly a quarter of a million mostly yellow cross (mustard) gas shells from the 12th to the 21st, causing 2000 casualties in the RND: Hawke and Drake lost between 400 and 600 men each.

The happenings of the next few dreadful days are sometimes sketchy, particularly for those Divisions which were virtually destroyed in the onslaught. The records of the RND, by good luck, good leadership, and the dogged resistance of the troops, are reasonably coherent. After a hurricane bombardment on top of the preparatory shelling of the previous fortnight, the Germans attacked in enormous strength through a heavy mist. By the end of the day, V Corps had suffered some loss on its front, and the RND, less seriously attacked than some, was planning a counterattack. However, the situation on the flanks was precarious where the adjoining Corps had been driven back, and the Division was forced to retreat in steps, first west through Bertincourt and Ytres, then to the Metz lines on the 23rd, then north through the old Somme battlefields when touch was lost with the left of the Fifth Army. At every stage from day one, the RND made a determined stand, and their artillery and machine guns made the Germans pay a high price for their advance. Until the 26 April, they bore the brunt of the attacks in this area with the 2nd Division to their north, eventually supported by the Reserve Unit, the 17th Division; from an early stage on the 23rd, the division on the right was separated, leaving a largely open southern flank. On the 26th, the RND came to a final halt in the old front line before Hamel in virtually the same positions they had occupied in July 1916, and went into reserve to counter an expected German thrust from Albert.

In a further series of defensive actions and counterattacks, some ground was given by the BEF, but the impetus of the Germans was now much less: their successes were fewer and their casualties greater. Static trench warfare returned to this part of the Somme by the time the RND handed over its part of the line on the Mesnil Ridge, and returned to civilisation after about 24 days of continuous action.

The cost had been high: between the preliminary bombardment and 27 March, the Division lost over 6000 men, including four

Battalion commanders killed, who between them had won one VC, three DSOs, and an MC: while small reinforcements reached them after the 27th, during the retreat most Battalions were in action with only about 250 men, including those drafted from transport and headquarters duties, and those 'invited' to serve from other broken units. A great deal of the credit for the Division's fine performance during the retreat was due to the leadership at all levels: the Divisional Commander had largely to operate without Corps orders, and a huge responsibility fell on the shoulders of the Brigade and Battalion Commander, whose initiative saved the situation on many occasions when communications with superiors were lost. But, as always, it came down to the determination and courage of the man with the rifle, and here, those many units which retained cohesion, and because of their *esprit*, refused to panic, fighting all the way, saved the British Army, and the RND was one of the chief among them.

By the end of April, losses had been replaced, and the RND was back to full strength in time for the final effort. They returned to the trenches around Hamel and Aveluy Wood on the Somme on 8 May. Until 4 June, the Division was involved in the old style of trench warfare for the last time: suffering strong German raids, and giving as good as they got with their own, on one occasion in brigade strength; this last raid on 24 May cost another 18 officers and 210 men. The heavy losses over a long period resulted in the amalgamation of the two RM Battalions, and the introduction of the 2nd Royal Irish Rifles to make up the 188th Brigade. Spells in the line, raiding and generally making life uncomfortable for the Germans, and training around Toutencourt filled the time until August. The RND did not fit in with the concept of 'live and let live' in the trenches: there were continual raids both to and from their lines when they were at the front.

By the middle of August, the Germans had had their 'Black Day' east of Amiens, and the RND was moved to take its part in the final offensive, arriving at Souastre on 19 August, now as part of IV Corps of the Third Army, after night marches. Their objective, starting at 4.55am on 21 August, part of the Battle of Albert – an excellent example of how infantry tactics had changed – was to follow the attack of the 37th Division, and, together with the 5th and 3rd Divisions, pass through and take the final objective, across the Achiet-Arras Railway. Despite much gallantry, the railway itself was not quite carried before the RND was relieved for a short rest. The new tactics involved attack followed by short periods of rest, before going back into the line again. Following these principles, after having advanced over two miles, and beaten off three determined enemy counterattacks, the RND was relieved during the night of the 22/23 August, and while they were resting, the advance was continued by others. Enemy resistance was still expert and energetic. By the time it was the RND's turn again on the 25th, the front line had moved east to the line between Loupart Wood and the Albert-Bapaume Road. The objectives were the villages of Ligny-Thilloy, Thilloy, and Le Barque. With the New Zealanders on their flank, the Division went forward with five Battalions: despite penetrating the villages, only Le Barque was taken. The total ground gained had been over three thousand yards. The next two days showed no further appreciable gains, and on the 28th the RND was relieved. For his conspicuous bravery, courageous leadership, and devotion to duty these battles, Commander Beak, of Drake Battalion, received the Victoria Cross. Thirty-seven German officers and nearly 1100 other ranks were captured. Casualties in August had been severe: 27 officers and 358 men killed, 88 officers and 2356 men wounded, and 9 officers and 486 men missing.

On being relieved the Naval Division was transferred on 30 August to Fergusson's XVII Corps to take part in the first of the battles for the Hindenburg Line, known as the Battle of Bapaume, which had opened on the 26th. From their start lines about three miles west of Hendecourt, the 188th Brigade was to pass through the right of the Canadians, cutting the Queant-Cambrai Railway. Queant was notorious as the southern end of the feared Drocourt-Queant switch line, which formed part of the Hindenburg defences. If this succeeded, reinforced by the 189th Brigade, the attack was to be carried through to the village of Inchy, this side of the Canal Du Nord. These were strenuous objectives, the distance to be advanced being over 10 miles! Starting at 7.45am on 2 September, with the Canadians on their left, the RND moved quickly forward under superb leadership by Commanders Buckle and Beak: on his own initiative, Beak led his Battalion across the railway and cut the Pronville-Inchy Road, barring the escape route for the Germans to the west. Chief Petty Officer Prowse, of his Battalion, won the VC for the most conspicuous bravery and devotion to duty. He already had a DCM. Meanwhile to the north, the 189th Brigade moved up to be prepared to attack the town of Inchy and attempt to cross the Canal Du Nord the following morning. On the 3rd, they took the Hindenburg support line fortifications and Inchy, joining up with Drake Battalion which by now on the outskirts of Moeuvres, and tried to storm the dried-out canal, but the position was too strong, and by the evening of the 4th, the Division had dug in just to the west of it, repelling strong German counterattacks.

Here the line was stabilised while other major battles to break the Hindenburg line further to the south took place. On the night of the 7/8 September, the Division was rested, and the advance on its front halted to allow the flanks to catch up. Commander Buckle's magnificent leadership led to the award of his second bar to his DSO, an average of about one per battle. Losses this time were under a thousand, due to the Corps policy of not pressing attacks when German resistance hardened, and also because, by now, the enemy performance had begun to decline.

On 26 September the RND returned to the positions around Mouevres to complete their unfinished business: this time the plan was to cross the canal, take the high ground the other side, then turn south and roll up the Hindenburg support line that ran parallel to it, before pressing on to the slopes above the Graincourt-Anneux line. The Canadians would again be on the left, attacking Bourlon.

At 5.05am on the 27th, the soldiers of the 190th Brigade crossed the canal and began to fight their way down the support line. Resistance was still strong, and the 52nd Division on the their flank was held up. Steadily, however, the Hindenburg support line was taken. Meanwhile, the sailors and marines of the other two battalions stormed Anneux and Graincourt, and consolidated. At dawn on the

28th, the 57th Division came through and secured the final objectives. It was decided to press on without delay. Hood Battalion would have to clear La Folie Wood, where significant German units still held out, while Drake would force the river. By 1 October, using battalions in sequence, the Division crossed the river, and had arrived in the very outskirts of Cambrai. In the four days of the engagements, the Division had advanced over seven miles, taking four prepared positions defended by dogged infantry: they had captured 63 officers, over 2100 men, 51 guns, 90 trench mortars and 400 machine guns; their losses were 21 officers killed and 83 wounded, and 400 men killed and 2000 wounded.

The Division was about to entrain for leave behind the lines, and the GOC was already on his way to England when General Fergusson decided to use it for one more push, to capture Niergnies, the key to Cambrai. The RND was promised leave on the day the town was taken. The start line ran from north east of Rumilly, and the naval brigades were given this critical task. Assisted by the artillery of other divisions, plus eight tanks, they went forward at 4.30am on 8 October, quickly taking the first objectives. However, at 9.30am the Germans counterattacked, supported by seven captured British tanks. The attack was defeated by Hood and Anson Battalions, whose commanding officers Pollock, and the inevitable Buckle, personally destroyed two tanks with captured German weapons. By 10.00am, the village was in RND hands: after beating off many counterattacks they were relieved in the line well to the east of Niergnies by the 2nd Division. As usual, Commander Buckle won a DSO, his fourth, and Pollock, recovered from his gassing at Flesquieres in April to take command of Hood, gained his second. They had lost 12 officers and 60 men, with a further 27 officers and 513 men wounded, but had captured a vital enemy position, taking 34 officers and 1155 men prisoner, and capturing 81 machine guns and 9 field guns. The way was now open to Cambrai which fell on 10 October.

So ends the major battle history of the Royal Naval Division; they retired to rest near St Pol. Never had they been so far from the front line since they were in France. On 6 November, they again took their place in the line as part of XXII Corps, west of the Bois d'Audregnies: while casualties were still incurred from sporadic incidents and chance shells, this was a pursuit rather than a battle. On the 8th, the Division liberated Witheries and Blaugies, on the 9th Quevy le Petit, Malplaquet (where Malborough had won a famous victory), and Harmignies, Villers St Ghislain and St Symphonien by the 10th. Here they temporarily halted on the Mons-Givry Road. Givry fell by 10.45am on the 11th. A quarter of an hour later, hostilities ceased, with the 188th and 189th Brigades alongside each other in the front line as so often in the past. Later that day, in the leading units of XXII Corps, the Division entered Mons, the nearest units of the BEF to the soil of Germany, where the British Army had begun its struggle four and a quarters years previously.

In many ways the experience of the RND was sadly not unique: 'Stormer' Divisions suffered very badly. The RND had 582 officers and 10,215 other ranks killed, and 1483 officers and 24,612 men wounded or captured, a total of just under 47,000 in all, not as great as some, but larger than most. Over 40 per cent of Royal Navy casualties in the Great War were suffered by the RND. More were killed and wounded in action in the Division on land than in the RN at sea. In April 1919, its eventful life came to a permanent end when the Division was disbanded.

On 25 April 1925, the tenth anniversary of the Gallipoli landings, Winston Churchill spoke at the unveiling in Horse Guards Parade of a magnificent memorial fountain designed by Lutyens, dedicated to the Division, and bearing the words of Rupert Brooke. During the Second World War, the Memorial was dismantled and stored to make way for the bunkers which were then being built: it now stands in the Royal Naval College Greenwich, where it was rededicated in 1951 in the presence of Lieutenant General Freyberg and Major General Beak. Arthur Asquith was not there: he died of Hodgkin's disease in August 1939. In his address in 1925, Churchill ended by saying, 'And this fountain to the memory of the Royal Naval Division will give forth not only the waters of honour, but the waters of healing and the waters of hope'.[13]

The Royal Naval Division Memorial, designed by Lutyens, at the Royal Naval College, Greenwich. (National Maritime Museum, London)

Select Bibliography

Unpublished Sources

The Private Papers of Brigadier General A M Asquith DSO, and Mrs Elizabeth Asquith. The Private Papers of Lady Asquith of Yambury, formerly Violet Bonham Carter.

Public Record Office: WO 95/3112, 95/3114, 95/3115, 95/3117, 95/3119
ADM 137/3064, 137/3088A
Imperial War Museum: Macmillan Papers, Archibald Paris Papers
Liddle Collection at Leeds University: Bentham Papers
The Private Papers of Bernard Freyberg

Published Sources
Cynthia Asquith, *Haply I May Remember* (James Barrie 1950)
---------, *Diaries of Lady Cynthia Asquith* (London 1968)
Violet Asquith, *Churchill as I Knew Him* (London 1965)
Glen Balfour-Paul, *The End of Empire in the Middle East* (Cambridge 1991)
Mark Bonham Carter and Mark Pottle (eds), *Lantern Slides, The Diaries and Letters of Violet Bonham Carter 1904-1914* (London 1996)
_____, *Champion Redoutable, The Diaries and Letters of Violet Bonham Carter 1915-1945* (London 1998)
Michael and Eleanor Brock (eds), *Asquith's Letters to Venetia Stanley* (Oxford 1985)
G Cornwallis-West, *Edwardian Hey-Days* (London 1930)
Anthony Farrar-Hockley, *Goughie* (London 1975)
Rev H C Foster, *At Antwerp and the Dardanelles* (London 1918)
Paul Freyberg, *Bernard Freyberg VC – Soldier of Two Nations* (London 1991)
Stair Gillon, *The Story of the 29th Division* (Nelson 1925)
Christopher Hassall, *Edward Marsh, A Biography* (London 1959)
A P Herbert, *A.P.H. – His Life and Times* (London 1970)
Roy Jenkins, *Asquith* (London 1988)
Douglas Jerrold, *The Royal Naval Division* (London 1923)
---------, *The Hawke Battalion, Some Personal Records of Four Years* (London 1925)
---------, *Georgian Adventure* (London 1937)
John Jolliffe, Raymond *Asquith Life and Letters* (London 1980)
Ronald Knox, *Patrick Shaw Stewart* (London 1920)
Angela Lambert, *The Unquiet Souls* (London 1984)
Lt-Col A B Lloyd-Baker, *A Gloucestershire Diarist* (Thornhill Press 1993)

Lyn Macdonald, *1914* (London 1987)

Jeanne Mackenzie, *The Children of the Souls* (London 1986)

Thomas Macmillan and James W Fry, *The Complete History of the Royal Naval Division* (Alnwick 1919)

Edward Marsh, *A Number of People* (London 1939)

Joseph Murray, *Gallipoli As I Saw It* (London 1965)

---------, *Call to Arms: From Gallipoli to the Western Front* (London 1980)

Jonathan Nicholls, *Cheerful Sacrifice, The Battle of Arras* (London 1990)

Christopher Page, *Command in the Royal Naval Division* (Staplehurst 1999)

Stephen Roskill, *Hankey: Man of Secrets* (London 1970)

Leonard Sellers, *Hood Battalion* (London 1992)

---------, *For God's Sake, Shoot Straight* (London 1995)

J A Spender and Cyril Asquith, *The Life of Herbert Henry Asquith, Lord Oxford and Asquith*, 2 vols (London 1932)

Nigel Steel and Peter Hart, *Defeat at Gallipoli* (Macmillan 1994)

Notes

1. The original battalions were: Hood, Hawke, Howe, Anson, Collingwood, Benbow, Drake and Nelson. The other battalions were initially made up from the Royal Marine Light Infantry. Later in the war, Army battalions served in the Division.
2. Douglas Jerrold, *The Royal Naval Division* (London 1923), pxiii. The Introduction was written by Churchill.
3. Report by GOC 63rd (Royal Naval) Division to GOC V Corps, dated 7 November 1916, PRO WO 95/3117.
4. Ibid.
5. Quoted in the *Official History: Military Operations in France and Belgium 1916, Vol II* (HMSO 1938), p527.
6. Report by GOC 63rd (Royal Naval) Division to GOC II Corps, dated 1 December 1916, PRO WO 95/3117.
7. Report by GOC II to GOC Fifth Army, dated 21 February 1917, PRO WO 95/3117.
8. Jerrold, *Royal Naval Division*, p209.
9. Ibid, p219.
10. Ibid, p230.
11. Ibid, p250.
12. *Official History: Military Operations in France and Belgium 1917*. The Battle of Cambrai (HMSO 1948), p277.
13. From an address given by Winston Churchill at the dedication of the Royal Naval Division Memorial on Horseguards, 25 April 1925.

CHAPTER 11

An Unlikely Encounter: Norway 1940

by Peter Hore

Perhaps one of the last occasions upon which a naval brigade of bluejackets and marines was called away was during the campaign in Norway between April and June 1940.[1] This campaign featured the classic elements of a struggle for sea control and of force projection, and many age-old lessons were bitterly relearned.

The winter of 1939-40 had been unusually cold and in the frozen Baltic the export of iron ore from Sweden was severely delayed, thus threatening the German war effort. While the Germans used the alternative route via Narvik in North Norway and along the Inner Leads, which was almost entirely in Norwegian territorial waters, Winston Churchill, then First Lord of the Admiralty, restlessly sought some opportunity for the Royal Navy to take the offensive – just as he had done in the First World War. Churchill's first idea was Operation 'Catherine', a plan for the British navy to outflank the Germans by entering the Baltic, a plan reminiscent of Admiral Fisher's when Churchill had been at the Admiralty in the First World War.[2] Later, when Russia had invaded Finland, 'Plan R4' called for a British and French army of nearly 100,000 men to land at Narvik and to pass along the railway (there was no road), through northern Sweden and so to help the Finns. However, the Scandinavians were unwilling to do anything which might have provoked the Germans. Captain Philip Vian's capture in February in HMS *Cossack* of the German oiler and prison-ship *Altmark* in Norwegian waters, spoke volumes of the attitude on all sides towards neutrality.[3] Only on 12 March, when the Finns capitulated, were the plans for 'R4' cancelled.

Meanwhile, the Admiralty was preparing plans to mine the Inner Leads and to force the iron ore carriers out into the open sea where they could be stopped. A strong German reaction was expected, and the British prepared to make pre-emptive landings at Stavanger, Bergen, Trondheim and Narvik, and assumed that these would be unopposed.

After delays by the British government in approving these plans, British destroyers laid three fields of dummy mines on 8 April 1940, while a covering force lead by the battlecruiser *Renown* stood out in the Norwegian Sea. Ironically, long-prepared German plans for the occupation of both Denmark and Norway were already underway, in part precipitated by Vian's rescue operation. By 6 April there were strong indications of enemy activity in the Baltic ports, and on the 7th the Admiralty was able to send to the Commander-in-Chief of the British Home Fleet an accurate account of German movements. However, these were interpreted as preparations for a breakout into the North Atlantic. When actual sighting reports of the enemy's northward movements were received, and the main forces of the Home Fleet sailed on the evening of 7 April, it was already too late. The speed and ruthlessness of German operations achieved complete tactical and operational surprise.

The weather in the Norwegian Sea was appalling and the British search for the German fleet brought only fleeting and accidental contacts. In the late evening of 8 April, the destroyer *Glowworm*, who had become detached from the fleet while searching for a man overboard, sent a sighting report on the heavy cruiser *Hipper* before heroically closing to attack and damage her. On 9 April, *Renown*, searching for the *Hipper*, found the battlecruisers *Scharnhorst* and *Gneisenau*, but despite damaging the latter, lost the Germans in a snowstorm. Also on the 9th, the Luftwaffe attacked the Home Fleet, without sinking any ships, while the British submarine *Truant* torpedoed and sank the cruiser *Karlsruhe*. The next day, Fleet Air Arm Skuas, at extreme range from their base in the Orkneys, sank the *Königsberg* in Bergen harbour, and the pocket battleship *Lützow* was torpedoed by the submarine *Spearfish* and put out of action on her way home. In a confused situation, Winston Churchill attempted to

The scene at Romdahl's Fjord, one of the Norwegian ports. (Imperial War Museum: K4017)

take charge and issue orders.4

Notable actions followed, particularly between the destroyers at the First and Second Battles of Narvik. In the first battle, several enemy destroyers were sunk for which Captain Warburton-Lee was posthumously awarded the Victoria Cross, and, in the second, on 13 April, the surviving German ships were annihilated. Standard naval histories tend to concentrate on these battles, but it is the work of the naval brigade ashore which interests us here. Unkindly, these operations merit only one sentence in Roskill's abbreviated history of the RN in the Second World War, and hardly more, proportionally, in his multi-volume official history of the war.[5] Fortunately, the Navy's operations ashore have been recorded in a naval staff history, *Battle Summary No. 17, Naval Operations of the Campaign in Norway: April – June 1940*.[6] The troops, who had been embarked in cruisers ready for unopposed landings in Norwegian ports, had been put ashore in Scotland when the cruisers were diverted to the mistaken mission of preventing a German breakout. Paradoxically, it was Churchill who had ordered this, to the disappointment of the Cabinet when they found the fleet was on a wild goose chase instead of the operations which they had intended.[7] Thus it was that armed seamen and Royal Marines from HMS *Glasgow* and *Sheffield* were transferred to destroyers and the first to be landed at dusk on 14 April to occupy Namsos, at the head of Namsenfjord.

On 15 April there was urgent consultation between the Army and the Navy. Admiral Lord Cork, flying his flag in the cruiser *Aurora*, met General Mackesy who had arrived in Vaagsfjord in another cruiser, the *Southampton*. In central Norway Major General Carton de Wiart VC arrived by flying boat at Namsos to discuss arrangements for the follow-on forces there with Captain Nicholson of the *Somali*. Two separate operations were planned, in the north and centre of the west coast of Norway, against Narvik and Trondheim. At both places the lodgements of German troops, whose supplies had been severely disrupted by the Royal Navy, were seemingly precarious. In the north, Operation 'Rupert' was to use 30,000 troops to take Narvik. In the centre, Operations 'Maurice' and 'Sickle', using 12,000 men, were to create a pincer movement against Trondheim. Further south, matters were to be left to the Navy, who were enjoying some success against the German Navy and the German Army's supply ships.[8]

Operation 'Rupert', the main effort by an allied army of British, French and Polish troops was haphazard. The first troops did arrive at Harstad in the Lofoten islands on 14 and 15 April, but reinforcements were spread out over a wide area, some as far as 100 miles away in

Major General Carton de Wiart (centre), who would write that the Royal Navy did not know the meaning of the word 'impossible'. (Imperial War Museum: N68)

Bodo and separated by Vestfjord, a part of the Inner Leads. Thus concentration and co-ordination was impossible. Added to the geographical difficulties, other delays, some caused by the appalling weather meant that the Allies were not ready to move against Narvik for over six weeks. They captured the town on 28 May, only to be evacuated by 8 June. The Germans had launched their blitzkrieg against Holland and France, thus forcing the Allies to abandon 'Rupert' and Norway – after a further, brief attempt to hold onto Bodo.

In the centre, Operations 'Maurice' and 'Sickle' were to be preceded by two enabling operations known, respectively, as 'Henry' and 'Primrose'. 'Henry' called for 350 seamen and marines from ships already operating off Namsos to forestall the Germans, and to prepare for unopposed landings by larger, follow-on forces. 'Primrose' was altogether a bigger operation, calling for 700 men from capital ships in dockyard hands in England to land with field howitzers, high-angle pom-poms and two 4in guns at Aalesund.[9] Again, both 'Henry' and 'Primrose' were given orders not to attempt any landing if the Germans were already in occupation. In passing, the similarity between this use of a naval brigade and Churchill's despatch to Antwerp of the Royal Naval Division, of which he was 'the creator and champion' in the First World War, is striking.[10]

Operation 'Maurice' and its precursor, 'Henry', were short-lived. General de Wiart's flying boat was strafed as it arrived and his ADC was wounded, but he was able to reach the destroyer *Somali* unharmed and set up headquarters onboard. The ships had a hard time defending against German dive bombers based only a few minutes' flying time away.[11] *Somali* soon expended all her ammunition and the General transferred with his staff to *Afridi*. Namsos came under continuous air bombardment and the berthing facilities for large troopships were inadequate, so that the troops were taken to Lillesjonafjord where two of the three battalions of troops were transferred to the smaller destroyers. The third battalion was brought to Namsos in the Polish destroyer *Chrobry* a day later. At no time were the ships safe from the attention of German aircraft, though fortunately they only scored near-misses, and the lack of air cover was to prove fatal to the success of the whole campaign.[12] In the face of fierce opposition, mostly by Junkers Ju88 bombers and later by Stuka dive bombers and despite the weather, with fog offshore and fresh falls of snow ashore, General de Wiart's forces, after achieving little, were evacuated from Namsos on 2 May, much equipment and transport being abandoned ashore.

In the south-centre, 'Primrose' and 'Sickle' in Romdalsfjord were relatively more successful. Although closer to the Germans, it took some days for the enemy to appreciate that landings had been made. According to the official history, '... plans for [British] landings in central Norway were only gradually evolved.' Apparently, landing parties from the battleships were ordered to make ready to land their seamen and marines only two days before the expedition was finally decided upon, and the general intention of these landings was only signalled on 13 April that '... a force of marines and seamen from *Nelson*, *Barham*, and *Hood*, about 800 strong, will land at Aalesund ... this will be known as Operation "Primrose".' Again, according to the battle summary, a signal on 11 April had stated that:

> ... marine detachments of 100 men from each ship and seamen field gun's crews may be required for a special operation to capture and occupy small islands for limited period shortly; parties would be required to be self-supporting for one month, and to land and mount 12-pdr gun or 3.7-in howitzer; necessary preliminary preparations are to be made — orders next day increased the size of each party by 70 men.[13]

However, examination of *Hood*'s log for the period reveals that preparations had been in hand for some days before. The battlecruiser had arrived in Devonport for routine maintenance on 31 March 1940 and she remained there until 27 May. There were several air raid warnings, many of short duration and evidently false alarms. Several ratings came and went on draft including some Maltese, and there were training or courtesy visits from the Royal Marines, the Army and ratings of the Polish Navy. There must have been some kind of warning, however, of the formal signal, because on 8 April 'higher gunnery rates and range party' went to breakfast at 6.30am and were mustered on the jetty an hour later. They were to do so every day until the 13th. Then, on Saturday 13 April, *Hood*'s log records in the first watch, '... 2130 Seamens Landing Party fall in ... 2145 No 1 Platoon fall in ... 2330 Seamens Landing Party landed ... 2350 RM detachment landed ...' and in the middle watch (Sunday 14 April) ' ... 0030 RM landing party landed ...'. This was *Hood*'s marines, howitzer crew, and seamen landing party preparing for their new role and entraining for Scotland and passage to Norway.[14]

According to Midshipman Browne who was in *Hood*'s landing party, he only learned:

> ... on Saturday afternoon [13th] that the ship was required immediately to provide a landing party of Royal Marines and seamen. Organised chaos resulted whilst a party of about 250 was got together from the limited numbers on board. The jetty alongside was rapidly filled with a hotch potch of stores and ammunition. Pride of place was taken by the ship's howitzer, an ancient piece of ordnance which few knew existed ...[15]

On the northbound midnight train, the Royal Marines from *Hood* were the largest contingent. Commanded by Major Lumley and Lieutenant Stroud, they had commandeered Hood's automatic weapons such as the Lewis guns, and '... appeared to know what they were about. [They] regarded the seamen with some tolerance bordering on condescension.'[16] The other elements of the naval brigade, as well as the men from *Hood*, were men from the battleships *Barham* in Liverpool and *Nelson* in Portsmouth, an anti-aircraft battery from Tynemouth and a searchlight detachment from Yeovil. Lieutenant Colonel Simpson was placed in command, first meeting his makeshift force at Rosyth as they arrived on 14 April. Simpson subsequently reported:

> Men and gear went onboard the sloops as they arrived, for the expedition had to sail the same day, so had not time for 'any pre-arranged and useful order' of stowage. For instance, the seamen and the marines from *Nelson* sailed in different ships [so too did the 'Hoods'], to make room for the anti-aircraft guns to sail in two ships also and avoid the risk of having all in one basket, but the 'Nelson's' had not expected nor prepared for this when loading their train.[17]

They embarked in four sloops, *Black Swan*, *Bittern*, *Flamingo* and *Auckland* which sailed heavily laden.[18] To make room, the expedition's victuals were left behind, to be replaced by rations drawn from the ships themselves. Other equipment was also left behind, including the searchlights. Even so the ships drew a foot more water than their normal draft and, besides the additional men, had topweight stowed on their upperdecks, notwithstanding the severe weather which was forecast. *Auckland* sailed first with the 'Barhams' and their 4in gun, intending to make an early lodgement at Aalesund. The other ships sailed at 3.30am on 15 April. Bad weather forced all the squadron to take shelter in Invergordon, from where Col Simpson wrote, '... It is for consideration whether in similar circumstances, a delay of some hours in sailing is not justifiable in order to allow a reasonable loading plan.' While at Invergordon, he also received a signal changing the destination of the expedition from Aalesund to Aandalsnes, further eastward and slightly closer to Trondheim. The delay at least gave Simpson time to meet his officers and explain his plans, though he lacked maps and knew little of the country for which he was bound. In fact his only sources of intelligence were the wartime newspapers and that essential guide to mariners, the *Norway Pilot*.[19] The despatch and embarkation of forces for Operation 'Primrose' within so short a space of time was a considerable feat of improvisation and of the railway timetables, but the expedition was showing many of the symptoms of failure which have dogged this type of operation repeatedly over the centuries.

Captain Poland, the senior naval officer in *Black Swan*, ignoring his orders to take a northerly route, and, turning the weather to his advantage, chanced discovery from the air by steering along the Norwegian coast. He arrived on the late evening of 17th and overnight the naval brigade landed at three small fishing-ports strung out along Romsdalsfjord, the fjord leading to Trondheim. The main force landed at Aandalsnes and smaller forces at Aalesund (the original destination) and Molde. At Aandalsnes, disembarkation was considerably helped by a 5-ton travelling crane on the jetty – which was not listed in the *Norway Pilot*. Captain Denny, the Naval Officer-in-Charge ashore, unaccountably established himself at Molde 40 miles away and on the opposite side of the fjord to Aandalsnes.

It was probably better for Colonel Simpson's equanimity that he

An Unlikely Encounter: Norway 1940

Howitzer battery in firing position near Namsos. (Imperial War Museum: N87)

had no maps. The significance of Aandalsnes was its railhead on the track leading from Dombaas, 60 miles away, on to Lillehammer and so to Oslo: the track up which the Germans were advancing. From Dombaas a branch line led off to Trondheim a further 100 miles away, and 150 miles further north by rail lay Namsos. All this was clear from a schoolboy's atlas, but the coast was deeply indented with long fjords and bordered by high mountains. In spring, the valley floors were flooded and the narrow, steep, winding, snowbound roads out of the small towns and villages were impassable to large formations of troops. Normal traffic between centres of population was by tiny, port-hopping ferries. The idea of using either Namsos or Aandalsnes as a base against Trondheim, still less of initiating a pincer movement from these two areas against the Germans, who had already established themselves, was clearly ludicrous. However, neither the

A typical fjord scene: although the German aircraft were able to attack with only a few minutes' warning, the ships were free to manouvre in deep water up to the cliff egde if necessary, to take shelter there.

battle summary nor Stephen Roskill, in three post-war analyses of the campaign in Norway, mention this little topographical difficulty.

The strategic significance of Dombaas being recognised by both sides, the marines of Simpson's naval brigade were ordered to advance, to capture the rail centre, and to cut off Trondheim. Whereas the British effort was dispersed, the Germans had no doubt about their main strategic objective and their operations were on a rather larger scale. Three days before the British naval bridge landed, the Germans had ordered submarines, each carrying 40 to 50 tons of small arms and anti-aircraft ammunition, to resupply Trondheim, paratroops to land at Dombaas to secure the rail junction, and the Luftwaffe to destroy any British troops who had landed. And Army Group XXI with its armour was ordered to advance along the railway to reinforce Trondheim.[20]

The 'Primrose' force, under the cover of the weather, was free from attack on its passage to Norway, but intelligence of what was happening ashore was poor. Lieutenant Donald, first lieutenant of *Black Swan* remembers saying at the time that it would have been '... nice to know if the ship was to be greeted by cheers and kisses from Norwegian blondes or a hail of gunfire.'[21] Despite reports of German seaplanes having forestalled them, the naval brigade disembarked without molestation. At 10.00pm on 17 April, *Black Swan* went alongside the jetty and *Bittern* berthed outboard of her, while *Flamingo* and *Auckland* stood off as guardships. After changing places, disembarkation was completed by 7.00am the next morning. Only then was *Auckland* released with *Bittern* in company to take the 'Barhams' and the 4in guns back down the fjord to Aalesund. At Aalesund, the Norwegians welcomed the British but not their large guns: they argued that the 4in guns would only attract German reprisals from the air. Major Lumley of the *Hood* caused gunpits to be dug and sent for high-angle guns, though no guns were ever mounted, not because of Norwegian objections, but because all the parts never arrived. One or two transports coaled at Aalesund but little else happened expect daily air-raids, and enemy bombing soon set the town on fire. Molde came off comparatively lightly until the last few days of the expedition, when it too was razed by the Luftwaffe.[22]

The German response at Aandalsnes was dilatory, the first air attacks only beginning on 20 April, and concentrating on the warships underway in the Romdalsfjord to give air defence to the naval brigade. Ashore, the 'Primrose' force was soon subsumed into 'Sickle', most of the troops and stores for this coming from the transport *Orion* and diverted from operations against Namsos. The initial force, under Brigadier Morgan, consisted of 1000 men in two territorial battalions and four anti-aircraft guns. Again, some of these forces were transported in warships, the cruisers *Galatea*, *Arethusa*,

Carlisle and *Curaçoa* and they were landed under cover of darkness overnight on 18/19 April. Morgan was also ordered to advance on Dombaas, and he was promised a second echelon of forces 48 hours later. Eventually some 4000 troops, with a divisional headquarters and a considerable volume of stores, under command of Major-General Paget, landed at Aandalsnes, with a small number dispersed to Molde, which was being used to land the troops rather than hold them in ships a moment longer than necessary, '... it [being] of great importance to get troops out of ships as soon as possible on account of air attack.'[23]

When Morgan sent his forces forward to Dombaas, the defence of the base at and around Aandalsnes became the principal object of the naval brigade. Simpson deployed his men in six posts with one in reserve at important tactical positions, including various bridges on the likely lines of approach of the enemy, and at outlying positions like the power station at Verma and at the erstwhile air base at Lake Lesjaswick. The seamen meanwhile made themselves useful around the base. 'It is fortunate', wrote Captain Denny, 'that the first party to be landed was a seaman and Royal Marines' force ... [in] the absence of any proper base personnel and equipment ... [the] situation ... was only mastered through the adaptability to be expected of naval units.' Indeed the sailors displayed their usual resourcefulness. On the one hand, a sailor commandeered a disused cookhouse and provided the force with round-the-clock hot food and drinks. On the other, when Midshipman Gallacher's Skua was forced to land on a remote lake (not Gladiator lake) through lack of fuel, the sailors cleared a runway for him so he could take off and fly back to *Ark Royal*. In fact, as the situation ashore worsened, '... the more uncomfortable and potentially dangerous things appeared to be, the more cheerfully and enthusiastically they were faced.' A start was made too on small-arms practice, but the sailors also found time to build a cresta run.[24] By night they slept in disused Norwegian army huts, but by day they dispersed into the hills and woods to watch the deadly duel between the ships in the fjord and the bombers. The ships suffered relatively little damage, but, sadly, the town was destroyed by fire. The six Oerlikon guns landed and manned by a party under Sub-Lieutenant

An Unlikely Encounter: Norway 1940

HMS *Black Swan* in 1940. Her high-angle 4in guns were to prove useful for air defence in the Norwegian fjords. (National Maritime Museum, London: Neg No N6731)

Goodale from Whale Island could only save the jetties and the railway station.

One notable action between the naval brigade and the German army did take place. The battle summary states, somewhat laconically, that, '... the *Hood*'s field howitzer went into action against some German parachute troops between Dombaas and Dovre the day after the landing, and helped the Norwegians in rounding them up.' *Hood*'s naval officers in the brigade were Lieutenant Commander Charles Awdry, brought back from retirement, Sub-Lieutenant D C Salter and Midshipman Browne. It was Salter who was ordered to take the ship's 3.7in howitzer and crew forward to the junction at Dombaas to reinforce the Norwegian army, and here he scored a major success. According to Browne, the ... first shot fell short, whereupon the best that [Salter] could think was to apply a simple spotting correction as if in a ship. Much to his and the crew's surprise [this] resulted in a direct hit and the surrender of the [Germans].' Browne modestly states that the landing party was totally insignificant: in truth this single action by the ship's howitzer probably delayed the Germans by several days. It slowed, though it did not halt, the German advance to reinforce Trondheim, and the delay enabled the King of Norway and his government to be evacuated to Britain. While these remained at liberty, albeit in exile, the political aim of the German invasion was doomed to failure.

However, as de Wiart at Namsos had already noted, further military operations under unopposed air attack were not practicable. Though losses were comparatively minor, the ships were running out of ammunition, and the Commander in Chief had already signalled for '... A.A. batteries and Royal Air Force fighters to counter enemy air action.' Now it was Paget's turn in the centre-south to request that '... arrangements to evacuate should be prepared if air supremacy is not assured forthwith.'[25] By 25 April, Aandalsnes began to receive the same aerial bombardment which had already almost obliterated Namsos, and, being built largely of wood, was soon set on fire. On 27 April, Captain Vian, now in the *Afridi*, reached Aandalsnes with a supply convoy including petrol for the army ashore: but, '... we found Aandalsnes on fire, and were met by the smoke-blackened Naval Officer in Charge. He informed us that the decision had been taken to evacuate.'[26]

The second and last action of Operation 'Primrose's' naval brigade was on the last day of the expedition when the Royal Marines manning the post at Verma fought a rearguard action against the advancing German army. Here Lieutenant E D Stroud RM and two marines '... were responsible for holding the last road block before successfully extricating themselves and catching the last ship to leave.'[27]

The post-war battle summary analysed the campaign in terms of the Principles of War as 'agreed between the three fighting services'.[28] The British aim had not been clearly thought-out, still less maintained, whereas the German aim was sustained: first taking the capital and then defending Trondheim. The constant change of orders had an effect on British morale, whereas the Germans' morale was maintained by their steady advance. Offensive action by Britain and her allies was impracticable without air power, and, while the enemy had almost unfettered use of the air, security of bases could not be achieved. Apart from some local incidents – like the 'Hoods' ability to deploy their howitzer so quickly on the front line – surprise was entirely on the German side. They also concentrated their forces, while the allies spread theirs out over great distances and difficult terrain. The Allies used 35,000 troops and considerable naval forces to evict the Germans from Narvik, the Germans used greater economy of effort and barely 9000 troops to occupy five strategic ports. The Allied plan was inflexible and could not take advantage of the destruction of German naval forces at Narvik. On the other hand, co-operation, of a sort, was achieved but '... weaknesses in the administrative arrangements revealed themselves as the campaign progressed.'[29]

Churchill's plans in this war were reminiscent of those he had supervised at Antwerp and Gallipoli in the First World War. The Navy's execution of these plans was a master-class in improvisation, the sailors demonstrating their customary versatility in landing and manoeuvring their guns into action. However, though well executed in detail, the plans were flawed. Neither the Navy nor the Army had paid any attention to the importance of tactical loading of men and equipment. Nor had either appreciated, until their forces were committed, that they could not operate where the enemy had air superiority. In any case, the plans failed to maintain any concentration of effort, intelligence was poor, and once again there were no maps.[30] Perhaps the Navy learned, too, that in modern warfare specialist arms are needed; certainly a similar naval brigade has not been landed since. On the positive side, the principle was established, which the world would see again at Dunkirk and at Crete, that the Royal Navy would never abandon the army. The gun action by the 'Hoods' at Dombaas 80 miles from the tiny port of

Seapower Ashore

Aandalsnes surprised the Germans and halted their advance, this allowed the army time to land and further delay the German attack. The time thus bought was not wasted: it enabled the King of Norway and his government to escape to Britain, more than a million tons of Norwegian shipping was added to British resources, and the German navy suffered heavily. The successful withdrawal from Dunkirk must owe something too to the campaign in Norway.[31]

No analysis can be complete without considering what might have been. The harebrained schemes for reaching the Baltic and Finland were Churchill's, but it was on his orders too that the troops in Scotland had been landed from their cruisers. Had they remained onboard they could have got to Stavanger before the Germans, or they would have been available to occupy Narvik as soon as the German navy there was destroyed on 13 April. Indeed, '... it is easy to see in retrospect what a very important role they might have played [had] the troops been kept embarked and had they been tactically stowed.'[32] Within days of the end of the campaign in Norway Churchill was Prime Minister and, under his leadership, Britain went on to victory in the war against Germany. Nevertheless, he later glossed over many of the details of the campaign in Norway. However, the battle summary, although it was highly classified and intended for reading in private by only the most senior naval officers, it does carry the caveat that its analysis is written '... in no spirit of criticism of Service Ministries or Staffs – still less individuals, all of whom were doing their best under circumstances of extraordinary stress and complexity.'[33]

The naval brigade's operations ceased with their evacuation on two nights, 1 and 2 May, when the Navy lifted more than 10,000 men from Namsos and the Romsdalsfjord ports. As General Carton de Wiart later wrote, '... I thought this was impossible, but learned a few hours later that the Navy does not know the word.'[34]

Notes

[1] Though referred to in this chapter as a 'naval brigade', the 700-800 seamen and marines (the number is not certain), who took part in Operation 'Primrose', were never called this in contemporary records or in official reports.

2 S W Roskill, *Churchill and the Admirals* (London 1977), p93. See also W S Churchill, *The Second World War* (London 1948), pp363-5 '... on the fourth day after I reached the Admiralty I asked that a plan for forcing a passage into the Baltic should be prepared by the Naval Staff.' He also brought back the 67 year-old Admiral of the Fleet Lord Cork and Orrery to command Operation 'Catherine'.
3 Admiral of the Fleet Sir Philip Vian, *Action This Day: a War Memoir* (London 1960), pp24-31 gives Vian's autobiographical account of this stirring incident in which he released 299 British merchant seamen who had been captured by a German raider, the pocket battleship *Graf Spee*, and held as prisoners onboard the supply ship *Altmark*. *Altmark* took refuge in Josingfjord in the Inner Leads, but Vian followed her in, in breach of Norwegian neutrality. Apart from anything else, the event is noteworthy for the original signal from the Commander-in-Chief, giving a wide remit, '*Altmark* your objective. Act accordingly' and the boarding officer's cry to the prisoners 'The Navy's here!' The episode is analysed more objectively in various editions of James Cable, *Gunboat Diplomacy 1919-1991, Political Applications of Limited Naval Force* (Basingstoke 1994).
4 Roskill, *Churchill and the Admirals*, pp93-103. See also S W Roskill, *The Navy at War 1939-1945* (London 1960), pp63-4 '... Small wonder that, with a stream of urgent, and sometimes contradictory orders, some of which bore the unmistakable imprint of the First Lord's language, emanating from London, Admiral Forbes [the Commander-in-Chief, Home Fleet] should have been faced by an extremely confused situation.'
5 Roskill, *The Navy at War 1939-1945*, p67 '... A few days later warships took across some 700 seamen and marines and landed them at the small ports of Aandalsnes and Molde, south of Trondheim.'
6 Historical Section, *Naval Operations of the Campaign in Norway: April - June 1940* TSD 57/50 (London 1950). First published in limited edition in 1950 as Confidential Book [CB] 3305(2) and subsequently declassified as Book of Reference [BR] 1736(46).
7 Roskill, *Churchill and the Admirals*, p99. When the Prime Minister asked if the cruisers had sailed with their troops for Norway, Churchill replied that they had been disembarked so that the cruisers could join the fleet. He looked decidedly sheepish and there was a 'distinct silence' round the Cabinet table.
8 Historical Section, *Naval Operations of the Campaign in Norway: April - June 1940*. See p48 for a summary of losses caused by the British and Norwegians amongst German supply ships: the battle summary concludes that initial supply arrangements for German forces at the two northern ports had 'virtually broken down'. They were however being supplied by rail and by submarine.
9 According to the battle summary, 45 officers and 680 men with three 3.7in howitzers, eight anti-aircraft pom-poms and two 4in guns.
10 Douglas Jerrold, *The Royal Naval Division* (London 1923). This is a near-contemporary account of the Royal Naval Division (RND), with a foreword by Churchill. For a more recent analysis of the RND see Chris Page's biography of Arthur Asquith, Christopher Page, *Command in the Royal Naval Division: a Military Biography of Brigadier General A M Asquith DSO* (Staplehurst 1999).
11 Vian, *Action This Day*, pp39-40. '... in narrow waters flanked by mountains, the card were held by the aircraft. There was too little sea-room for full freedom of manoeuvre, and the aircraft's approach was screened by the rock walls. As often as not, when they did come into view it was at such an angle that our 4.7-inch guns, whose maximum elevation was only forty degrees, could not reach them.'
12 Vian, *Action This Day*, p 41 '... The effect of even a token fighter protection, which at one stage took the form of an occasional old Gladiator or Skua, was most remarkable. So long as even one of these aircraft was about, every bomber kept clear.'
13 Historical Section, *Naval Operations of the Campaign in Norway: April - June 1940*, p78.
14 PRO ADM 53/112446 HMS *Hood* Ship's Log for May 1940.
15 Browne, Ian Commander, 'A Low Tech Naval Landing Party', *The Naval Review* (July 1989), pp263-66.
16 Browne, Ian Commander, letter dated 6 February 2000 to the author. For example 'a few of the Tars were wearing "go ashore" shoes, a fact they regretted when they landed in the snow at midnight! I think we got them Norwegian army boots.'

17 Historical Section, *Naval Operations of the Campaign in Norway: April - June 1940*, pp79-80.
18 As it turned out the sloops were well suited to their eventual task of air defence ships in the narrow fjords, being armed with three twin 4in high-angle guns.
19 The Pilot is a guide to mariners, so it was as if Simpson was trying to navigate the streets of London equipped only with a map of the Underground.
20 Historical Section, *The German Campaign in Norway* Book of Reference 1840(1) German orders translated and quoted in another British naval staff history. The Germans were more focused: from their point of view the fate of Narvik depended on holding the Trondheim area further south, which was thus 'the pivot of all operations'.
21 William Donald, *Stand by for Action: a Sailor's Story* (London 1956), p20. He also records that the sailors didn't think much of the name of their force, but were reassured by Captain Poland that '... whatever happens it will not be a pansy affair ...', p18.
22 Historical Section, *Naval Operations of the Campaign in Norway*, pp80-1 and 83.
23 Historical Section, *Naval Operations of the Campaign in Norway*, p81.
24 Browne, 'A Low Tech Naval Landing Party'. The Skua landed not on 'Gladiator Lake' but another. See also Browne, 6 Feb 00 '... I am sure that the majority [of the Tars] had received no military training (including me).'
25 Vian, *Action This Day*, p43. British Gladiator (biplane fighters) were based on the frozen Lake Lesjaswick, or 'Gladiator Lake', but this base was soon bombed out of existence '... though not before the gallant operations of this handful of aircraft had shown how even a few fighters might have wrested air superiority from the German bombers.'
26 Vian, *Action This Day*, p44. After a hazardous passage up the fjord, Vian was told, '... there was no need, therefore, for the supply ships, least of all the petrol tanker ... would we please take them away.'
27 Browne, 'A Low Tech Naval Landing Party'. For which all three were decorated.
28 Naval War Manual, 1947, pp6-8.
29 Historical Section, *Naval Operations of the Campaign in Norway*, pp139-41.
30 A J P Taylor, *English History 1914 to 1945* (Oxford 1965), pp462-71. '... The decisive argument was simply the need for some action, never mind where or who against ... the plans were run up in the slapdash spirit which had so characterised the expedition to the Dardenelles.'
31 Taylor, *English History 1914 to 1945*, p471.
32 Historical Section, *Naval Operations of the Campaign in Norway*, p138.
33 Historical Section, *Naval Operations of the Campaign in Norway*, p140 f2.
34 Carton de Wiart, *Happy Odyssey* (London 1950) p 240. See also Vian, *Action This Day*, p46. This British, French, Polish naval operation seems to have been conducted without serious problems of command or communications. However, by daylight the ships had not made sufficient offing and the French destroyer *Bison* and HMS *Afridi* were sunk.

CHAPTER 12

Assault on Walcheren: 1944
by Ivor Howcroft

The context of the amphibious assault on the Dutch island of Walcheren in November 1944 was the strategic need to open the port of Antwerp to supply Allied armies on their drive into Germany. The port had been occupied since September but access from the North Sea up the River Scheldt was denied by mines laid in the river and. before they could be cleared, the Germans had to be overcome on the island of Walcheren which dominated the western side of the river from the sea.[1]

Two amphibious assaults were involved, codenamed 'Infatuate I' and 'Infatuate II', the first to take Flushing and, then, the main assault at Westkapelle (see Map 1). In concept, they were not like Operation 'Neptune' at Normandy, which had been based on those hallmarks of combined operations in the latter part of the war, long-term planning and training. In contrast, the Walcheren operation was unscheduled, hastily put-together, using whatever resources that were available at the time: one of improvisation and expediency.

The operation related primarily to a conflict of priorities in the aims of the principal Allied commanders. General Eisenhower, as Supreme Commander, had a policy of an advance extended on a broad front expanding out of Normandy, whereas the British commander, Montgomery, was all for a narrow spearhead thrust to push towards the heart of the German industrial area of the Ruhr, an ambition which led to the unsuccessful Operation 'Market Garden', the attempt to secure Arnhem by an airborne assault. Eisenhower conceded by allowing Montgomery to pursue his goal at the expense of the tactical need to open up and safeguard a secure supply route for his army through the port of Antwerp.[2] As a consequence the port stayed closed. The Allied Naval Commander-in-Chief Admiral

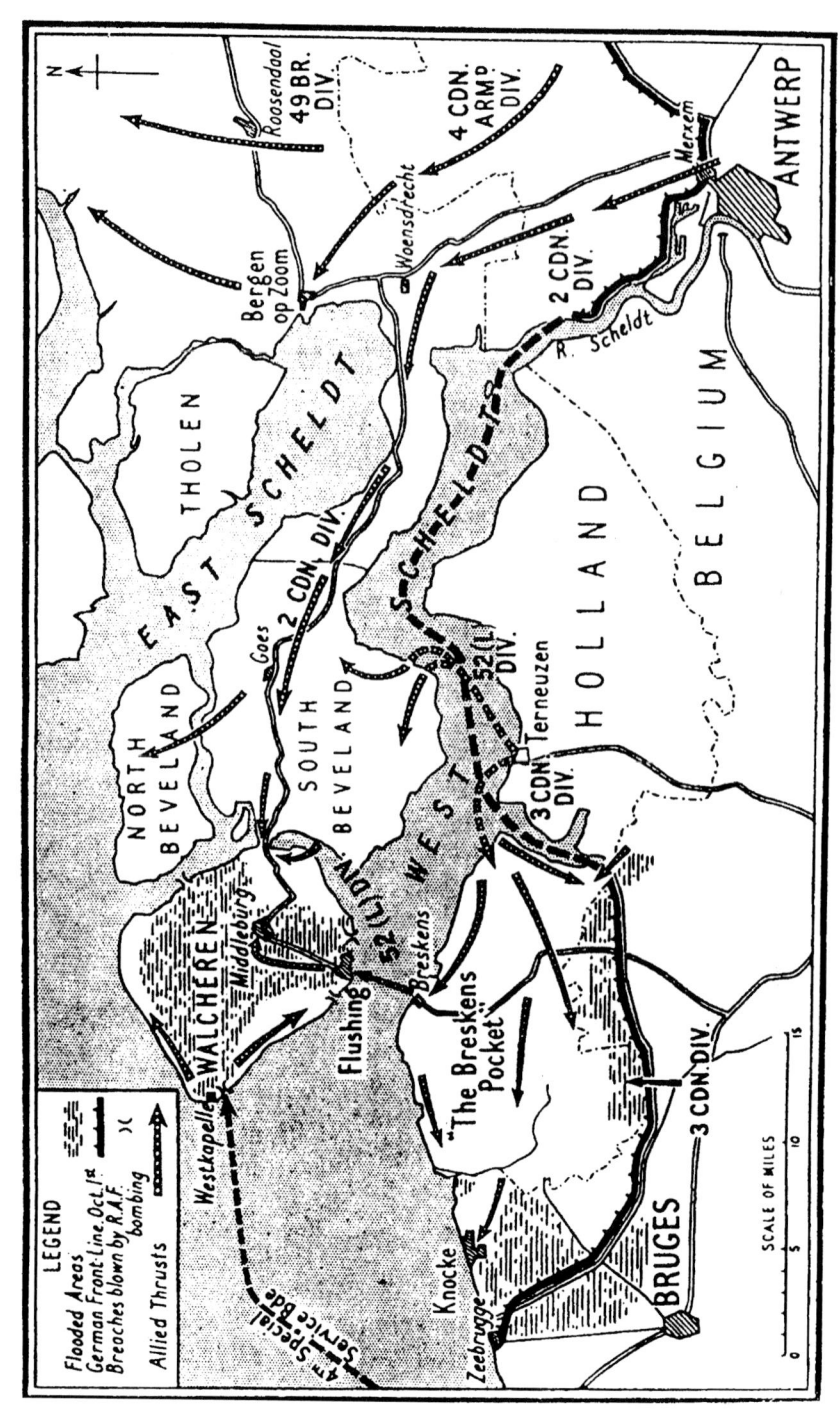

Map 1: Opening the Scheldt Estuary, October–November 1944 (From C Wilmot, *The Struggle for Europe*).

Sir Bertram Ramsay saw the folly in such neglect and repeatedly pressed for priority to be given to take the Scheldt estuary leading to Antwerp through a landward advance.[3] Churchill was also aware of the need to open Antwerp.[4]

By November the supply position was critical. The overland route from the beachhead at Normandy was far too extended, and there was a real danger of the Allied advance in the northern area coming to a grinding halt. Port supply facilities were vital and the Germans had to be cleared from the banks of the Scheldt, and this meant the capture of Walcheren. The island of Walcheren, all of which was below sea level and whose protecting sea dykes gave it a saucer shape, had been turned into a military fortress over a construction period of four years. Complex and formidable beach obstacles, underwater defences, and dense mining of the beaches and their exits, pill boxes, flame throwers, barbed wire and rocket projectiles complemented nearly thirty batteries of guns from 3in to 8.7in sited to cover the entrance of the West Scheldt. Fourteen of these batteries totalling sixty guns were in the Westkapelle area (see Map 2), manned by German naval personnel in heavily-protected casemates to engage ships at sea by direct fire.

It is interesting to note that the Germany navy and army differed in their ideas about the siting of coastal batteries.[5] The Navy favoured them being sited forward on the coastline in heavily protected casemates of steel and concrete to engage ships at sea by direct fire, whereas the Army considered that they should be sited further back, concealed by ground and in open casemates, able to bring indirect fire on to the beaches and on to any craft approaching them. At Walcheren the naval system was adopted, which sacrificed the field of fire for protection in closed casemates: as will be shown it was the right choice.

In taking Walcheren there could be little element of surprise, the Germans fully realising the Allies' need for Antwerp: Ultra intelligence provided clear messages that Hitler intended to resist the opening of the port.[6] A German author, Ansgar Dürnholz maintains that Field Marshal von Rundstedt believed that there would be an easterly landing on Walcheren once the Allies had a foothold in

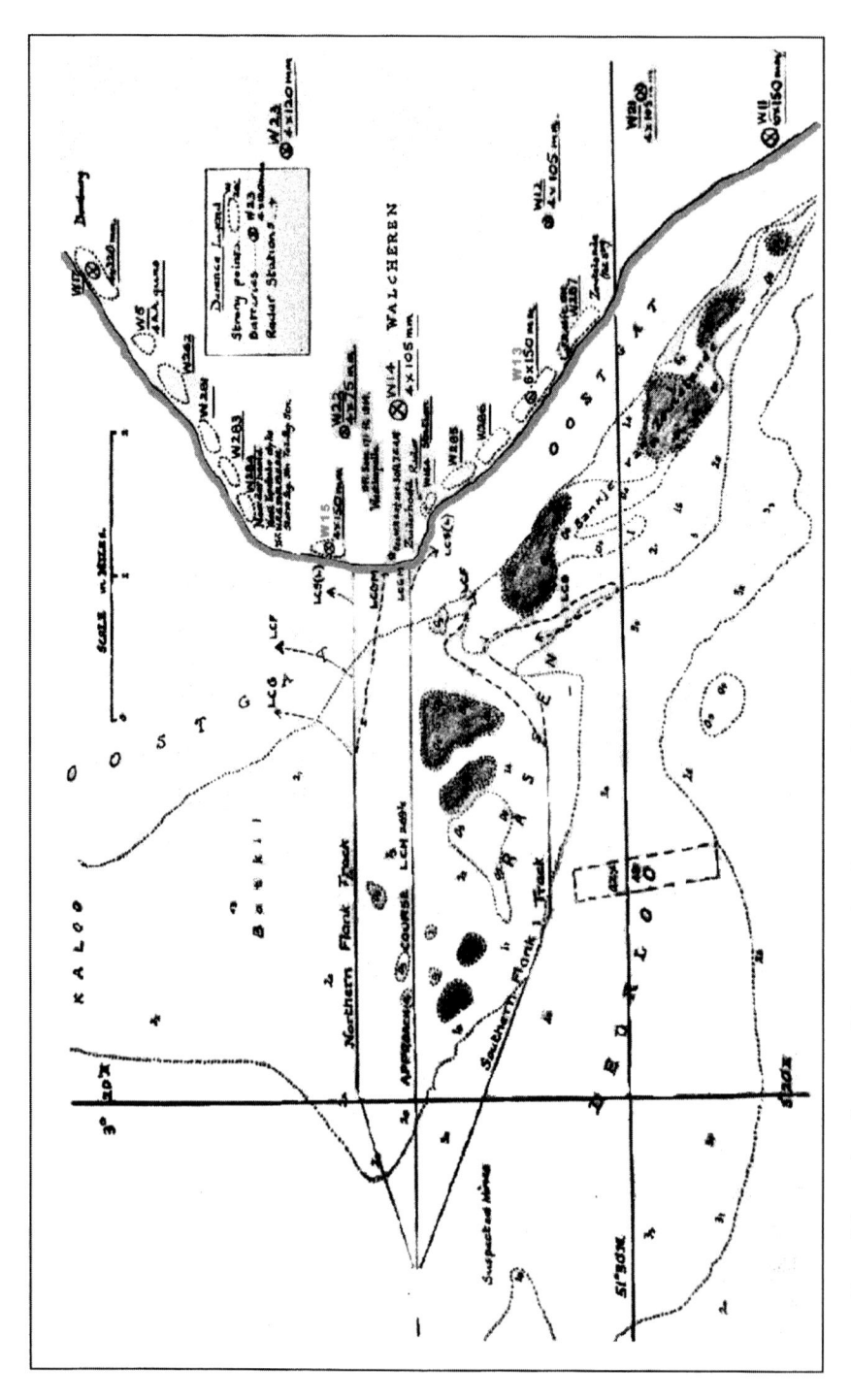

Map 2: Chart of the Westkapelle Approach by Support Squadron Eastern Flank. (WO 205/865A - XC 14768)

Europe.[7] In contrast, General Daser, the local commander, expected the main assault from the landward side and kept a substantial number of his troops facing South Beveland. From the Allies' point of view the weather was going to be the decisive factor, with October running out and the November fogs, overcast skies and rough seas ahead. One very positive benefit was that the island's 'saucer' had been flooded. Notwithstanding the reluctance of the senior RAF commanders, Leigh Mallory, Tedder and 'Bomber' Harris, to devote Lancaster heavy bombers to Walcheren, a concentrated bombing offensive had been undertaken in October, leading to the breaching of the dykes in four places (see Map 3).[8] Consequently all gun emplacements on low ground had been drowned, eliminating any indirect fire, though leaving the large-calibre naval gun sites still intact around the perimeter. It was in one of those breaches, at Westkapelle, widened by the action of the tide, that the principal assault was to go in.

The choice of the assault date was a crucial one: it would have to be in daylight to allow the large number of assault and support craft to work through very tricky shallow waters, and to spot for fire support. It would also be necessary to land before half-tide in order to force the beach obstacles, but assault craft would be unable to cross the numerous sand banks until one and a half hours after low water. Two tidal windows were available – 1 to 4 November and 14 to 17 November. The decision was to be left in the hands of the two on the scene commanders, Captain A F Pugsley, Royal Navy, and Brigadier B W Leicester, Royal Marines, who had a close working relationship.

Expediency and improvisation were inevitable factors but the Navy's objective was quite clear and specific: '... the reduction of the Walcheren defences in support of the capture by the 4th Special Service Brigade and 155 Brigade', the former were primarily the Royal Marine Commandos at Westkapelle, whilst the latter were the Army units at Flushing.[9] The bombardment force comprised the old battleship *Warspite*, well past her prime, with only three of her four twin 15in turrets in commission, together with another First World War veteran, *Erebus*, a monitor with two 15in guns, and the modern monitor *Roberts*. All previous Allied planning had been based on the

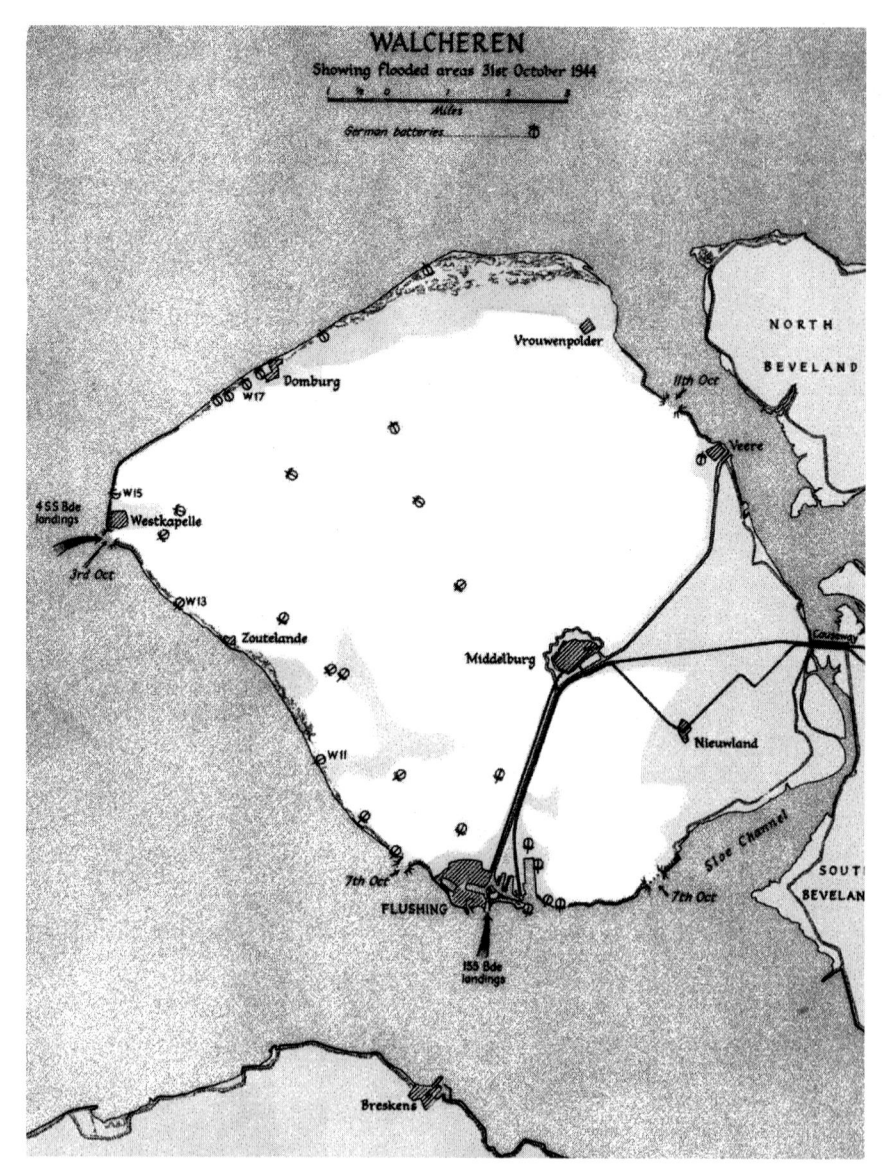

Map 3: Walcheren, showing flooded areas, 31 October 1944.

assumption that any ports or pockets of resistance on the Channel coast would be taken from landward, and so no amphibious reserve had been kept to exploit the Allied command of the sea.[10] However, Admiral Ramsay was able to turn to the Support Squadron Eastern Flank, only some three months old, having been formed at

Normandy from a mixture of support craft created as a defensive ring, 'the Trout Line', to protect the eastern flank of the invasion beaches against German E-boats, midget submarines and explosive motor boats. The squadron comprised of Landing Craft, Gun (LCG), Landing Graft, Flak (LCF), Landing Craft, Support (LCS), and Motor Launches (ML) supplemented by some Landing Craft, Tank (Rocket) (LCT(R)). Many of them were worn out. Thirty-six were rejected and a frantic repair job was organised to produce a mixed fleet of twenty-five vessels for Walcheren.

A desperate hunt was mounted to find assault vessels. After Normandy all the American landing craft had been taken away to be used for Operation 'Anvil' (the landing in the South of France) or for the Pacific war, but a group of Landing Craft, Assault (LCA), Landing Craft, Infantry (Small) (LCI(S)) and Landing Craft, Tank (LCT) were assembled in time to meet the minimum requirements. The planning and co-ordination of the assaults were far from easy: the principal commanders were scattered geographically – Ramsay at Granville, Simonds at St Omer, the LCT Squadron at Southampton, the Support Squadron at Poole, and the Royal Marines at Ostend and Terneugen. The issue of orders was a headache with the bombardment squadron only getting their copies minutes before sailing.[11] The local Dutch residents were warned of the impending assault by leaflets dropped on 2 October and with philosophical resignation, these Zealanders said that seawater (from the breaching of the dykes) was at least preferable to the Germans.[12]

Some training was undertaken, but no comprehensive rehearsal was possible at such short notice, and it was fortunate that the Support Squadron under Commander 'Monkey' Sellar, Royal Navy, was already a band of brothers from their Normandy experiences. Furthermore, the LCTs involved in the assault landing had, to some extent, worked as an integrated unit.[13] Pre-assault activities included minesweeping ahead of the bombardment squadron by the 18th Minesweeping Flotilla: no mines were found but it was an essential task nonetheless. It was to prove a very different story in the shallow shoal waters and beach approaches outside the scope of the Flotilla's *Algerine* minesweepers, the mines in the inshore waters causing

The gap at Westkapelle, 3 October 1944. (Imperial War Museum: C4668)

grievous losses. Data gathering by 'Tarbrush' (Intelligence) beach parties working in dories from Motor Torpedo Boats (MTB) was obtained on the state of the breached gap in the dyke at Westkapelle, and very strong surface streams southward off Westkapelle after low water were discovered. This meant that the shallow draft assault vessels would need to be prepared to steer upwards of 40 degrees off course to tideward to maintain the correct approach bearing.[14]

The initial assault, Operation 'Infatuate 'I, at Flushing, was with the Navy providing forty LCAs which sailed before dawn from Breskens on the far shore of the Scheldt. Three waves brought over the Naval Landing Craft Obstacle Clearance Unit (LCOCU) and the Beach Signals Sections and No. 4 Army Commando to form a beachhead, consolidated and developed by 52 Division in amphibious Buffaloes (Landing Vehicle, Tracked). Quite a degree of stealth was employed with the attack going in at 4.45am in the dark, surprise being achieved by the first two waves and the Navy's first amphibious task at Walcheren was completed with very few casualties.[15] The larger-scale attack at Westkapelle was a very different operation, both in its conception and execution. There was absolutely no chance of surprise, the attack involving a long approach run in daylight, enabling the enemy to fire at the oncoming vessels from their very well protected positions. It was therefore considered necessary for a pre-assault bombardment, complemented by close support action to divert the German gunners' attention from the assault vessels.

Offshore, the shallows, the maze of shifting sandbanks and the tidal runs, heavily mined, prevented large vessels, such as destroyers, from working close inshore. The support bombardment had to be from beyond the 10-fathom line (60 feet) and so the battleship and monitors engaged the enemy gun batteries at a range of 20,000 yards. The bombardment by *Warspite*, *Erebus* and *Roberts* was based on a fireplan intended to neutralise the coastal batteries and beach defences during the approach and initial assault, and then to remain on call for indirect bombardment from sightings by Forward Observers, Bombardment (FOB) ashore or spotting aircraft. Problems included a temporary turret failure in *Erebus* and the lack of competent spotting aircraft in the forenoon.[16] It was planned to use Spitfires based in England which had trained with the fleet but bad weather hampered their availability, and. until noon on the first day, the lack of reports from the Army's Air Observation Post (AOP) aircraft, which were not used to working with the fleet and with poor communications, meant that most of the bombardment was by direct fire from the ships' own observations.[17] Given the flat nature of the terrain, effective spotting from the ships at 20,000 yards was almost impossible. *Warspite* was in action on the first day, with the two monitors again shooting on the second day. Captain Kelsey of the *Warspite* saw an immediate improvement in speed and accuracy of shoots once the professional spotting Spitfires were in action and supplemented by FOBs ashore.[18] The fall of shot was not, however, very effective: in a subsequent analysis of their effectiveness on five principal gun battery sites, it was determined that a total of 636 rounds were fired, of which *Warspite* contributed 353, for just two hits achieved.[19]

Whilst the bombardment was in progress the Support Squadron Eastern Flank carried out their own vital role of close support.[20] It was one of great valour and fortitude: the vessels being lightly armoured and with small calibre guns. Six Landing Craft, Gun (Large) (LCG(L)) had two 4.7in guns each, two smaller Landing Craft, Gun (Medium) (LCG(M)) each had two 17-pounders, the Landing Craft, Support (Large) (LCS(L)) each had one 6-pounder whilst the Landing Craft, Flak (LCF) were armed with four 2-pounder anti-aircraft guns – never designed for taking on a fixed land site.[21] The main destructive weight was in the five Landing Craft, Tank (Rocket) (L.C.T.(R)) vessels which mounted 800 5in rockets, a deadly salvo to saturate the beach, but these were 'one-shot' platforms.

On a grey and miserable 1 November morning, with fair visibility and an acceptable sea state, with the code word 'Nelson' as the affirmative signal, the assault on Westkapelle was led in by the Support Squadron. It split into two equal groups either side of the gap breached in the dyke wall to face the full onslaught of the coastal batteries (see Map 2 and photograph). Rocket salvoes were fired, sadly two salvoes falling amongst our own vessels, whilst gun and flak vessels went closed the range to 1000 yards.[22] The two LCG(M) actually beached, as ordered, on either shoulder of the gap to take on pre-selected pill boxes, supported very closely by the LCS(L)s. It was a gallant action but a very costly one.[23] The southern vessel LCG(M) 102 and her three escorts were all destroyed and 101, whilst coming off the beach, also sank.[24] Under such point-blank fire, heavy casualties in men were inevitable: reports from veterans when the writer joined them at their reunion on Walcheren in November 1994 spoke of the Support Squadron being 'a forfeit', 'a sacrificial decoy', 'a bait for the German guns'.[25] By 12.30pm, of the twenty-five ships that had met the enemy at 8.30am, only six were fit for action, and one-third of the ships' companies of 297 men were casualties, 172 of whom were dead.

The sacrifice of the Support Squadron Eastern Flank on 1 November 1944 has to stand out as the most significant and costly contribution made by the Navy in the action. Captain Pugsley in his report as Naval Commander Force 'T' was concise and precise in evaluating its role:

> ... the operation was a success in that the troops were landed and achieved their objective. The success would NOT have been achieved without the outstanding gallantry and determination displayed by all officers and men of the Support Squadron under the command of Commander K.A. Sellar, Royal Navy, who led the attack and engaged the extremely active enemy batteries.[26]

The conception of their role was quite straightforward and deliberately planned: they were indeed to distract the enemy batteries and so to allow the assault craft to land the commandos relatively unscathed. It was a ploy taken by Sellar from his experience of German gunners in the assault at Normandy in June: the Germans fired at those vessels which fired at them. Indeed the key German battery, W13, had run out of ammunition, the German gunners having used their limited supply on the support craft, destroying LCT 37, LCS(L) 252, 256 and 258 and LCG(M) 102: the naval plan had been conceived bearing in mind the likely nature of the German reaction.[27]

The other roles of the Royal Navy at Westkapelle related to the assault itself. The Royal Marines went in behind the close support vessels as the principal units of the 4th Special Service Brigade. They were embarked in twenty-nine Landing Craft, Infantry (Small) (LCI(S)) assault vessels with Landing Craft, Tank (LCT) carrying amphibious Buffaloes (Landing Vehicle, Tracked) (LVT) and Weasels (cargo carriers), together with special assault flail tanks and armoured bulldozers. They landed, as already indicated, at what was seen to be the Achilles' heel of the German defence – on either side of the breached gap in the dyke (see photograph). There were many problems for the vehicles in the wet and muddy conditions and the marines were to face some hard fighting in the flank attacks, but it was infinitely preferable to trying to storm the heavily-defended high dyke itself. Naval beach parties were prominent in controlling the flow of traffic and so enabling the marines to spread in both directions along the rim of the flooded saucer, to attack and take each defended gun battery one by one. Movement was restricted by the flooded landscape and the Germans did not surrender until 8 November.

After putting the troops ashore, there was need to keep them supplied. For two days after the landing the tiny area of the breached dyke was under heavy and accurate German shell fire and the depleted Support Squadron was unable to maintain its diversionary role during the supply phase of the operation. These supply needs were met by the LCTs. When one sank, having struck a mine, the Principal Beach Master, Commander Prior had a difficult decision to make and he ordered two others off. The pressing need for supplies was being weighed against heavy German fire, when the weather then took a hand in the events, deteriorating to such an extent that beaching was impossible. On 4 November two LCTS did beach in high winds, one broaching to and the other driving against a groyne: but the vital supplies were off-loaded before the vessels were totally lost. Supplies were eked out by a parachute drop but the high degree of determination and seamanship by the crews of the LCTs did most to overcome the supply problem. Subsequently other vessels took off the wounded troops.

Summarising the action, the role of the Royal Navy was integral and focal to the combined operation, conceived to meet the strategic priority of opening the port of Antwerp. Whilst initially inter-service co-operation was lacking – Montgomery doing his own thing, and senior RAF commanders showing reluctance to assign their heavy bombers, and the Canadian General Simonds was left to his own devices on the far bank of the Scheldt – there were good communications and liaison in the operation phase. In particular, there was a dynamic and positive sense of co-operation established between the on-the-spot commanders, Pugsley and Leicester, who were properly delegated the responsibility for the assault on Walcheren. The RAF's contribution was the sinking of the island by breaching the dykes with Spitfire and Typhoon attacks during the day. Pre-assault and supporting bombardments by *Warspite* and the two monitors were of limited benefit, though they helped to demoralise the German gunners. The most heroic action was the close support of the Support Squadron Eastern Flank, an unselfish sacrifice which enabled the assault troops to land to secure the island.

As in all amphibious assaults, even at this late stage in the war in Europe, there were lessons to be learnt from Walcheren. Better and longer-term planning and more training would have been desirable, and more suitable bombardment ships and more support and assault vessels. There were limitations in the operation of the LCT(R)s – the subsequent inquiry hearing that too much reliance had been placed on radar fixes, especially with a low-contour coastline, and simpler navigational methods being ignored.[28] The LCFs were totally unsuitable for the task in hand and should not have been used. The bombardment was strongly criticised by the AORG, but the essential problem was the lack of proper spotting facilities for indirect fire. Admiral Ramsay later proposed that an aircraft carrier should have been used, the Navy thereby taking its own air support.[29] Captain Pugsley claimed that he had urged in vain that the spotters should be based on the Continent, as fog so often formed on one side of the Channel and not the other. In the absence of suitable aircraft he also, in his battle narrative, advocated that the Landing Craft, Headquarters (LCH) would have been a good location for FOBs as these vessels were close inshore – some 2000-3000 yards off the beach – to spot the fall of shot.[30] In essence, however, success was achieved by using the available forces to the best advantage, albeit built up in haste for an unscheduled task.

In 1809 there had been an attempt involving 250 warships and 40,000 troops to occupy Walcheren and deny Napoleon the use of

Seapower Ashore

Antwerp and Flushing.[31] Sadly inter-service liaison and co-operation were absent; the two commanders, navy and army, were at loggerheads and it was a disaster. The Walcheren action in the Second World War proved to be a very positive success, and was a significant element in the prosecution of the war into the German heartland; the last seaborne amphibious assault of the war in Europe. Major General Julian Thompson recently summed up the assault on Walcheren, a little-known event elsewhere called Cinderella operation, as '... the classic example of the employment of amphibious forces to unlock the door to a strategic objective.'[32] The price paid in casualties by the Royal Navy was very high, but the Senior Service carried out yet again its traditional role of putting troops ashore and sustaining them. It is an action that should be remembered for its commitment, valour and sacrifice.

NOTES

1 The port of Antwerp was taken largely intact, no demolitions having occurred thanks to the 'spoiling' efforts of the Belgian 'underground' forces.
2 D D Eisenhower, *Crusade in Europe* (London 1948), p337.
3 W S Chalmers, *Full Cycle: The Biography of Admiral Sir Bertram Ramsay* (London 1959), p252.
4 W S Churchill, *The Second World War* (London 1954), Vol VI, p844. A full description of the command problems is covered by R W Thompson, *The Eighty-Five Days* (London 1957), pp38-43.
5 G Blummentritt, *Von Rundstedt: The Soldier and Man* (London 1952), pp253-4. Hitler had made no decision on the matter but he tended to favour the naval system.
6 R Bennett, *Ultra in the West – The Normandy Campaign of 1944-45* (London 1979), p143.
7 A Dürnholz, Manuscript. The information is taken from the manuscript of a book to be published relating to the German view of the battles of North West Europe following the Normandy landing in June 1944.
8 Lord Tedder, *With Prejudice – the War Memoirs of Marshal of the Royal Air Force* (London 1966), p606. A Harris, *Bomber Offensive* (London 1990), p266. Harris' only concern was his 'Bomber Command' which he believed would win the war with strategic bombing of Germany; naval and army operations were seen to be of secondary importance. He failed to appreciate that, for example, the fuel for his aircraft had to be conveyed by the Royal Navy's protection across the Atlantic.
9 PRO, DEFE 2/308, Force 'T' Naval Operations Orders Appendix F, Orders for Naval Bombardment.
10 C Wilmot, *The Struggle for Europe* (London 1952), p607. Apart from one scare during the night of 1 November of suspected E Boats and explosive motor boats – which was groundless – no enemy naval vessels were encountered during the action.
11 A F Pugsley, *Destroyer Man* (London 1952), p185.
12 J L Moulton, *Battle for Antwerp* (London 1978), p121.
13 PRO ADM 116/5053, Naval Commander Force 'T' HMS *Squid*, Southampton No 82/255 Operation Infatuate II, Report to Allied Naval Commander Expeditionary Force 17 November 1944, p2.
14 PRO, DEFE 2/308, Force 'T' Naval Operational Orders (OIN two) Appendix C Operation Infatuate.
15 PRO, WO 205/865A, Report of Proceedings 10 Nov 1944 Captain C Maud, Royal Navy,

Assault on Walcheren: 1944

Deputy Naval Commander, Infatuate I.
16 PRO ADM 53/119407 and 119408, Ship's logs HMS *Erebus*. ADM 53/110734 and ADM 53/11935, Ship's logs HMS *Warspite*. ADM 116/5053, Reports of Proceedings HMS *Warspite*, HMS *Erebus* and HMS *Roberts*. Record of events 1st November HMS *Warspite* – bombardment of enemy gun batteries on Walcheren Island.
17 Armitage D. A., Museum of Army Flying, Middle Wallop – correspondence with the writer 2 Nov 1995, – 660 Squadron had conducted a shoot with coastal guns at Dover, but had no working relationships with the bombardment unit.
18 PRO ADM 116/5053. Report of Proceedings 7 November, p2.
19 PRO, DEFE 2/310, Army Operational Research Group report No 299.
20 PRO, DEFE 2/308, Force 'T' Naval Operational Orders (OIN two) Appendix G Orders for close support.
21 PRO, ADM 116/5053, Flotilla Officer, 332nd Support Flotilla, Enclosure No 24 to Commander, Support Squadron Eastern Flank's letter No 162/94/1 14 Nov 1944, p5.
22 PRO, ADM 116/5053, Operation Infatuate II. Erroneous firing of rockets during the assault – Report by Commander K A Sellar RN, Letter by Captain A F Pugsley RN and Report and recommendation by Admiral B H Ramsay.
23 PRO, ADM 116/5053, Commander, Support Squadron Eastern Flank, Letter No 162/94/1 14 Nov 1944 p6.
24 PRO ADM 202/407, Report on the use of LCG(M) 101 and 102 in Operation Infatuate, Captain S M Peritz RM.
25 Conversations with W H Cheney and P W Sharp on 4 Nov 1994, together with Aerogramme letter from T Sharkey, 23 Feb 1995.
26 PRO, ADM 116/5053, Operation Infatuate 81/1/255, 17 Nov 1944. Report by Captain A F Pugsley RN.
27 PRO, ADM 116/5053, Commander, Support Squadron Eastern Flank's letter No 162/94/1.
28 See Note 24.
29 PRO, ADM 116/5053, Report on Operation Infatuate, 22 Dec 1944. Bombarding Squadron and air liaison section. Admiral B H Ramsay, Allied Naval Commander-in-Chief, Expeditionary Force.
30 See Note 15.
31 G C Bond, *The Grand Expedition* (Athens, Georgia 1979).
32 E Grove, and P Hore (eds), *Dimension of Sea Power – Amphibious Operations: Projecting Sea Power Ashore* (Hull 1998), p105, and G Rawling, *Cinderella Operation* (London 1980).

CHAPTER 13

From *Tigre* to Tomahawk: the Adriatic Revisited, 1999
by Dr Lee Willett

On 18 November 1998 the British submarine HMS *Splendid* fired Britain's first live Tomahawk land attack cruise missile on the United States Navy's Naval Air Weapons Pacific Fleet Test Range at Point Mugu, off the coast of California. On 3 March 1999 she sailed from her home base at Faslane for deployment to the Persian Gulf before being diverted to the Adriatic. There, in Operation 'Allied Force', on 24 March 1999 *Splendid* fired Britain's first Tomahawk in anger. It was not only a very clear demonstration of the mobility and versatility of naval forces, but also, by any standards in peace or war, it was a remarkably speedy introduction into service of a new weapon system. In attacking Serb forces in land-locked Kosovo, a country otherwise seemingly inaccessible from the sea, *Splendid* was one of the first NATO units into action.

Seaborne artillery has always been used in attacks on the land, the Navy building when necessary special ships for the purpose.[1] The British Navy used Congreve rockets for shore bombardment in its 1805 attack on the French invasion forces at Boulogne, and through most of the nineteenth century, naval brigades deployed ashore used a variety of rockets.[2] Even the concept of using submarines for land attack is not new: in the First World War a British submarine bombarded Constantinople with torpedo and naval gun fire, prompting Sir Winston Churchill to enthuse that British naval history contained '... no page more wonderful than that which records the prowess of her submarines at the Dardenelles'.[3]

By the end of the twentieth century, the British navy itself no longer has the manpower to send ashore large naval brigades from its lean-manned ships, still less its submarines. Instead the Royal Marines have evolved, especially since the Second World War, into a specialist corps for amphibious and other landing operations. As for the Navy, for nearly 50 years, its declared policy has been to concentrate on its anti-submarine role in what was perceived would be the decisive battle against Soviet forces for the control of the North Atlantic. There were probably three factors, however, which lie behind the acquisition of a weapon like Tomahawk. First was the end of the Cold War and the search by the Navy for a new role; second was the availability of the weapon system: and third was the importance of the special relations with the United States, which is nowhere closer than it is between the two communities of submariners on each side of the Atlantic.

The Royal Navy's search for a role after the Cold War has been illuminated by the development of doctrine and a new look at the theories of deterrence and coercion. Much of this work originated in the Army, but was eagerly adopted by the Royal Navy. Further, since 1997 the government's Strategic Defence Review (SDR) has provided a backdrop against which the armed services have developed and articulated their roles, the Navy's particular thinking being embodied in its maritime doctrine, published as *BR1806*. Reflecting the strategic emphasis on expeditionary warfare, *BR1806* expounds a new operational concept called the Maritime Contribution to Joint Operations or MCJO.[4] MCJO postulates a national maritime military capability as the mainstay of British defence policy. Aircraft carriers, amphibious forces and Tomahawk-capable nuclear-powered attack submarines (SSNs) are the principal platforms in the MCJO framework, forming an effective triad for projecting maritime power ashore from the sea.[5] Broadly this triad was strengthened by the SDR. What Tomahawk missiles bring to the MCJO is an increasing ability within Britain's submarine flotilla to prepare the battlespace so as to enable the joint and combined arms campaign ashore in the land battle. To quote *Splendid*'s current commanding officer, Commander Richard Barker, *Tomahawk* '... provides the UK with a unique ability to contribute to the land campaign from long range, at any time, and potentially across all levels of warfare'.[6]

Tomahawk being launched from a submerged submarine. (MoD)

The new strategies and concepts of operations place particular emphasis on conventional deterrence and coercion. The theory of coercion has been understood by military thinkers from Sun Tzu to Thucydides, from Machiavelli to Giulio Douhet and Thomas Schelling.[7] Coercion was recognised as integral to the relationship between military means and political ends.[8] To modern writers like Sir James Cable coercion is 'the bread and butter of diplomacy'.[9] In the Navy's mind coercion is '... threat or use of limited offensive action ... to deter a possible aggressor or to compel him to comply with a diplomatic demarche or resolution'.[10] Given that successful coercion is based on four criteria − capability, credibility, commitment and intent to use force − a key issue raised by the development of these new strands of strategic thought is whether or not the Navy has all the weapons it needs.

In this context, successive Secretaries of State for Defence have noted the usefulness of Tomahawk. While nuclear-powered ballistic missile-carrying submarines (SSBNs) provide the ultimate deterrent, SSNs can also contribute to peace and security by providing coercive force for conventional deterrence.[11] Malcolm Rifkind, Defence Secretary when the British were negotiating to buy Tomahawk from the USA, said that Tomahawk offered a much improved stand-off capability which would '... be of value both in high-intensity conflict and in the coercive use of force as an instrument of policy'.[12] Rifkind's successor Michael Portillo saw the Tomahawk missile's range and precision as enabling Britain '... to threaten limited action against selected targets as a means of persuading an aggressor to desist from hostile activity'.[13] Other commentators clearly saw Tomahawk for what it was, as an '... example of employing a highly accurate sea-based weapon as a deterrent rather than relying on nuclear weapons which ... would be almost impossible to justify using'.[14] And Sir Patrick Duffy, one of the last – and most distinguished – Ministers of State for the Royal Navy, clarified for the British public how cruise missiles and submarines would fit into the wider concept of operations:

> ... the 'loiter' ability of a military force offshore [is essential as] a potent influence for conflict resolution. That military force will need to be mobile, flexible, stealthy, capable of forward deployment and well equipped. The introduction of Tomahawk submarine-launched cruise missile will enable the SSN to meet these requirements.[15]

In fact, Britain had first shown, in the wake of the Gulf War 1990-1, an interest in acquiring a capability for what was then called, in a paper prepared for the then Secretary of State Tom King, 'long-range bombardment'. Existing statements of requirements looked to air-launched missiles, but Tomahawk's successes in 'Desert Storm' focused some minds on a possible purchase from the Americans. Tomahawk even seemed to be a relatively cheap option compared to many of the alternatives such as stand-off airborne missiles. Eventually, under the 1994 *Front Line First* Defence Costs Study,

A Royal Navy Tomahawk in flight. (MoD)

Britain bought sixty-five missiles and enough fits of control equipment to arm seven of her *Swiftsure* and *Trafalgar* class submarines, for an initial programme cost of £100m. Subsequently, SDR mandated that Tomahawk would be fitted to all *Trafalgar*, *Swiftsure* and *Astute* classes of SSN. This wider fit would '... extend [Britain's] ability to use [*Tomahawk*] for deterrence and coercion'.[16]

A technical description of the weapon seems appropriate. Of the different launch options, the British chose the torpedo-tube method.[17] The missile is available in a number of versions, and the British bought the version known as Block III TLAM/C. Block III Tomahawk carries a 750lb WDU-36/B reactive titanium PBXN 107 high explosive/incendiary warhead out to a range of 1000 miles. A solid propellant booster gives initial thrust until it reached the cruise phase. The missile is given its initial position by an Inertial Navigation System (INS) and is navigated in flight along a pre-planned route by a satellite-based global positioning system (GPS), which is updated by Terrain Contour Matching (TERCOM) and a Digital Scene Matching Area Correlator (DSMAC) guidance system. TERCOM uses a radio altimeter to measure the contours beneath the flight path and DSMAC uses an electro-optical sensor to compare a stored image of the target area with what the sensor actually sees. Each operation is planned at Britain's own Cruise Missile Support Activity (CMSA), located underground at the headquarters of the Commander-in-Chief Fleet at Northwood in Middlesex, north west of London.[18] Technically such a system would have been unimaginable to Sir Sidney Smith at the siege of Acre in 1799, acting under his own initiative several weeks' sailing away by letter and sailing-packet from the Admiralty with his ship's guns and their shot and powder.

The procurement time-scale from the decision to acquire Tomahawk in 1994 to its first firing in 1999 is something of a record for any new equipment in recent years. Under the initial command of Commander Ian Corder, the system was fitted to *Splendid* during a six-month Capability Update Period (CUP). It was installed, tested, and set to work while a large number of other maintenance and capability work-ups also took place onboard the submarine. Once at sea again a full programme of safety and operational training was completed before further trials of the system could proceed. *Splendid* then deployed to Point Mugu for further tests and trials of the Tomahawk system, culminating in the live test firing on 18 November 1998. With both the First Sea Lord and the Flag Officer Submarines watching the firing, the live missile flew 612 nautical miles over the sea to San Clemente Island and destroyed a concrete bunker specially built to resemble a communications building. As one naval officer described it, '... if you can imagine the spot in the centre of a football pitch, a Tomahawk will land within the circle around it'.[19] Commander Richard Barker, known by an epithet which might have been chosen by sailors of two hundred years ago as 'Mad Dog' Barker, said:

> Little did many of those watching at the time realise that within a few short months, *Splendid* would be deployed to the Adriatic and be firing live weapons at selected and approved targets in support of NATO initiatives against the Former Republic of Yugoslavia.[20]

By the new year of 1999 *Splendid* had returned to her home base in Faslane and was due to take in exercises in the Mediterranean. She sailed arriving on 3 March, when it was reported that she had been assigned to the HMS *Invincible* task group in the Persian Gulf which was maintaining deterrent pressure on Saddam Hussein.[21] However, as the situation in Kosovo deteriorated, *Splendid*'s patrol was changed to the Adriatic. Showing remarkable flexibility in the ease of her redeployment, *Splendid* was to spend some 100 days in the theatre of operations as part of the Royal Navy's contribution to Operation 'Allied Force', the allied attack on Serb forces in Kosovo and Serbia. There she was employed from the first day to the last, with 100 per cent serviceability, demonstrating unequivocally British and especially the Navy's ability to project power on a world stage and, in particular, to influence the land battle. The air strikes on 24 March, the first day of the operation, only began after a wave of over 100 Tomahawks were fired from four US Navy warships, two American submarines and *Splendid*.[22] *Splendid* contributed an undisclosed number of rounds throughout the entire operation, and British fears about the replenishment of missiles while on patrol were allayed by *Splendid*'s two visits to the Italian naval base at Augusta, Sicily.[23]

Tomahawk proved to be appropriate for use against a wide range of political and military targets. Stated British policy is that Tomahawk is a tool for coercion, although in Kosovo repeated firings suggest a potential evolution in the weapon's rationale. Tomahawk evolved from a weapon with the high-level function of strategic coercion and the shaping of the battlespace to a weapon equally useful for immediate tactical purposes. NATO forces 'were able to bridge the distance from strategic to tactical application ... [Tomahawk] was the most responsive of all the weapons available to the task force commander'.[24] Militarily, *Splendid* and her Tomahawk missiles achieved everything required of them. However, experience from deployment and operations, and from working in closely with the USA does suggest the possibility of exploiting Tomahawk's tactical applications. Tomahawk proved to be a relatively inexpensive weapon that would supplement or supplant manned aircraft with minimal risk of loss and of collateral damage. Indeed, it turned out to be a more useful and usable weapon, across the strategic, operational and tactical spectrum, than previously envisaged. However, effective

Despite concern as to the practicalities, HMS *Splendid* was able to realod with Tomahawk missiles alongside in Agusta, Sicily, during Operation 'Allied Force' in 1999. (MoD)

and long-term tactical use is not something that can be achieved with just sixty-five rounds.

So, if the Strategic Defence Review was designed to remodel British forces and to 'maximise their effectiveness in today's strategic environment', perhaps there is a case for a wider fit of Tomahawk.[25] A wider fit in greater numbers of missiles and types and platforms would certainly improve political choice and the capabilities for coercion and sea-based bombardment.

Although rejected by Britain in the early 1990s, a surface fit is still a possibility. Surface ships provide visibility so crucial in coercive diplomacy. Surface ships can also carry more missiles than submarines. Current surface options include: building a Tomahawk-capable VLS into the new Type 45 destroyer; retro-fitting a VLS system into the *Invincible* class carriers and the Batch 3 Type 42 destroyers, and fitting aircraft carriers or some auxiliary surface ships with box-launched Tomahawk.[26] The Royal Air Force has even talked of fitting Tomahawk to aircraft, including Hercules transports.[27] Currently, the USN is considering the possibility of fitting Tomahawk into four otherwise redundant *Ohio* class SSBNs.[28] A nearer-term option for extending Britain's Tomahawk fit would be to procure greater numbers and types of missiles for the submarine force. Since Kosovo, Britain has entered into agreement with the USA to purchase twenty further submarine-launched rounds and is in discussions with the USN to develop a torpedo-tube version of the new Tactical Tomahawk (TacTom).[29]

Britain's purchase of Tomahawk from the USA and its rapid deployment at sea certainly maintained the Navy's reputation for responding to political changes and technical opportunities. The Tomahawk-armed SSN significantly enhances the political and strategic flexibility, reach and poise offered by carrier task groups and amphibious forces. A Tomahawk-capable SSN force provides Britain with new options for projecting carefully tailored levels of military force commensurate to the political context. Tomahawk will provide Britain an autonomous, balanced, flexible and discreet power projection capability to punch above its weight. There will be options for strategic coercion, for shaping the spatial and temporal dimensions of the operational battlespace and for tactical targeting. In short, Tomahawk is a classic maritime weapon and a core capability in future joint maritime operations.

In the words of the First Sea Lord, Admiral Sir Michael Boyce, in opening a new chapter for the Navy, Tomahawk gives Britain's attack submarines '... an even more pivotal role in de-fusing crises in the future'.[30] Tomahawk is a weapon of political and military choice which addresses the strategic realities of the modern world. It also a direct descendant in theory if not in technology of the guns which Sir Sidney Smith landed from his flagship, HMS *Tigre*, at Acre 200 years ago. Through weapons such as Tomahawk the '... political application of limited naval force is likely to remain an economic expedient ... and, by comparison with other forms of coercion, to seem an even better bargain in the years ahead'.[31] Former British

Defence Secretary Lord Robertson of Ellen noted, as *Splendid* returned to Faslane on 9 July 1999, that, as 'the first British submarine to fire cruise missiles in action, HMS *Splendid* will occupy a unique place in naval history'.[32]

NOTES

1. See C Ware, *The Bomb Vessel: Shore Bombardment Ships in the Age of Sail* (London 1994); A Preston, and J Major, *Send a Gunboat!: a Study of the Gunboat and its Role in British Policy, 1854-1904* (London 1967); I Buxton, *Big Gun Monitors: the History of the Design, Construction and Operation of the Royal Navy's Monitors* (Tyne & Wear 1978). The British navy built special ships for the purpose: bomb vessels in the eighteenth century, gunboats in the nineteenth century and monitors, which saw action in two world wars, in the twentieth century, being some examples. Operations such as these gave rise to the quotation from Prime Minister Lord Palmerston ... every country that has town within cannon shot of deep water will remember the operations of the British Fleet on the Coast of Syria in September, October and November 1840, whenever such country has any differences with us ...'. See A Lambert, 'Stopford: Acre, 1840', in E Grove (ed.), *Great Battles of the Royal Navy* (London 1994), p160.
2. R Brooks, *The Long Arm of Empire: Naval Brigades from the Crimea to the Boxer Rebellion* (London 1999), pp161-2. Congreve rockets were used until the mid-century when they were replaced by Hales rockets. Congreves came in different sizes from 3- to 24-pounders: they were 'area weapons', essentially inaccurate but good for bombarding forts and harbours, and for terrorising enemies who had not seen such things before.
3. E Gray, *The Underwater War: Submarines 1914-1918* (New York 1971), p145. Inevitably Admiral Sir Jackie 'Radical' Fisher went further and in 1915 proposed fitting a 12in gun, taken from a battleship, to a submarine. From this 'battleship-submarine', the *M 1*, was born.
4. See MOD, *The Strategic Defence Review* (Cm 3999. Presented to Parliament by the Secretary of State for Defence by Command of Her Majesty. July 1998. London: The Stationery Office); BR1806; *British Maritime Doctrine* (Naval Staff Directorate – NSD -, RN. 1999. D/NSD/2/10/1. By Command of the Defence Council. Second Edition. London: The Stationery Office – TSO); RN. Four papers were crucial in establishing the Navy's future direction and in setting the tone of public debate. See: Admiral of the Fleet Sir Benjamin Bathurst KCB (former First Sea Lord). (1995). 'The Royal Navy – Taking Maritime Power into the New Millennium', *RUSI Journal* (August 1995), p10; Rear-Admiral T Loughran, 'Projecting Power from the Sea: the RN Contribution to the Air Battle', in *RUSI Journal* (October 1996), p28; Admiral Sir Peter Abbott, 'The Maritime Component of British and Allied Military Strategy', *RUSI Journal* (December 1996), p9; Admiral Sir Jock Slater KCB, 'The Maritime Contribution to Joint Operations', *RUSI Journal* (December 1998), p20.
5. See BR1806. RN. *Maritime Contribution to Joint Operations*. Available on-line: <www.royal-navy.mod.uk>.
6. Cdr R D J Barker, RN, 'Precision Strike from the Sea: HMS *Splendid* and *Tomahawk*', *RUSI Journal* (August 1999), p75.
7. See Sun Tzu. *The Art of War* (Translated, with an introduction by Samuel Griffith) (Oxford 1971), p40; Thucydides. *The Peloponnesian War* (Introduction by M.I. Finley) (New York 1972), p57; Machiavelli. *The Art of War*. Book I. (Introduction by Neal Wood) (New York 1965), p30; GpCapt A Lambert, 'Air Power and Coercion', in GpCapt. S Peach (ed), *Perspectives on Air Power: Air Power in its Wider Context*. Defence Studies (RAF), Joint Services Command and Staff College (London: TSO 1998), p267.
8. This point was noted by Robert Osgood in *NATO: the Entangling Alliance* (Chicago 1962), p5.
9. Sir J Cable, *Diplomacy at Sea* (London 1985), p3.
10. BR 1806, p58.
11. RN. 'Frequently Asked Questions', in *Today's Royal Navy*, p2. Available on-line on the RN's home-page: <http:// www.royal-navy.mod.uk/today/faq.htm>.
12. Hon. M Rifkind, Speech at Centre for Defence Studies, King's College, London. 15 February 1994.

13 Hon. M Portillo, *Statement to House of Commons on Defence Equipment,* 13 July 1995. London: Hansard; Statement to House of Commons, 14 July 1995. London: Hansard.
14 C Bellamy, *Knights in White Armour: the New Art of War and Peace* (London 1997), p235.
15 Sir Patrick Duffy, Ph.D. (Parliamentary Under-Secretary of State for Defence, Navy, 1976-9), 'Nuclear Submarines.' Letter to *The Times,* 5 March 1998.
16 *The Strategic Defence Review,* p37.
17 The are four methods of launch for sea-based Tomahawk missiles: from submarines, torpedo tube or vertically launched (VLS); and, from surface ships, VLS or box-launched.
18 Barker, 'Precision Strike from the Sea: HMS *Splendid* and *Tomahawk*', pp73-5.
19 Quoted in M Evans, 'Allies on Full Alert for Retaliation', *The Times,* 25 March 1999, p5.
20 Barker, 'Precision Strike from the Sea: HMS *Splendid* and *Tomahawk*', p75.
21 M Evans, J Sherman, and I Brodie, 'British Nuclear Watch on Iraq.' *The Times,* 21 December 1998, p1.
22 American B-52 Stratofortress strategic bombers (flying from RAF Fairford in Gloucestershire) and B-2 Spirit stealth bombers (flying from Whiteman Air Force Base in Missouri) were also involved in the opening strikes.
23 See: '"Allied Force' Applied to Serbia', *Jane's Defence Weekly* (31 March 1999), p3.; I. Kemp. '£600m Added to UK Defence Budget', *Jane's Defence Weekly* (9 February 2000), p13; B MacIntyre,. 'Alliance Plans Three Key Stages', *The Times,* 24 March 1999, p5; 'NATO Attacks'. Features, in *The Sunday Times,* 28 March 1999, p13; T Walker, M Evans, and P Webster, 'The Heart of Belgrade Burns'. *The Times,* 3 April 1999, p1; M Evans, 'Splendid Job, Sub's Crew Told.' *The Times,* 10 July 1999, p1.
24 Vice-Admiral D Murphy USN, 'NATO Naval Forces in the Kosovo Operation.' Paper cited by K Strauss, 'The Notion of Precision Land Attack: a Case Study on the Tactical Tomahawk.' Paper presented to conference on Naval Land Attack Weapons, London, 1-2 December 1999. SMi Defence conferences.
25 *The Strategic Defence Review,* Chapter 11, para 203, p54.
26 It is apparent that the carrier and Type 42 options have, for the time being, been ruled out. As far as box launchers are concerned, suitable for a British Tomahawk fleet of relatively limited numbers, the author's research suggests that the only costs payable by Britain to the US government would be for delivery of the boxes and for launcher and fire control systems.
27 See, for example: N Friedman, 'Airborne Tomahawks: World Naval Developments', in USNI *Proceedings,* Vol.125/4/1,154, p6; P Almond, 'RAF 'To Arm Hercules with Cruise Missiles''. *The Sunday Telegraph,* 12 June 1998, p12. It is understood that Boeing have designed and manufactured the magazine for such a fit.
28 The USN is considering fitting its first four *Ohio* class SSBNs (to be decommissioned as SSBNs under the Strategic Arms Reduction Talks) with up to 154 Tomahawks, which each could be discharged in as little as six minutes.
29 Capt J Kirkpatrick RN OBE, 'Tomahawk Cruise Missile: UK Requirement and Procurement Programme', Paper presented to conference on Naval Land Attack Weapons, London, 1-2 December 1999.
30 Boyce, *First Sea Lord's Message.* Available on-line: <www.royal-navy.mod.uk> 25 February 1999.
31 Sir J Cable, 'Gunboat Diplomacy 1919-1991', International Institute for Strategic Studies: Studies in International Security, no.16. London, p146.
32 Robertson. Quoted in M Evans, 'Splendid Job, Sub's Crew Told', *The Times,* 10 July 1999, p1.

Index

Page numbers in *italics* refer to illustrations

Abbreviations
Adm = Admiral; Capt = Captain; Cdr = Commander; Cdre = Commodore; Fr = France; GB = Great Britain; Ger = Germany; HMS = His (Her) Majesty's Ship; L/Cpl = Lance-Corporal; Lt = Lieutenant; Lt-Cdr = Lieutenant-Commander; Lt-Col = Lieutenant-Colonel; Lt-Gen = Lieutenant-General; Neth = Netherlands; R/A = Rear-Admiral; Rus = Russia; V/A = Vice-Admiral

Aalesund 246, 248-51
Aandalsnes 248-52, 254-6
Abbott, Adm 22
Abercromby, General Sir Ralph 40, 47
Abu Klea, HMS *166*, 170, 172, 178
Acre
  bombardment of (1840) 13, 84-93, *88*, *90*
  siege of (1799) 9-10, 23, 28-37, *32*, *36*, 279, 282
Active, HMS 131
Aeolus, HMS 103, 107, 126
Afghanistan 79, 124
Afridi, HMS 245, 254
Agamemnon, HMS 53, 55, 63
Aigle (Fr) 126
Aigrette (Fr) 126
Alacrity, HMS 175
Åland Islands 97-8
Albania 79
Albert, battle of 232-3
Alexander, Capt John 157-8
Alexandra, HMS 168
Alexandria 42
  blockade of (1840) 80, 84, 91
Algerine, HMS and class 176, 265
Alma, battle of 133
Altmark (Ger) 240
Amorha, battle of 140
Amphion, HMS 106-7, 111-12, 114, 121, 125
Amsterdam (Neth) 156-7
Ancre, battle of the 221-2
Antwerp 18, 209-11, *210*, *213*, 245, 255, 259, *260*, 261, 270, 272
Arethusa, HMS 251-2
Argus, HMS 149-50, 156-9
Ark Royal, HMS 252
Arrogant, HMS 107, 112, 125
Asia, HMS 81, 84
Asquith, Arthur 208, 212, *215*, 218, 223, 225, *227*, 228-9, 236
Astute class submarines (GB) 278
Atbara, battle of 172-3
Auckland, HMS 247-8, 251
Aurora, HMS 167, 243
Austerlitz (Fr) 126
Australia 214
Austria 26-7, 35, 49-50, 83-4, 86, *90*, 91, 93
Avalanche (Fr) 126
Awdry, Lt-Cdr Charles 253

Bacchante, HMS 47-50
Badger, HMS 114, 116, 126
Balta-Liman, Treaty of 80
Baltic Sea 13, 96-126, 240, 256
Bandierea, R/A 93

Bapaume, battle of 233-5
Barbados 40
Barfleur, HMS 164-5, 169, 176
Barham, HMS 246
Barker, Cdr Richard 275, 279
Barossa (Fr) 155-6, 161
Bastia 59-60
  siege of 45-7, 55
Bayly, Capt Edward 176-7
Baynes, R/A 102
Beacon, HMS 117, 126
Beak, Cdr 233-4, 236
Beatty, Adm David 15, 164-79, *166*
Beirut 82, 84
Belleisle, HMS 126
Bellerophon, HMS *90*, 93
Belmont 194, 206
Benbow, HMS 89, *90*, 93
Bennett, Cdr Sterndale 225
Beresford, Adm Lord Charles 20
Bergen 241
Berkeley, Adm Sir Maurice 93, 98
Biter, HMS 126
Bittern, HMS 247, 251
Black Sea 102, 119, 122
Black Swan, HMS 247-8, 251, 253
Blazer, HMS 126
Bloemfontein 198, 200-1, 203
Boadicea, HMS 131
Boer War (1899-1900) 9, 15, 177, 181-207
Boharsef, battle of 84
Bomarsund 98-100, 121
Bombe (Fr) 126
Bonaparte, General Napoleon 11, 26-7, 30
  at Acre 9-10, 27-8, 31-7
Borneo 146
Botha, General 188, 191, 204-5
Boulogne 42, 49, 63, 274
Bouncer, HMS 156, 161
Bowen, Capt Richard 65, 70-1, 73, 76
Boxer, Capt Edward 85, 93
Boyce, Adm Sir Michael 282
Boyes, Midshipman Duncan 158
Brenton, Capt Edward 42-3
Brooke, Rupert 208, 212, *215*, 236
Browne, Midshipman 247, 253-4
Buckle, Cdr 230, 234-5
Buenos Ayres 51
Buller, General Sir Redvers 184-93, 205
Burma 131, 146
Burrows, Midshipman Montagu 89-90
Byam Martin, Adm of the Fleet Sir Thomas 97

Ça Ira (Fr) 53
Cadiz 37, 63

Caffin, Capt RC 125
Calcutta 131-2
Calcutta, HMS 103, 107, 126
Caldwell, Capt 114, 117
Calvi, siege of 11, 55, *58*
Cambrai, battle of 230
Campbell, Field Marshal Sir Colin 132, 134, 136-7, 142
Canada 229-30, 233-4, 265, 270
Canrobert, Marshal 122
Cape St Vincent, battle of 63, 70, 77
Capraia, island of 59-62, 64, 66-7, 76
Capt, HMS 57, 59-61
Carlisle, HMS 252
Carron, HMS 126
Carysfort, HMS *90*, 93
Castor, HMS *90*, 93
Cawnpore 131, 136-8, 142
Censeur (Fr) 53
Centaur, HMS 10
Cherbourg 96, 99, 124
China 13, 146, 153, 182, 193
  Boxer Rebellion 164-70, 174-7, *177*
  First China War (1840-2) 79, 146
  Second China War 131
Christian, Adm 47
Chrobry (Poland) 245
Churchill, Winston 178
  in First World War 178, 208-9, 211, 218, 223, 236, 240, 245, 274
  in Second World War 240, 241-2, 243, 245, 255-6, 261
Cochrane, Adm Lord 11, 41, 51
Cockburn, Capt George 60-1
Codrington, Capt Henry 85, 89, 93
Cold War 20-3, 275
Colenso 184, 187, *187*, 188, 191
Collier, Capt Edward 93
Colville, Stanley 164-5, 167-9, 172, 179
Conqueror, HMS 153, 156-7, 161
Constantinople 26-7, 30, 35, 80, 82, 92, 274
Cook, Capt 44-5
Cooper-Key, Capt A 106-7, 118-19, 124-5
Coquette, HMS 146, 149, 155-6, 157, 160
Corbett, Julian 21, 23-4
Corder, Cdr Ian 279
Cork and Orrery, Adm Lord 243
Cornwallis, HMS 107, 111-12, 114, 125
Corsica 40, 43-5, *44*, 48, 51, 55-7, *58*, 67
Corunna 11, 51
Cossack, HMS 112, 125, 240
Cowen, Adm Sir Walter 168, 178-9
Cradock, Adm Christopher 178
Crawford, Capt 40, 51
Crete 255

285

Crimean War *12*, 13-14, *14*, 15, 97, 99, 102, 122, 132, *133*, 138, 146, 170
  see also Alma, Sevastopol
Cronje, General 198-200
Cronstadt 99-100, 102-3, 106, 119, 121-4
Crook, Surgeon AH *213*
cruise missiles 23-4, 274-83
  see also Tomahawk missiles
Cruiser, HMS 112, 125
Culloden, HMS 65
Cunningham, Adm of the Fleet Lord 15, 201
Curacao, HMS 252
Cuxhaven 18

Dalmatia 47-50
Dapper, HMS 126
Daser, General 263
de Burgh, General 59, 64
de Casembroot, Capt 157
De La Rey, General 204
de Lisle, General 222
De Wet, General 202
de Wiart, General Carton 243, *244*, 245, 254, 256
Denmark 119, 241
Denny, Capt 248, 252
Deschenes, Adm Parseval 98
Dew, Cdr R 125
Diamond Rock, HMS *10*, 10-11
Dido, HMS 63
D'Jambi (Neth) 155, 160-1
Djezzar Pasha 28, 30-1, 33-5
Dogger Bank, battle of 164
Dombaas 249-56
Donald, Lt 251
Doris, HMS 182, 198
Douglas, Cdr GH 125
Douglas, General Sir Howard 105-6, 124
Dragon, HMS 108-9, 125
Dragonne (Fr) 126
Drake, HMS 104, 120, 125-6
Dubrovnik 49-50
Duffy, Sir Patrick 277
Duke of Wellington, HMS 107-8, 114, 125
Duncan, Major John 57, 59
Dundas, General 44-5
Dundas, R/A Sir Richard Saunders 99, *100*, 101-3, 107-9, 111, 113-14, 116-19, 121-2, 125
Dundonald, Lord 191-2
Dunkirk, evacuation of 255-6
Dupleix (Fr) 155, 160
Duquesne (Fr) 126
Durban 186, 191, *195*
Dürnholz, Ansgar 261

Edinburgh, HMS 86, 89, *90*, 93, 107-8, 121, 125
Egypt, 15
  Napoleonic Wars 9, 26, 34, 37, 40, 42, 51
  1840 campaign 79-80, 82-90, 92
  1896-8 campaign 164-7, 170-1, 173-4, 177
Eisenhower, General DD 259
El Arish 27-8, 36
El Teb, battle of 17
El Teb, HMS 171, 178
Elba 57-9, *60*, 61, 64, 66, 76
Elliot, Cdr Charles 93
Elliot, Sir Gilbert 44-5, 55, 57, 61, 67
Emerald, HMS 65, 73
Erebus, HMS 263, 267
Eupatoria 14-15
Euryalus, HMS 107-9, 114, 118, 125, 146-51, 156-7, 160-2
Excellent, HMS 89, 105

Exmouth, HMS 107, 125
Fanshawe, Capt EH 125
Fanshawe, Capt Robert 93
Fashoda, battle of 174, 177
Fateh, HMS 174, 177-8
Fergusson, General 235
Finland 97-8, 101-2, 122, 124, 240, 256
First World War 15, 18, 164, 177, 208-39, 274
Fisher, Adm Sir John 15, 240
Flamingo, HMS 247, 251
Fleet Air Arm 241
Flesquieres, battle of 230-1
Forte, HMS 193
Fournaise (Fr) 126
Fowler, Mr 140
Fox, HMS 65, 70-1
France 80-1, 83-5, 92, 96-9, 101-4, 107-9, 114, 117-18, 120, 122-4, 126, 174, 178
  in Japan 153, 155, 156-8, 160-1
  in Napoleonic Wars 9-11, 26-53, 53, 55-7, 274
  in First World War 210, 214-15, 217, 219-36, 225-6
  in Second World War 240, 243, 245, 265
Frederick, Archduke 93
Fremantle, Capt Thomas 65, 70-1, 73
French, General 198
Freyberg, Lt-Gen Bernard 208, 212-13, *215*, 221-3, 225, 236
Fry, Brigadier 23
Fulminante (Fr) 126

Galatea, HMS 251-2
Gallacher, Midshipman 252
Gallipoli 18, 212-19, *216*, *218*, 227, 236, 255, 274
Gatacre, General 186
Gauthier, General 48-9
Gavrelle 224-7
Genoa 59, 61, 63
Germany 17, 47
  in First World War 209-11, 211, 221-2, 224-33
  in Second World War 19, 240-3, 245-6, 249, 249-56, 250-6, 259-72
Geyser, HMS 107-8, 125
Gibraltar 64
Gladstone, WE 98
Glasgow, HMS 243
Glasse, Capt FHH 125
Gleaner, HMS 126
Glowworm, HMS 241
Gneisenau (Ger) 241
Good Hope, HMS 177
Goodale, Sub-Lt 252-3
Gordon, General Charles 164
Gordon Highlanders 184, 186
Gorgon, HMS 59-60, 89, *90*, 93
Gough, General 223, 230
Gourly, Lt 60-1
Graham, Sir James 97-101, 105, 119
Grant, Cdr WL 198-200, 202-3
Grappler, HMS 126
Graspan 194-6, 206
Greece 79-80
Greenwich 21
Grey, Earl 105
Growler, HMS 110, 120, 126
Guadeloupe 40-1
Guerriere (Austria) 86, 93
Gulf War 274, 277, 280
Gurkhas 130, 139-40, 142-3
Gurriera (Austria) *90*
Gutiérrez, General Don Antonio 66, 68-70, 74-6

Hafir 165, 170, 172, 177

Haifa 31
Haig, Field Marshal Earl 220
Haine, 2nd Lt 226-7
Hamilton, General 185
Hanover 42
Hart, General 188-9
Hastings, HMS 86, 107, 111-12, 114, 125
Havoc, HMS 116, 120, 150
Havock, HMS 126
Hayes, Capt John 155
Hazard, HMS 90, 93
Hedderwick, Cdr *216*
Hedworth-Lambton, Capt 184, 186
Helsingfors 98-9, 107, 113, *115*, 118, 122
Henderson, Capt William H 93
Henderson, Cdr Thomas 93
Herbert, AP 208
Hewlett, Capt RS 108, 111, 115, 125
Hezekiel (Rus) 117
Highland regiments *17*, 197, 200-2, 222
Hildyard, General 188
Hipper (Ger) 241
Hitler, Adolf 261
Hobart, Lt Augustus 108
Hong Kong 131-2
Hood, Adm Herbert 178
Hood, Adm Viscount Samuel 51
Hood, HMS 246-7, 251, 253, 255-6
Hood, V/A Sir Samuel 65, 70, 74-5
Hoste, Capt William 11, *46*, 47-51
Hotham, V/A William 53
Hughes, Reverend 118

Ibrahim Pasha 80, 84
Imperieuse, HMS 42
Implacable, HMS 84
Inconstant, HMS 57
India 26-7, 146
  Indian Mutiny 13, 130-45, 177
Invincible, HMS and class 280-1
Iraq 280
Irish Brigade 188
Istanbul *see* Constantinople
Italy 27, 30, 51, 57-62, 280

Jacob, General 223
Jaffa 28, 34
Japan 13, 146-63
Jaurès, Adm *154*, 156, 160-1
Jellicoe, Adm Sir John 15, 164-6, 178
Jervis, Adm Sir John *see* St Vincent, Adm Lord
Josling, Capt John 150, 152
Jutland, battle of 164, 177

Kagoshima, battle of 146-53, *148*, 156, 162
Karlsruhe (Ger) 241
Keith, Adm Lord 40, 42
Kelsey, Capt 268
Keppel, Colin 168, 174
Keyes, Adm Roger 178
Khartoum 164-5, 167-8, 174
Kimberley 186, 193, 198
King, Tom 277
Kingston, Cdr Augustus 149, 155, 157
Kitchener, Field Marshal Lord 164-5, 167-8, 171-4, 177, 198-9, 203, 209
Kléber, Marshal 33-5, 37
Koehler, Major 43-4
Koniya, battle of 80
Kosovo 274, 280, 282
Krithia, third battle of 214-17
Kruger, President 181, 201, 205-6
Kuper, R/A Augustus 146-61, *154*

Ladysmith, siege and relief of 181-93
Lark, HMS 126
Lasalle de Louisenthal, Capt 47
Lawrence, Capt 108

Index

Lawrie, General 223
Le Havre 30
Leicester, Brigadier BW 263, 271
Leopard (Fr) 155, 161
Lightning, HMS 118, 125
Lipsia (Austria) 86, *90*, 93
Livorno 57
Locust, HMS 125
Logan, Major James 59-61
London, HMS 121
London, Treaty of (1840) 83
Long, Colonel 188
Louis Philippe, King of France 83
Lucknow, relief of 130-45, 133
Ludendorff, Field-Marshal 223
Lumley, Major 247, 251
Lützow (Ger) 241
Lyons, Adm Sir Edmund 119

Mackesy, General 243
Mafeking 186
Magersfontein 188, 196-9
Magicienne, HMS 107-9, 125
Magpie, HMS 111, 120, 126
Mahan, Capt Alfred Thayer 15, 17, 21, 77
Mahmud, Emir 170
Mahmud II, Sultan 79-80, 83
Malaya 146
Malik, HMS 178
Mallet, Robert 121
Manly, HMS 126
Mansel, Cdr George 93
Marines *see* Royal Marines *and under* USA
Martin, Capt Henry 93
Martinique 11, 40, 43
Mastiff, HMS 126
Matalen Kruis (Neth) 160
Maurice, Lt James 10-11
Medalen Kruis (Neth) 155
Medea (Austria) 86, *90*, 93
Medusa (Neth) 156-7
Mehemet Ali 79-81, 83-4, 91-2
Melbourne, Lord 83
Merlin, HMS 103, 107, 109-10, 116-17, 125
Metemmeh, HMS 171-2, 178
Methuen, General 186, 193-4, 196-8
Miller, Capt Ralph 31, 34, 64-5, 68, 70-1, 74-7
Milner, Sir Alfred 181
Minerve, HMS 60-1
Minto, Lord 81, 83
Modder River 196-8, 200
Monarch, HMS 182
Montagu, Midshipman 139
Montenegro 47
Montgomery, Field Marshal BL 259, 270
Moore, Colonel Sir John 11, 43-4
Moresby, Capt John 156-61
Morgan, Brigadier 251-2
Mori Idzuno 160
mortars and mortar vessels 97-9, 102-11, 114-15, *115*, 116-21, 124-6
Mount Tabor, battle of 34

Nagato, Daimyo of 153, 155, 160
Namsos 243, 245-6, 249, *249*, 251, 254, 256
Napier, V/A Sir Charles 81, 84, *86*, 87-8, 91-3, 97-101
Napoleon I *see* Bonaparte
Napoleon III, Emperor 97
Napoleonic Wars 9-11, 18, 26-52, 81, 105, 271-2, 274
Nargen 102-3, 107, 118-19
Narvik 241-6
Nasir, HMS 178

NATO 22, 274, 279-80
Navarino, battle of 80
Navy Records Society 14
Neale, Lt-Col Edward 147, 151
Nelson, HMS 246-7
Nelson, V/A Horatio 13, 26-8, 30, 37, 53-78, 56
 at Bastia 59
 at Calvi 11, *58*
 at Cape St Vincent 54, 70
 on Capraia 59-62, 64, 66-7, 76
 in Corsica 48, 54, 55-7, 67
 in Egypt 9, 26, 54
 on Elba 57-9, *60*, 61, 64, 66, 76
 in Nicaragua 54
 at Santa Cruz de Tenerife 51, 54, 62-77
 at siege of Bastia 45, 47, 55
 wounds 11, 53-4, 55, *58*, 63, 71-3, *72*, 76-7
Nesbit, Josiah 71-2, *72*
Netherlands 51, 80, 153, 155, 158, 161, 210, 245, 259-73
 see also Antwerp, Ostend
New Zealand 130-1, 233
Nezib, battle of 80
Nicaragua 54
Nicholson, Capt 243
Niger, HMS 131
Nile 164-5, 168-71, 177-9
 battle of the Nile 9, 26, 31, 37, 77, 170
Nisbet, Josiah 71-3, *72*
Normandy landings 20, 259, 261, 265, 269
Norway 19, 240-58
Nugent, Capt 102, 106

Ogilvie, Lt FCA 190-1
O'Hara, General 64
Ohio class (US) 282
Oldfield, Capt 74-5
Oldfield, Major Thomas 34
Omdurman, battle of 165, 168, 174, 177
Operation Allied Force 274, 280
Operation Anvil 265
Operation Desert Storm 277
Operation Henry 245-6
Operation Maurice 243, 245
Operation Primrose 245-54
Operation Rupert 243-5
Operation Sickle 243, 245-6, 251
Orion, HMS 251
Orlando, HMS 167, *173*
Oscar I, King of Sweden 97
Osprey, HMS 161
Ostend 51, 265
Ottoman Empire *see* Turkey

Paardeburg 198-200
Paget, Major-General 252, 254
Palamos raid 41
Palmerston, Lord 13, 80-1, 83-4, 91-2, 121-2
Paoli, Pasquale 55
Paris, General 211-12, 214, 217, 220
Paris, Peace of (1856) 123
Parker, L/Cpl 214
Parker, William 147, 149
Passchendaele, battle of 227-30
Pearl, HMS 130-4, 138-41, *141*, 142-5
Pearl, HMS 149
Peel, Capt William 132-3, *133*, 135, 136-7, 144
Pelham, Cdre 103, 108-9, 116
Pelican (Fr) 118, 126
Pelorus, HMS 131
Pelter, HMS 109-10, 120, 126
Pembroke, HMS 107, 117, 125
Pembrokeshire, HMS 153

Penaud, Adm 101-3, 107, 117-18, 121, 126
Peninsula War 11, 39, 41-2
Perry, Cdre 146
Perseus, HMS 149, 155-8, 161-2
Peterel, HMS 57
Phélippeaux, Colonel Louis-Edmond 30-2, 34
Phoenix, HMS 87, *90*, 93
Pickle, HMS 109, 126
Pincher, HMS 126
Pique, HMS 85, *90*, 92-3
Poland 85, 124, 243, 245-6
Poland, Capt 248
Pole-Carew, General 206
Pollard, 2nd Lt 226
Porpoise, HMS 126
Portillo, Michael 277
Portugal 80-1
Powerful, HMS 9, 15, 81, 87-8, *90*, 93, 182-3, 186, 193, 201
Preedy, Cdr 111
Pride, Thomas 158
Princess Alice, HMS 126
Princess Charlotte, HMS 81, 85, 88, *90*, 93
Prior, Cdr 270
Prompt, HMS 126
Prothero, Capt 194-5
Prowse, CPO 234
Prussia 27, 83
Puerto Rico 51
Pugsley, Capt AF 263, 269, 271
Pyramids, battle of the 26

Quiberon Bay 51

Racehorse, HMS 149-50, 152, 162
Raglan, Field Marshal Lord 15
Ragusa 49-50
railways 14, 18
Ramsay, Adm Sir Bertram 259, 261, 264-5, 271
Ramsay, Capt G 108-9, 116, 118, 125
Redbreast, HMS 126
Redwing, HMS 126
Renown, HMS 241
Reval 97, 102, 107, 121
Revenge, HMS 87-8, *90*, 93
Rhodes 34
Richardson, Charles 147, 151
Rifkind, Malcolm 277
RMA (Royal Marine Artillery) *see under* Royal Marines
Roberts, Capt 120
Roberts, Field Marshal Lord 198-206
Roberts, HMS 263, 267
Robertson, CH 168
Robertson of Ellen, Lord 283
Rocket, HMS 126
rockets 13-14, *14*, 48-9, 84, 96, 114, 116-17, 121, 136, 268
 Congreve rockets *14*, 42, 49-50, 114, 274
 Hale's rockets *173*
Rodney, HMS 121
Romdalsfjord *242*, 248-51, 256
Rose, HMS 60-1
Rosenberg, David 21
Roskill, Stephen 243, 250
Rossiya (Rus) 111, *115*
Rowcroft, Colonel 139-40
Royal Artillery 188-9, 206
Royal Engineers 156, 158
Royal Horse Artillery 189
Royal Marines 11, 14-15, 18, 21, 23, 32-4, 40-2, 64-5, 67-9, 74, 84, 91, 104, 131-2, 136-7, 139, 143, 153, 156-7, *159*, 166-7, 176, 195, 198, 201, 203, 221, 274-5

287

RMA (Royal Marine Artillery) 105, 108-11, 172-3, 202, 211
  in First World War 208-9, 212-14, 217, 221-2, 225, 227-8, 232
  in Second World War 243, 246-7, 252, 254, 263, 265, 269
Royal Naval Division 18, 208-39, 245
  memorial 236, *237*
Royal Navy Field Gun Competition 9
Rundstedt, Field Marshal von 261, 263
Russell, Lord John 83
Russia 9, 13-14, 27, 80-3, 92, 97-9, 101, 108-9, 111-24, 168, 240, 275
  see also Cronstadt, St Petersburg

Saddam Hussein 280
Salter, Sub-Lt DC 253-4
San Juan River 54
Sans Pareil, HMS 119
Santa Cruz de Tenerife 51, *62*, 62-77
Saran Field Force 139-40, 142
Satsuma, Daimyo of 147, 149, 151
Scapa Flow 177-8
Scharnhorst (Ger) 241
Schomberg, Capt 108
Scott, Capt Percy 9, 176, 182-3, 186
Seahorse, HMS 65
Second World War 19-20, *24*, 240-73, 275
Seely, William 158
Sellar, Cdr KA 265, 269
Sémiramis (Fr) 156
Sevastopol 14, 97, 99, 120, 143
Seymour, Capt GH 117, 125
Seymour, R/A Sir M 125
Shah, HMS 131
Shannon, HMS 130-2, 134, 136, 138, *138*, 142-4, 176
Sheffield, HMS 243
Sheik, HMS 178
shells, introduction of 105-6, 110, 121, 139-40
Shimonoseki, bombardment of 153 *62*, 154-5, *159*
Shute, General Cameron 220, 223
Sicily 27, 30, 280
Sidon 84, 86, *86*
Sikhs 130, 139, 142
Simonds, General 265, 270
Simpson, Lt-Col 247-9, 252
Sims, Mr 184-5
Sinbad, HMS 104, 125-6
Singapore 131
Skylark, HMS 126
Slater, Adm Sir Jock 23
Smith, Cdre Sir Sidney 9, 13, 27-37, *29*, *36*, 279, 282
Smith, Sir Charles 85
Smith, Spencer 27, 30
Snap, HMS 111, 126
Snapper, HMS 111, 126
Soanpur 139
Somali, HMS 243, 245
Somme, battle of the 231-2
Sotheby, Capt Edward 132, 134, 138-9, 142-3
South Africa 13, 15, 181-207
Southamtpon, HMS 243
Spain 41, 54, 63-76
Spearfish, HMS 241
Spicer, Lt James 61
Spion Kop, battle of 185, 190
Splendid, HMS 23, 274-5, 279-80, *281*, 283
St Lucia 47

St Petersburg 13, 99, 101, 122
St Vincent, Adm Lord 31, 40, 43, 57, 59, 61-6
Starling, HMS 109-10, 111, 126
Stavanger 241, 256
steam propulsion, introduction of *19*, 87, 93, 96, 99, 105, 124, 131, 150, 153, 161-2
Stewart, Capt Houston 93
Stewart, Capt WH 125
Steyn, President 181, 205-6
Stopford, Cdr Robert 93
Stopford, V/A Sir Robert 81-5, *82*, 87-8, 90-1, 93
Stork, HMS 111, 115, 126
Stormburg 193
strategy 11, 13-15, 18, 21-3, 274-83
  MCJO (Maritime Contribution to Joint Operations) 275
  SDR (Strategic Defence Review) 23, 275, 278, 281
Stromberg, battle of 188
Stromboli, HMS *90*, 93
Stroud, Lt ED 247, 254
Stuart, General 11
Stuart, Lord Dudley 98
submarines 18, 250, 274-5
  SSBNs 275, 277, 282
  SSNs 282
Sudan *17*, *19*, 164-73, 177
Sulivan, Capt BJ 100, *100*, 101, 103, 106-12, 114, 117-18, 120-2, 124-5
Sultan, HMS 178
Surly, HMS 120, 126
Suther, Lt-Col William 157-8
Svarto 108, 111, 114, 116-17
Sweaborg 96, 98-103, 106-7, *110*, 111, *113*, 115, 119-26
Sweden 29, 30, 97-8, 121, 240
Swiftsure class submarines (GB) 278
Syria 9-10, 13, 27-8, 34-5, 79-95, 92, 279
  see also Acre

Talbot, HMS 85, 89, *90*, 93
Tamai, HMS 172, 178
Tancrède (Fr) 156, 161
Tantia Topi 136
Tartar, HMS 155, 157, 160
Tedder, Air Marshal 263
telegraph *19*
Tempete (Fr) 126
Tenerife *see* Santa Cruz de Tenerife
Terpsichore, HMS 63, 65
Terrible, HMS 9, 176, 182-3, 186, *192*, 193
Terror, HMS 65
Theseus, HMS 31, 65-6, 69, *72*, 73-4
Thiers, Louis-Adolphe 83
Thistle, HMS 109-10, 126
Thompson, Capt 70, 73
Thompson, Major General Julian 272
Thunderer, HMS 81, *90*, 93
Tientsin 164-7
Tigre, HMS 23, 30, *32*, 282
Tisdall, S/Lt 213
Tocsin (Fr) 126
Tomahawk missiles 274-83, *276*, *278*
  launch and control 278-9
  TacTom 282
Tonnerre (Fr) 126
Torche (Fr) 126
Toulon 27, 40, 51, 53, 57, 124
Tourmente (Fr) 126
Tourville (Fr) 117, 126
Trafalgar, battle of 11, 37, 77

Trafalgar class submarines (GB) 278
Trafalgar, HMS 168
Trombe (Fr) 126
Trondheim 241, 243, 248-51, 254-5
Troubridge, Capt Thomas 65, 69-70, 73, 75-6
Troubridge, General 64-5
Truant, HMS 241
Tsientsin 168, 170, 174-7, 177
Turkey 13, 26-8, 30, 34, 34-5, 35, 79-84, *90*, 92-3, 97, 124
  in First World War 212-19, 274
  see also Constantinople
Turquoise, HMS 131

Unkiar Skelessi, Treaty of 80
USA 20, 54, 59, 124, 146, 176, 265
  Civil War 79, 120
  postwar 21-2, 274-5, 277, 279-80, 282
  US Marine Corps 21

Vaal Krantz, battle of 185, 190-1
Vanneau, HMS 60-1
Vansittart, Capt N 125
Vargon 107-8, 112, 114, 116, 118
Vesuvius, HMS *90*, 93
Vian, Capt Philip 240, 254
Victoria Cross *12*, 14-15, 242
Victoria, Queen *16*, 103, 122
Victory, HMS 81, 178
Villeneuve, Adm 11
Volcano, HMS 116-17, 125
Vulture, HMS 107-9, 114, 117, 125

Walcheren
  1809 39, 51, 271-2
  1944 20, 259-73, *260*, *262*, *264*
Waldegrave, Capt William 88, 93
Walker, Capt Baldwin 84, 87, *88*, 90-1, 93
Waller, Capt Thomas 65, 70, 73
Warburton-Lee, Capt 242
Ward, M1 117
Warren, General 190
Warspite, HMS 263, 267-8, 271
Wasp, HMS *90*, 93
Wauchope, General 197
Weasel, HMS 126
Wee Pet (GB) 118
Wellesley, Capt George 111-12, 125
Wellington, Duke of 11, 39
Wemyss, Capt (RM) 106-11, 113, 117-18, 120, 124
West Indies 10-11, 27, 40-1, 47
Westkapelle 259, *260*, 261, *262*, 263, *264*, 266, *266*, 267-9
Whale Island 9
White, General Sir George 181, 186
Wilhelm II, Kaiser 17
Wilhelmshaven 124
Williams, Cdr WJ 93
Wilmot, Cdr Edward 150, 152
Wood, Adm Sir Charles 102-3, 117, 119, 121-2
Woodlark, HMS 131
Wright, Capt John 30-1, 37

Yelverton, Capt H 112, 125
Yugoslavia 47-50, 274, 279-80, 282

Zafir, HMS 167, 177-8
Zealous, HMS 65, 71
Zebra, HMS 92
Zeebrugge 177
Zulu Wars 131

288